Cross-country comparisons of sectoral balance sheets offer crucial indications of differences in overall financial structure, which in turn underlie contrasts in financing and economic behaviour. In this context, this book aims to confront theory and extant empirical work with aggregate financial data across the G-7, covering the period from 1970 to 2000. Viewed in the light of the main theoretical and empirical results in the economic literature, it explores the contrasting patterns and development of financial structures in the UK, the US, Germany, Japan, Canada, France and Italy. It uses as raw material sectoral balance sheet data published by national statistical authorities across the corporate, household, general government, foreign, financial, banking and institutional-investor sectors.

Joseph P. Byrne graduated with a PhD from the University of Strathclyde in 2000 and since then has been employed by NIESR, where he is at present a Senior Research Officer. His research is mainly concerned with applied economics and he has publications in Economic Modelling and the Oxford Bulletin of Economics and Statistics. In addition to balance sheets and financial structure, he has recently worked on consumption, investment, exchange rates and price determination.

E. Philip Davis is Professor of Economics and Finance, Brunel University, West London and a Visiting Fellow at NIESR. He is also an Associate Member of the Financial Markets Group at LSE, Associate Fellow of the Royal Institute of International Affairs and Research Fellow of the Pensions Institute at Birkbeck College, London. Prior to taking up his Chair at Brunel, Davis studied at Oxford during 1975–80, before spending the period from 1980 to 2000 as a central banker at the Bank of England, BIS and European Monetary Institute. Davis's research interests cover the broad field of applied economic analysis of financial institutions and markets. Besides numerous articles, he has published the following books: *Debt, Financial Fragility, and Systemic Risk* (Oxford, 1995), *Pension Funds* (Oxford, 1995) and *Institutional Investors* (MIT Press, with Benn Steil, 2001).

THE NATIONAL INSTITUTE OF
ECONOMIC AND SOCIAL RESEARCH
XLIII




2 DEAN TRENCH STREET, SMITH SQUARE, LONDON, SW1P 3HE


The National Institute of Economic and Social Research is an independent, non-profit-making body, founded in 1938. It has as its aim the promotion of realistic research, particularly in the field of economics. It conducts research by its own research staff and in cooperation with universities and other academic bodies.

# Financial Structure
## An investigation of sectoral balance sheets in the G-7

JOSEPH P. BYRNE AND E. PHILIP DAVIS

CAMBRIDGE
UNIVERSITY PRESS

PUBLISHED BY THE PRESS SYNDICATE OF THE UNIVERSITY OF CAMBRIDGE
The Pitt Building, Trumpington Street, Cambridge, United Kingdom

CAMBRIDGE UNIVERSITY PRESS
The Edinburgh Building, Cambridge, CB2 2RU, UK
40 West 20th Street, New York, NY 10011-4211, USA
477 Williamstown Road, Port Melbourne, VIC 3207, Australia
Ruiz de Alarcón 13, 28014 Madrid, Spain
Dock House, The Waterfront, Cape Town 8001, South Africa

http://www.cambridge.org



First published 2003

Printed in the United Kingdom at the University Press, Cambridge

*A catalogue record for this book is available from the British Library*

ISBN 0 521 83180 6 hardback

# Contents

# Tables

# Figures

# ACKNOWLEDGEMENTS

The authors thank Paul Ashworth, Alistair Barr, Ray Barrell, Olivier de Bandt, Charles Goodhart, Sylvia Gottschalk, Florence Hubert, Nigel Pain, Fran Robinson, Albert Teplin, Martin Weale, Desirée van Welsum and staff of the Commissariat Générale du Plan for helpful suggestions. Sections 4.1 and 5.1 are largely drawn from Davis's book, *Debt, Financial Fragility, and Systemic Risk*, the publishing rights in which are held by Oxford University Press.

To my parents, Patricia and John

*J.P. Byrne*

To my children,

Rhiane, Elwen and Kenrick

*Philip Davis*

# Introduction

The balance sheet structure of the main economic sectors in the major industrial countries is a key indicator of differences between them in overall financial structure, while differences in financial structure in turn underlie contrasts in financing and economic behaviour. In this context, the aim of this book is to confront theory and extant empirical work with evidence from aggregate financial data on financial structure across the major industrial countries. Viewed in the light of the main theoretical and empirical results in the economic literature, it explores the contrasting patterns and development of financial structures across the major OECD countries since 1970, using as raw material sectoral balance sheet data published by the national statistical authorities. Such a cross-country confrontation of theory and evidence across the full range of sectors fills an important gap in the literature. Cross-country comparisons, and indeed analyses of sectoral financing behaviour *per se*, are rare outside the areas of household assets and corporate liabilities.

Concerning theory and extant empirical evidence, the book provides a critical *tour d'horizon* of work on economic issues and findings relating to comparative financial systems, determinants of structural differences between them and judgements about their optimality. It also assesses implications of balance sheet composition for real economic activity in the long term. In this context, the aim of the work is not to provide a comprehensive assessment of the literature on all fields of financing. Nor are we seeking to analyse cyclical behaviour or financial stability matters,[1] except in passing. Rather, we aim to be selective, giving a flavour of the

1 See Davis (1995b, 1999a) and Oxford Review of Economic Policy (1999) for surveys of financial stability theories and underlying issues, also Kiyotaki and Moore (1997) for recent theoretical work.

factors underlying the evolving long-run equilibrium portfolio compositions and related structural aspects of financing behaviour of the various economic sectors, as well as the cross-country differences and their long-term economic implications.

Against the background of the survey, we offer a set of data illustrating the financial and balance sheet structure in the G-7 countries. The raw material is the national balance sheets provided by the central banks of the US, France, Germany, Italy and Japan, and by the statistical agencies of Canada and the UK. The main focus is on a comparison of sectoral patterns for the years 1998 and 2000, with historical perspective being given by data for 1970, 1980 and 1990.

Sectors covered are the main macroeconomic aggregates, namely households/personal sector, companies, financial institutions, the general government and foreign sectors. We also provide balance sheet information for three subsectors of finance, namely banks, insurance/pension funds and mutual funds. The main instrument breakdown is between deposits/notes and coin, money market instruments, bonds, loans, equities, mutual funds, foreign direct investment (FDI), central bank reserves and insurance/pension claims. Data are shown both as a proportion of the portfolio (gross assets or liabilities) and as a percentage of GDP.

We maintain that such a set of data as presented here can provide powerful insights into the main differences in financial structure, which can be interpreted in the light of economic theory and empirical work in the literature. The differences in the structure of assets and liabilities are indicators of the key underlying differences in financing behaviour. Besides commenting on results for individual countries, we seek to assess whether it is justifiable to group countries in some way, for example, between bank-dominated and market-based countries. The data are also used to show whether such differences have tended to diminish in recent years owing to factors such as deregulation and the growth of institutional investors. We include some tentative suggestions as to whether differing balance sheets are important to overall economic performance.

The book is structured as follows; we begin in Chapter 1 with an overview of financial structure issues in general (which largely link the financial sector and corporate sector financing), for which six areas of work seem to us particularly useful:

- general portfolio theory, which helps explain choice of financing by any agent in the economy over both assets and liabilities;
- the 'exceptions' to Arrow-Debreu complete markets which justify the existence of the financial system, and the theory of intermediation which

justifies the existence of financial intermediaries;
- work on the functions of the financial system highlighted by Merton and Bodie (1995);
- work on the arguments relating to the differences between Anglo-Saxon and continental financial systems, see Allen and Gale (2000), Carlin and Mayer (1999) and Schmidt *et al.* (1999, 2001). This focuses on comparative advantages in intertemporal risk sharing. Work on legal systems which accompany financial structures is also important (La Porta *et al.* 2000), linking for example to the argument that relationship banking accompanies weaknesses in the legal and accounting infrastructure which fail to protect non-bank equity investors;
- work on the evolution of financial systems from those based on banks to securitised systems, as summarised in Rybczinski (1997).

In Chapter 2, we detail some of the main statistical differences between the national balance sheets, in terms of sectoral definitions, instrument definitions and accounting practices, and note how these affect the exercise of providing comparable information which is the aim of the work.

Chapter 3 provides key macroeconomic and demographic data as further background for understanding the balance sheet composition of the sectors. For example, low inflation in Germany, as well as historic losses on shares, help to explain relatively high usage of bond finance in that economy.

At the level of individual sectors, the subsequent chapters focus briefly in each case on the underlying theory and also on the empirical work that has been undertaken comparing patterns in the G-7 countries. This is then complemented by the data on balance sheets of the individual sectors. Reflecting the principal focus of extant theoretical and empirical work, we begin our sectoral analysis in Chapter 4 with an overview of the theoretical and empirical literature on the structure of corporate sector financing (Modigliani-Miller and its further developments, asymmetric inflation and agency costs) and the corresponding data, including information on flows and the ownership of equities. In presenting the data, we seek to show insights from theory rather than presenting only numerical comparisons.

The household sector has also been studied in some depth, and is covered in Chapter 5, although we note that the composition of household liabilities is less well covered in the literature than assets.[2] Subsequent chapters cover the assets and liabilities of other sectors; Chapter 6 addresses the general government, Chapter 7 the foreign sector, Chapter

2 Work of Jappelli and Pagano (1994) is an exception.

8 the financial sector, Chapter 9 banks, and Chapter 10 pension funds/life insurance and mutual funds.

Finally, in Chapter 11, we examine the degree to which the data conform to the stylised facts which are often adduced of a clear divide between balance sheets in bank-dominated and market-based financial systems, as well as examining rough indicators of convergence of financial structure and considering whether financial structure makes a major difference to behaviour and economic performance at a macro or micro level. We also offer an analysis of equity financing and equity holding in France compared with the G-7, which illustrates the many analytical uses to which the data in the book may be put.

The concluding section notes some of the broad issues arising, notably the tensions between the aggregate and sectoral economic analyses and between the theory and data, and also draws out some policy issues.

# 1 System-wide issues

In this chapter we address topics which arise for the financial system as a whole, namely portfolio theory, the justification for the existence of a financial system; corporate governance; the functions of the financial system; bank and market-based systems; financial development and financial structure; and recent developments affecting the financial system. All of these cast light on factors underlying the differing size and balance sheet structures of national financial systems. As background, we show data in Figures 1.1–1.8 relative to GDP of corporate liabilities and the financial assets of households, general government, the foreign sector, the financial sector, banking and institutional investors. These aggregates and their portfolio composition are discussed in detail in Chapters 4–10. What becomes immediately apparent is the diverse size of balance sheets of the different sectors across industrial countries at comparable levels of income and economic development. One key aspect of the book is to help explain why portfolios differ in magnitude as well as composition.

Note that, apart from portfolio theory, which is of quite general application, the systemic issues deemed of broader economic interest link largely to the corporate sector and financial sectors, and to a lesser extent the household sector. The analysis of financial systems has less to say regarding the behaviour of the public and foreign sectors, although there is of course a specialised literature on these matters.

## 1.1 THEORIES OF PORTFOLIO CHOICE

Since the overall aim of the book is to illustrate the patterns of portfolio holdings by the main economic sectors, it is appropriate to begin with an

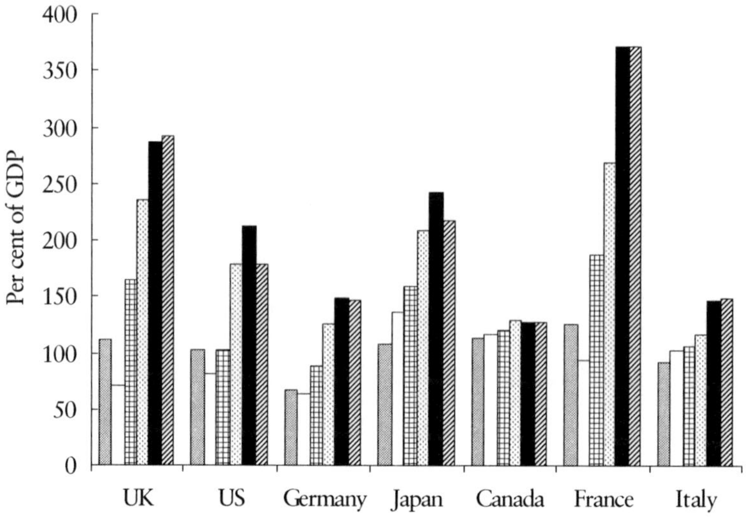


Figure 1.1 *Corporate sector liabilities*
Note: For each country each group of bars represents (from left to right) 1970, 1980, 1990, 1998, 1999, 2000.

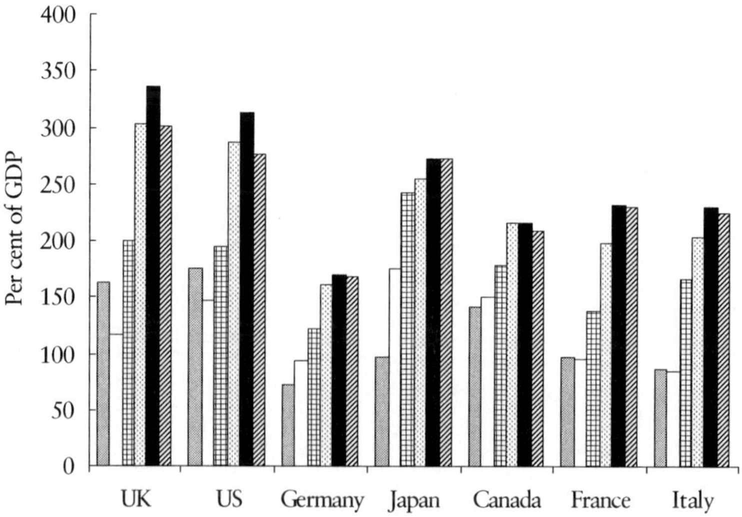


Figure 1.2 *Household sector financial assets*
Note: As Figure 1.1.

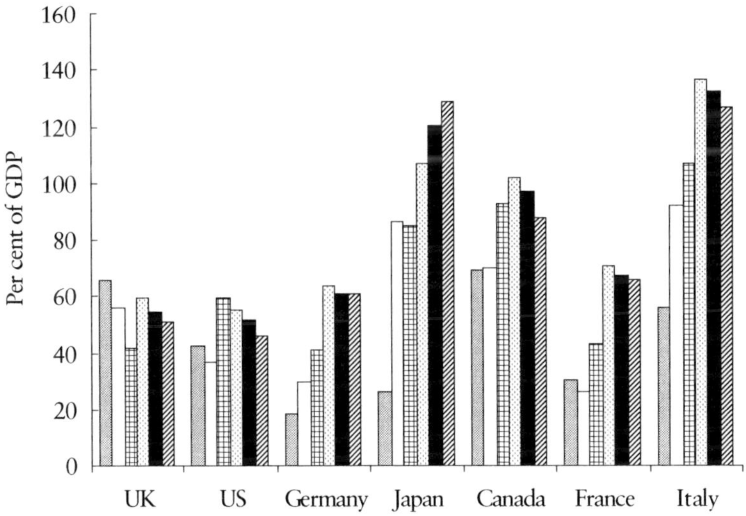


Figure 1.3 *General government liabilities*
Note: As Figure 1.1.

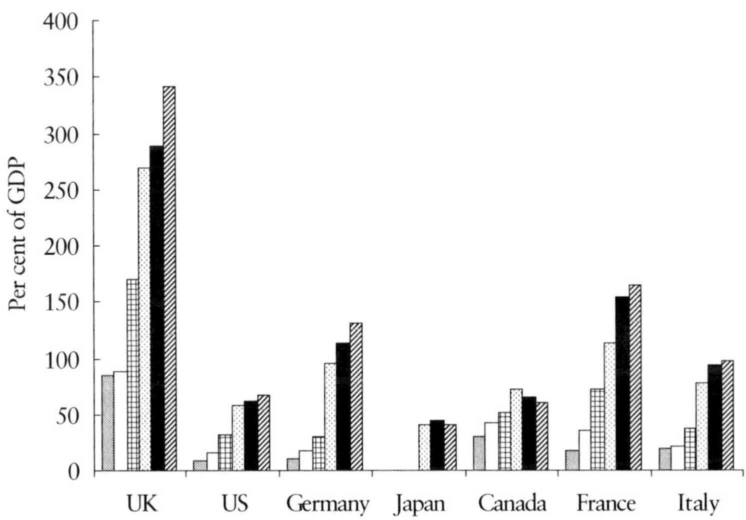


Figure 1.4 *Foreign sector financial assets*
Note: As Figure 1.1.

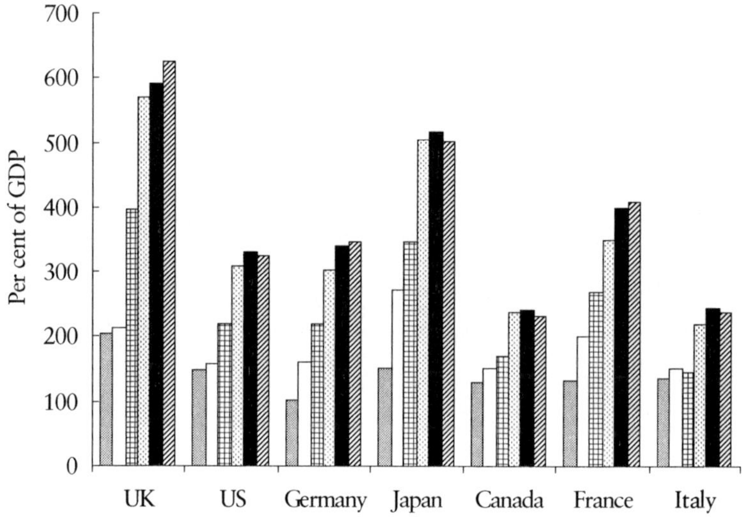


Figure 1.5 *Financial sector financial assets*
Note: As Figure 1.1.

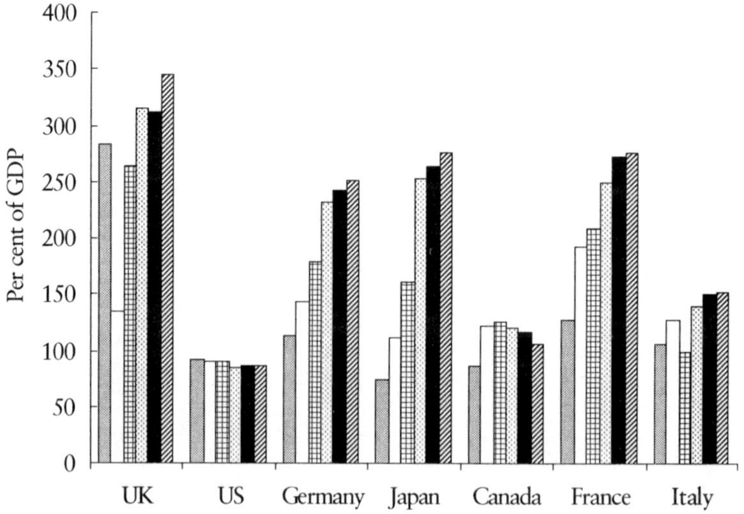


Figure 1.6 *Banking sector financial assets*
Note: As Figure 1.1.

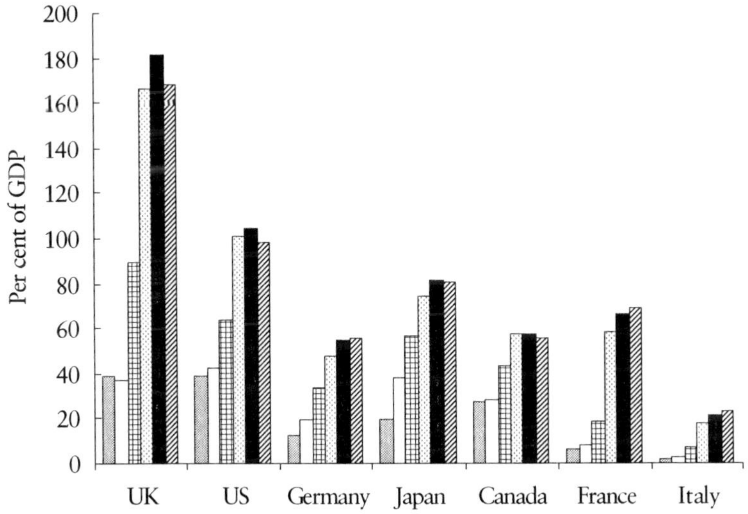


Figure 1.7 *Life insurance and pension fund sector financial assets*
Note: As Figure 1.1.

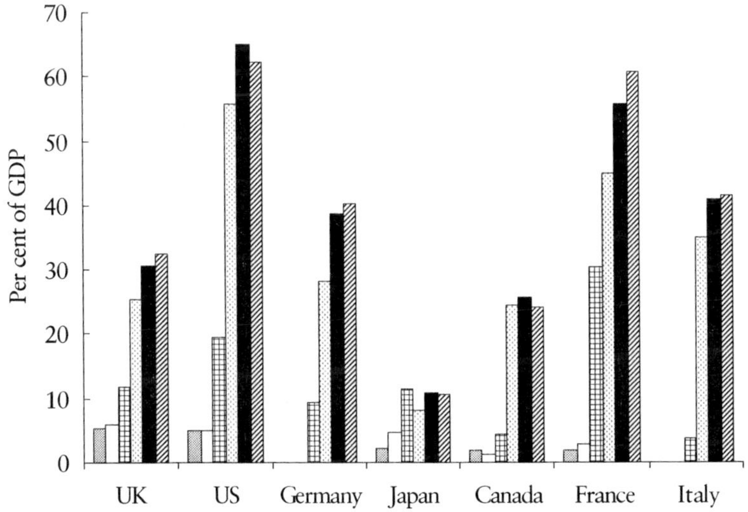


Figure 1.8 *Mutual funds' financial assets*
Note: As Figure 1.1.

overview of the main lines of economic theory which seek to explain portfolio distributions. Whereas the discussion is set in terms of risky and risk free assets in general terms, note that in practice the key distinctions between types of asset include:

- those between equity and debt (where the former are residual claimants on income with no guaranteed return, and the latter are senior claimants with a fixed, guaranteed return);
- those between private and publicly issued debt (where the latter are risk free in terms of nominal value in domestic currency while the former are subject to wider credit risk);
- those that are traded in markets (bonds, equities, money market instruments) versus those not traded (deposits and loans), although loan securitisation makes this formerly sharp distinction a less clear one;
- domestic assets and those in foreign currency, bearing exchange rate risk for domestic investors;
- financial assets – the focus of this book – and tangible assets, where the latter include non-tradable human wealth as well as capital and inventories;
- underlying assets – the focus of this book – and derivative financial instruments.[3]

Assuming there is more than one asset available, an investor holding non-human wealth faces a problem of portfolio choice, i.e. selection among a range of instruments to maximise utility. Under certain assumptions (that the utility function is additively separable), the decision concerning the form in which to hold wealth in a given period can be separated from the decision as to how much wealth to accumulate. This assumption allows a simplification of the more complex problem that would be derived from the more basic neoclassical theory of lifetime optimisation (see Lancaster, 1971). Derivation of portfolio choice then faces the problem that as long as all assets are not risk free, the investor faces uncertainty over the exact return to be received from the portfolio. The investor may also be risk averse. Even cash is not risk free in real (inflation adjusted) terms.

A general approach to portfolio selection under uncertainty and risk aversion is that of time-state preferences (Arrow, 1964; Debreu,1959), which is again hard to give empirical content. On special assumptions, however, the problem can be reduced to two parameters, where portfolio

3 Long runs of data are not available on derivatives in the flow of funds balance sheet tables.

choice depends solely on the mean and variance of return in an expected utility maximising framework (Tobin, 1958; Markowitz, 1952). Sufficient conditions are a quadratic utility function, joint normally distributed asset rates of return, or a logarithmic utility function and a lognormally distributed portfolio rate of return.

Each of these conditions is subject to objections. A quadratic utility function implies that for sufficiently high incomes, utility falls as income rises, and if there is only one risky asset and one safe one, the investor holds less of the risky one as he grows richer. Observation suggests that risk is not an 'inferior good', as the rich hold riskier and higher yielding portfolios than the poor. The importance of the normality assumptions is that if each security has a normal distribution of returns, then, whatever portfolio is chosen, the distribution of the asset holders' total income is also normal. All possible distributions have the same shape, differing only in mean and variance, so the investor may concentrate on his desired combination of these. The mean-variance approach is again best seen as an approximation; asset returns are empirically not found to be normal, being rather leptokurtic, with fatter tails than the normal distribution.

Using these assumptions, one may derive a set of linear homogeneous portfolio demand functions (Tobin, 1969; Friedman, 1977).

$$\frac{A^*_{it}}{W_t} = \sum_k^N \beta_{ik} r_{kt} + \sum_h^M \gamma_{ih} X_{ht} + \pi_i \tag{1.1}$$

where $A^*_{it}$, $i = 1, \ldots N$ is the investor's desired equilibrium holding of the $i$th asset at time period $t$ ($\sum_i A^*_{it} = W_t$), $W_t$ is the investor's total portfolio size (wealth) at time period $t$; $r_{kt}$, $k = 1, \ldots N$ is the expected holding period return on the $k$th asset at time period $t$ (net of taxes); and $X_{ht}$, $h = 1, \ldots M$ the values at time period $t$ of additional variables which influence the portfolio allocation.

These equations give a desired portfolio towards which the investor's decisions are directed. In a real world of transactions costs, habits and lags in expectation formation, the investor may not maintain these holdings precisely at a given time. The constant $\pi_i$ ensures the equation captures the normal share of the asset when other variables are at average levels (including average levels of risk and tax effects). If investors do not suffer from money illusion, then relevant yields would be in real terms, deducting expected inflation from expected returns. Returns should include capital gains and losses, as well as income flows such as interest and dividends, and should be after tax. The variables $X$ would include indicators of time varying risk and risk aversion, as well as other variables influencing portfolio decisions, such as income in the case of assets held for transactions or precautionary purposes (i.e. 'liquidity'). This income effect will be important when substitution between assets is costly in terms of transactions costs, meaning there will be a demand for low-yielding assets easily transformed into expenditure items.

This formulation is quite general, but clearly, separate factors will influence specific sectors' asset demands. For example, for households the $X$ variables might also include demographic variables if asset demands vary over the life cycle due to differing risk aversion of individuals at different ages, see also Section 5.2. For firms, leverage may be important (Section 4.1), and for government, the fiscal position is relevant (Section 6.1). Tangible wealth such as housing may influence financial asset demand, especially if it is relatively liquid and hence usable as a store of value, as is the case in some countries.

The relationship depicted implies homogeneity in wealth – the share of the asset does not depend on the size of the portfolio. This is a result of separability – but in practice, there may be assets whose holdings are dependent on wealth. The set of such equations sums to one by the wealth constraint. It is plausible that individual equations will be characterised by interest rate homogeneity, that the sum of interest rate terms is zero, so that a rise in all rates together does not change the portfolio composition. Symmetry implies that the coefficient of asset $i$'s return in the equation for asset $k$ is equal to that of $k$'s return on $i$. It may also be expected that an investor's demand for a given asset depends positively on its own yield and negatively on the yield of other assets, so called gross substitutability. In fact some assets may be complements.

The framework is set out above in terms of financial assets, but liabilities may also be integrated (the aggregate would then be net wealth with liabilities entered negatively), and where the expectation would be that the own-rate would have a negative sign. In this context, it is likely that non-price constraints on borrowing are often important, and would need to be introduced separately into the framework. Such 'credit rationing' may be related to asymmetries of information between lenders and borrowers, as discussed in Sections 1.2, 4.2 and 5.1, even in a liberalised financial system. Prior to liberalisation it may also have linked to direct or indirect controls on credit expansion or allocation imposed by government (see Section 1.7).

The framework as set out above takes into account only portfolio demands, and takes supplies as given. However, the latter can be integrated by setting out a similar framework for all economic sectors, where the supply of assets is equivalent to overall demand for liabilities held in the same form.

In the context of these equations, cross-country differences in asset holdings may be related to a combination of two different aspects. One is variation in risks and returns (net of taxes and inflation) and the other is variation in the characteristics of portfolio demands (relating to aspects of overall financial structure such as the system of industrial, housing or pension financing as well as differing regulations and attitudes to risk). Which of these dominates is an empirical matter, addressed in Chapters 4–10 below.

Given the separability assumption, the overall size of the wealth portfolio is exogenous. The determination of this depends on the cumulated difference between income and expenditure, plus or minus any capital gains and losses, and in real terms taking account of the impact of inflation. For each sector, different considerations arise, which we deal with at greater length in the sectoral chapters below. For example the household sector is typically assumed to accumulate net financial wealth according to a life-cycle pattern with accumulation over working life, and possible decumulation in retirement (Section 5.1).

The determination of asset returns is also omitted by the framework, although it results in effect from the combination of asset demands and supplies from each sector. The simplest approach to asset price determination is the capital asset pricing model (CAPM), which we now outline briefly (see Bodie *et al.*, 1999, and Cuthbertson, 1996, for more detail). The rationale for holding a portfolio of risky assets rather than a single risky asset is that, by combining different assets whose returns are not perfectly positively correlated, the variance of the return of the overall portfolio is reduced by holding several assets. It is indeed optimal to hold a certain proportion of all risky assets (the global portfolio) in order to minimise risk on the portfolio of risky assets.

The simplest form of the CAPM (the two-fund or mutual fund separation theorem) then suggests that the individual investor's choice can be separated into two decisions. First, there is the share of wealth to hold in the risky portfolio, determined by risk aversion, needs for liquidity, transaction costs and so on. Second, there is the proportion of each risky asset to hold in the risky portfolio, which is independent of preferences. According to this simplification, all investors would hold assets in the same proportion in the risky portfolio, due to homogeneous assumptions about expected returns, variances and covariances of risky asset returns. Note that the share of assets held in each form is only entirely freely determined when borrowing and lending at the market rate are feasible. Then the equilibrium expected return on each asset relative to the risk free rate $(ER_i - r)$ will depend on the expected excess return on the risky market portfolio (chosen by all investors) $(ER^m - r)$ modified by $\beta_i$, the covariance of the asset's return with the market portfolio divided by the variance of the market portfolio. Thus

$$(ER_i - r) = \beta_i(ER^m - r) \tag{1.2}$$

or

$$ER_i = r + \beta_i(ER^m - r) \tag{1.3}$$

where

$$\beta_i = \text{cov}(R_i, R^m) / \text{var}(R^m) \tag{1.4}$$

In general , the expected return on risky assets has to be greater than that on a risk free asset, to induce investors to accept willingly the corresponding risk. Clearly, for assets which move in line with the markets $(\beta_i = 1)$ the return is equal to the market return. For instruments that have $\beta_i > 1$ the return has to exceed the market return. However, risky assets that have a low correlation with the market portfolio $(\beta_i < 1)$ will be willingly held at a lower return than the market owing to diversification benefits.

Considering the analysis in terms of a risk/return trade-off, each asset can be represented as a point on a graph showing its own risk and return characteristics. Assets can be combined into portfolios with superior risk/return characteristics to individual assets, owing to diversification. Then one can derive the 'frontier of efficient portfolios' composed of a variety of such portfolios, where one cannot obtain a higher return for the same risk or a lower risk for the same return. The frontier shows portfolios that eliminate idiosyncratic risk associated with individual assets, but not systematic risk due to the market as a whole. There is only one efficient frontier for a given set of assets. Assuming, as set out above, that the investors' choices depend on risk and return, it is optimal to choose a point on the frontier depending on preferences.

If there is no lending or borrowing permitted, the agent must choose a point on the frontier. If however, the agent is allowed either to borrow to lever returns, or to lend at a risk free rate, there will be a single optimal point on the frontier which they will hold as a 'risky asset', varying their risk and return by such borrowing or lending along the 'transformation line' according to their preferences, see Figure 1.9. In effect, such a line gives better risk and return combinations than are available from any other point on the frontier. Risk averse investors choose a point to the left of the tangency by lending and risk lovers a point to the right by borrowing. The slope

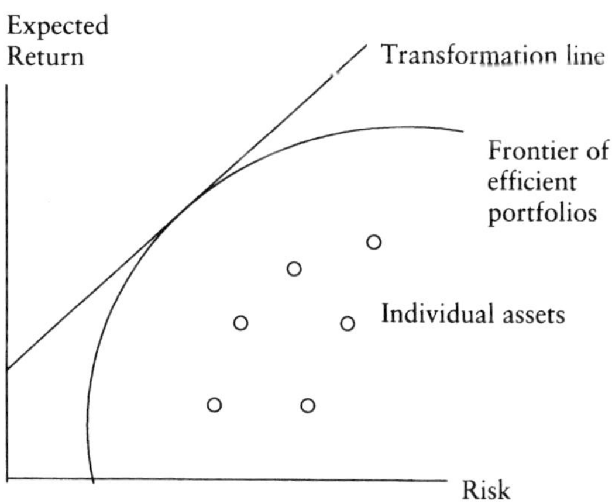


Figure 1.9 *The frontier of efficient portfolios*

of the transformation line or capital market line shows how individuals trade off risk for return and is often called the market price of risk. In order for this result to hold, again with all agents holding risky assets in the same proportion, all agents must have the same expectation of risk and return for each asset, as derived from the equations above.

Note that the CAPM does not imply that returns are constant. Rather, they will vary with their changing covariance with the market portfolio. The model can be extended to allow for borrowing or lending being possible but not at the risk free rate (due to credit constraints). Then the individual chooses a different optimal portfolio along the frontier by an appropriate combination of an arbitrary mean-variance efficient portfolio and a 'zero beta' portfolio whose return is both uncorrelated with that portfolio and a minimum variance portfolio along the frontier. One can also allow for differing borrowing and lending rates, non-marketable assets, taxes and inflation (in the absence of indexed assets), with broadly similar results to the standard model, although transactions costs limiting individual stock holding or heterogeneous expectations make the model intractable (Cuthbertson, 1996).

The mean-variance approach and the CAPM both imply a choice between assets which depends on the mean and variance of the return on the assets. The mean-variance approach can in principle be made into a model of asset returns where the excess return depends on variance, risk aversion and the exogenous supply of the asset in question – or, as noted,

Table 1.1 *Annual real asset returns and risks over 1967–1995*

| Average real return (and standard deviation) | Short-term assets | Loans | Domestic bonds | Domestic shares | Real estate | Foreign equities | Foreign bonds | Memo CPI inflation | Memo Average earnings |
|---|---|---|---|---|---|---|---|---|---|
| Canada | 2.7 | 4.2 | 2.0 | 5.0 | 9.4 | 8.2 | 5.1 | 5.7 | 1.5 |
| | *3.3* | *3.1* | *13.3* | *15.8* | *8.3* | *17.8* | *15.0* | *3.4* | *2.3* |
| France | 2.9 | 3.3 | 2.5 | 7.7 | 4.3 | 6.9 | 3.8 | 6.3 | 2.9 |
| | *3.4* | *3.3* | *15.8* | *18.4* | *14.5* | *17.2* | *14.5* | *4.2* | *2.4* |
| Germany | 3.1 | 6.8 | 3.9 | 10.8 | 10.9 | 5.5 | 2.4 | 3.5 | 3.0 |
| | *2.1* | *2.0* | *15.7* | *23.8* | *11.5* | *21.4* | *17.4* | *1.9* | *2.8* |
| Italy | −0.3 | 4.3 | −2.0 | 4.1 | na | 7.9 | 4.9 | 9.4 | 3.3 |
| | *4.4* | *3.7* | *20.8* | *32.5* | na | *16.3* | *14.5* | *5.9* | *4.4* |
| Japan | −0.2 | 1.4 | 3.1 | 8.5 | 11.5 | 7.8 | 4.4 | 4.7 | 3.5 |
| | *4.5* | *4.7* | *19.5* | *20.9* | *19.4* | *20.4* | *12.8* | *5.1* | *3.7* |
| UK | 2.1 | 1.7 | 1.0 | 8.3 | 1.5 | 8.0 | 4.1 | 8.1 | 2.8 |
| | *4.6* | *6.1* | *14.9* | *17.8* | *15.3* | *17.7* | *15.7* | *5.4* | *2.2* |
| US | 2.0 | 3.8 | 1.2 | 2.0 | 5.6 | 8.5 | 5.5 | 5.5 | −0.1 |
| | *2.3* | *2.3* | *15.2* | *2.3* | *22.1* | *18.7* | *14.9* | *3.0* | *1.8* |

Source: Davis (2002c). Note: na = not available.

by deriving demands by all sectors. The difference between CAPM and mean-variance is that the mean-variance approach uses a representative individual who has subjective preferences for the rate at which he will substitute risk for return. Hence the above-mentioned need for a given form of the utility function. In the CAPM, the separation theorem allows the portfolio choice between risky assets to be separated from the investor's preference about risk, so that all investors hold the same risky portfolio, and asset demands depend on the additional return on the market portfolio per unit of risk on the market portfolio.

In a global market with no transaction costs, one can apply the international CAPM, implying that all investors hold the global portfolio (see also Chapter 7). Barriers to capital mobility, taxation, transactions costs (for example, of hedging exchange rate risk) and heterogeneous expectations help to explain why both asset returns and portfolio shares vary across countries in a way not predicted by the CAPM.

In this context, Table 1.1 shows average asset returns and risks on the main asset categories in the G-7 since 1967. Note that these are real returns and their corresponding risks. Nominal returns will be boosted by the corresponding rate of inflation in the country concerned. They are also total returns, with estimated capital gains and losses on bonds, equities and real estate being added to the yield. Foreign asset returns are calculated by use of a simple weighting scheme of nominal total returns to G-7 country equities and bonds, based on rough estimates of world capitalisation weights.[4] These weighted returns are then derived in domestic currency in real terms by subtracting the change in the nominal effective exchange rate and the domestic inflation rate.

It is shown that the highest real returns are typically from (domestic) equities, which also have the greatest volatility. Other high-return assets are property and foreign equities, followed by bonds and loans, and finally short-term assets. As regards standard deviations, risks on foreign assets are generally lower than for domestic assets of the same type. This is because of the diversification benefits of foreign assets, which more than offset exchange rate risk. Meanwhile, contrary to the expectations of finance theory, the volatility pattern is not entirely congruent with the pattern of real yields, with total returns on bonds showing a relatively high volatility despite rather low real returns. This is partly linked to the fact that, in the 1970s, bond yields rose sharply with high and volatile unanticipated inflation, a pattern that was unique in history and has been much less characteristic of the 1980s and 1990s. Table 1.1 also shows inflation and real average earnings. The latter has been an average of 2 per cent for the countries shown. Inflation averaged 6 per cent over the period shown, although levels for individual countries vary significantly. Further data on asset returns and inflation are provided in Chapter 3.

Summarising the CAPM, the most basic aim of economic agents on both the asset and liability side is to achieve an optimal trade-off of risk and return by allocation of the portfolio to appropriately diversified combinations of assets (and in some cases liabilities, i.e. leveraging the portfolio by borrowing). The precondition for such an optimal trade-off is the ability to attain the frontier of efficient portfolios, where there is no possibility of increasing return without increasing risk, or of reducing risk without reducing return. Any portfolio where it is possible to increase return without raising risk is inefficient and is dominated by a portfolio with more return for the same risk. The exact trade-off chosen will depend on objectives, preferences and constraints.

In terms of objectives, there is a need to assess where on the above-mentioned optimal risk return trade-off the agent wishes to be, in other words his risk tolerance in pursuit of return. As regards constraints, these

4 A cross-check with the MSCI world index revealed similar risks and returns.

may include liquidity, investment horizon, inflation sensitivity, regulations, tax and accounting considerations and unique needs:

- liquidity based constraints link to the need to withdraw funds as a lump sum, or for regular disbursement;
- the investment horizon relates to the planned liquidation date of the financial investment, and is often measured by the concept of effective maturity or duration;[5]
- inflation sensitivity relates to the need to hold assets as inflation hedges;
- tax considerations may change the nature of the trade-off separately from underlying returns and risks;
- accounting rules can generate different 'optimal' portfolios;
- finally there is the influence of financial regulations, which affect, in particular, financial institutions but generally do not affect the non-financial sectors.

We now turn to an overview of economic theory relevant to financial structure *per se*.

## 1.2 JUSTIFICATIONS FOR THE EXISTENCE OF THE FINANCIAL SYSTEM

A key question to arise from a broad examination of comparative balance sheets of the G-7 is why sectoral balance sheets feature intermediated as well as non-intermediated claims, and why securities have the features they do? Why, in other words, do financial intermediaries exist, and what explains the type of instruments traded in financial markets?

We can define the financial system as encompassing (i) financial markets and institutions, and (ii) the overall balance sheet and flow relationships between the different sectors. These entail not merely flows and stocks of assets, but also the relationships and related flows of information and influence (Schmidt *et al.*, 2001).

The existence of financial systems needs to be justified in economic terms because in the Arrow-Debreu world, and indeed in the simpler portfolio and asset pricing theory set out in Section 1.1, the financing of firms (and governments) by households would occur directly in a frictionless manner – there are no information asymmetries or transactions costs. This leaves no role for financial intermediaries, nor for most of the familiar features

5 Duration is the average time to an asset's discounted cash flows.

of real world financial markets. There would exist a full set of contingent markets in which all can participate to obtain any form of insurance that is required. Credit markets also being perfect, individuals would not face credit rationing and could always borrow to attain their life-cycle optimum level of consumption. Allocation of resources would be Pareto optimal and there would be no role for intermediaries to add value. In addition (employing Modigliani-Miller, 1958, see Section 4.1), balance sheet structure would be irrelevant. This is because in a world such as that described, households can construct portfolios which offset the actions of an intermediary or corporation, and intermediation cannot add any value (Fama, 1980).

As noted by Allen and Santomero (1998), the traditional theory of financial intermediation is focused on the real-world market features of transactions costs and asymmetric information.[6] Intermediaries in this context include not only banks but also institutional investors such as insurance companies, pension funds and mutual funds.

The idea of transactions costs, first developed in the context of the theory of the firm by Coase (1937), was introduced as a key form of friction in financial markets by Gurley and Shaw (1960). Accordingly, economies of scale which benefit intermediaries result from indivisibilities and nonconvexities in transactions technology which restrict diversification and risk sharing under direct financing. Examples include fixed costs of evaluating assets, and declining average trading costs which mean intermediaries may diversify more cheaply than individuals. The 'liquidity insurance' which banks provide to depositors and borrowers (whereby deposits can be cashed on demand while banks' assets are mainly long-term and illiquid) also results from scale economies in risk pooling (Diamond and Dybvig, 1983). Active securities markets also provide forms of risk pooling, via market liquidity. Both banks and markets are vulnerable in this context to forms of liquidity failure caused by runs, although only in the case of banks can such illiquidity lead on directly to insolvency.

The existence of asymmetries of information between borrowers and lenders, combined with the inability to write complete contracts, specifying behaviour in all circumstances, gives rise to difficulties in financing. Specifically, there are problems of screening the quality of entrepreneurs and firms to avoid adverse selection (Leland and Pyle, 1977) and monitoring their performance to minimise moral hazard (Diamond, 1984). Adverse selection is an *ex ante* problem (arising before the contract is agreed). It can be defined as a situation where a pricing policy induces a low average quality of sellers in a market, where asymmetric information prevents the

6 For a summary, see Bhattacharya and Thakor (1993).

buyer from distinguishing quality. Moral hazard is an *ex post* issue (after the contract is agreed). It relates to the incentive of the beneficiary of a fixed value in the presence of asymmetric information and incomplete contracts, to change behaviour after the contract has been signed, to maximise wealth to the detriment of the provider of the contract.

In terms of debt finance, adverse selection may arise from the fact that those taking loans at high interest rates will be those less likely to pay back. So there is a conflict between the need to charge a risk premium over the risk free interest rate (to cover the risk of default) and the fact that the average quality of borrowers is lower, the higher the interest rate. Moral hazard can be viewed in terms of conflict between holders of debt (such as banks lending money to a firm) and of equity. Equity holders prefer a riskier investment plan although it does not maximise the overall value of the firm and is contrary to the lender's interests. Note that moral hazard is distinct from fraud. Moral hazard increases, the higher is the debt/equity ratio, or correspondingly the lower is net worth (assets less liabilities) or capital adequacy (equity as a proportion of assets).

If moral hazard and adverse selection problems are not overcome, borrowers may be subject to credit rationing in the sense of Stiglitz and Weiss (1981), with some borrowers of a group that are otherwise identical being unable to access credit. Intermediaries are considered to cope better than securities market investors with asymmetric information. Leland and Pyle (1977) suggested that intermediaries could communicate proprietary information at lower cost than borrowers, and then sell claims to diversified portfolios of these assets to investors. Diamond (1984) suggests that financial intermediaries act as delegated monitors to overcome asymmetric information, whereby diversification reduces monitoring costs. Non-traded bank loans based on private information are the likely preferred option in terms of instruments.

The advantage of intermediaries making non-traded loans is reinforced by the free-rider problem to which markets are subject. Investors in securities, who undertake information acquisition, find that others can profit from their findings at no cost to themselves. Inadequate provision of information leads to adverse selection (overvalued securities are most likely to be offered for sale) and moral hazard (inability of markets to monitor and enforce to the extent desirable).

A corollary is that market finance tends to be available only to borrowers with a reputation. Hence, small firms with low levels of public information will be served by banks, while larger firms, with a higher degree of public information, will have the option to be served by debt-securities markets, if they exist in the country concerned, or if firms can access international capital markets.

The issues of moral hazard, adverse selection and free riding are of pervasive importance in the financial sector, underlining as they do the importance of incentives in financial contracts (see Chai and Johnston, 2000). Other examples of such incentive issues arise for corporate governance (Section 1.3), the counterpart of the above-mentioned debt-related problems for the equity market, as well as such features as:

- Contagion, whereby trading in one market affects another, as investors cannot distinguish cross-market hedging and information based trades; or for banks where there is uncertainty over balance sheet structure, so depositors run from banks that are perceived to have similar loan portfolios to others that are in difficulty;
- Rational herding – whereby either (i) the payoff of a lending or investment strategy increases with the number adopting it; (ii) there is safety in numbers in an imperfectly informed market – no-one will blame a trader or lender if all make the same mistake; or (iii) traders or lenders assume others have superior information and follow their actions, ignoring their own information.

The theories of transactions costs/economies of scale and information asymmetry are not the only bases for intermediation (Davis and Mayer 1991). Under 'commitment' or 'relationship banking', banks can offer long-term relationships to borrowers not available in the debt-securities markets (often underpinned by bank equity stakes). These reduce information asymmetry and moral hazard, and may allow a lesser incidence of credit rationing in recessions for firms benefiting from such insurance (Allen and Gale, 2000). This concept is discussed further in Section 1.5 below.

Meanwhile, theories of intermediation based on 'control' also highlight the incompleteness of loan contracts and suggest that intermediaries are better able than markets to influence the behaviour of borrowers while a loan is outstanding, and seize assets or restructure in the case of default (Bolton and Freixas, 2000). The corollary of control theory is that a higher degree of risk in a transaction will tend to be accompanied by bank financing, as banks are better able to influence the behaviour of borrowers while a loan is outstanding, and seize assets or restructure in the case of default.

## 1.3 CORPORATE GOVERNANCE

Apart from transactions costs, the above paradigms broadly justify the existence of intermediaries as a response to market failures of adverse selection and moral hazard in debt finance. These market failures may be yet more severe in equity finance, raising the issue of corporate governance. Given the divorce of ownership and control in the modern corporation, shareholders cannot perfectly control managers acting on their behalf. Hence principal-agent problems arise. Managers (agents) have superior information about the firm and its prospects and at best a partial link of their compensation to the firms' profitability.[7] As a consequence, they may divert funds in their own interests and to the disadvantage of shareholders (principals), reducing dividends (payment of which is discretionary). Forms of diversion of funds may include expropriation or diversion of cash flow to unprofitable projects.[8]

Evidence for such agency costs includes the frequent observation that share prices of bidder firms fall when acquisitions are announced (Roll, 1986), resistance of managers to take-overs that threaten their positions (Walkling and Long, 1984), and the premium offered to shares with voting rights (Zingales, 1995). As Schleifer and Vishny (1997) noted, shareholders are much more vulnerable than other stakeholders in the firm, such as workers and creditors. Workers can withdraw labour, and creditors can refuse debt finance and apply pressure on the managers by those means. Whereas it may be argued that managers' desire to maintain reputation in the market will help to protect shareholders (Kreps, 1990), it may not be sufficient.

Principal-agent problems in equity finance imply a need for shareholders to exert control over management, while also remaining sufficiently distinct from managers to let equity holders buy and sell shares freely without breaking insider trading rules. If difficulties of such 'corporate governance' are not resolved, equity finance will tend to be unduly costly and often subject to quantitative restrictions.[9]

---

7 Performance-related pay, the use of share options, and similar devices may help to align managers' and shareholders' interests. But such contracts may themselves worsen the governance problem by leading to heightened incentives for self-dealing, with managers negotiating such contracts when they know that performance may improve.

8 Beyond theft, transfer pricing, and asset sales, expropriation may take forms such as perquisites, high salaries, diversion of funds to pet projects, and general entrenchment even in cases in which managers are no longer competent or qualified to run the firm.

9 Investor overoptimism may play a periodic role in the provision of external finance. See, for example, evidence on the overvaluation of junk bonds used to finance US takeovers in the 1980s in Kaplan and Stein (1993) and of new equity issues by Ritter (1991). But this sentiment tends to be highly cyclical.

As outlined in Davis and Steil (2001), a key to all successful forms of corporate governance is mechanisms for legal protection of shareholders. These include the right to vote on important corporate matters, notably mergers, as well as elections of boards of directors. There may also be a legally enforceable duty of loyalty by managers to shareholders (see Schleifer and Vishny, 1997). Boards of directors, in particular non-executive directors, act as shareholders' representatives in monitoring management and ensuring that the firm is run in their interests. Shareholder influence is ensured by their right to vote on choice of directors (as well as other elements of policy proposed by management). On the other hand, if boards are weakly supervised by shareholders, they may act in managers' interests rather than those of shareholders (Jensen, 1993), or they will be passive in all but extreme circumstances (Kaplan, 1994).

Hence effectiveness of corporate governance typically also requires the presence of large investors, be they banks, other companies, or institutional investors. They will have the leverage to oblige managers to distribute profits to providers of external finance. They are needed because individual investors may find it difficult to enforce their rights, even if these are legally enshrined. Underlying these difficulties are information asymmetries vis-à-vis managers, the difficulty of forming coalitions to act in a concerted manner against management, and free rider problems. Large investors may find it easier than small investors to enforce their rights in court.[10]

There is also a downside to large investors, as they may override the interests of minority shareholders (La Porta *et al.*, 1999). Consistent with this downside, Morck *et al.* (1988) found that profitability is higher for firms with shareholders that have up to 5 per cent stakes; beyond that, profitability falls. This pattern may indicate that larger, block-holding investors seek to generate private benefits of control that are not shared by minority shareholders. Institutional shareholders are often limited, either by regulation or by a desire to maintain liquidity, to holding a maximum 5 per cent of a firm's equity. Davis (2002a) shows that a rise in institutional-investor shareholding is linked to improvements in aspects of corporate sector performance at a macro level.

## 1.4 A FUNCTIONAL APPROACH TO THE FINANCIAL SYSTEM

A further issue is why national financial systems fulfil similar functions

10 Note that this argument suggests that households will be justified in being more willing to provide equity finance via institutions than they would directly.

while having very different institutional and balance sheet structure, as revealed in the financial accounts.

Consideration of the overall functions of the financial system in effect encompasses the reasons for existence of intermediaries and markets set out in Section 1.2, and allows a richer menu of activities to be covered by the subject of intermediation. It is particularly helpful in assessing financial development. A functional approach to the financial system seeks to isolate constant features both of long-term trends and of more recent developments. In effect, whereas the institutional form taken by financial systems is subject to evolution through time, the functions fulfilled by the financial system are relatively fixed.

The evolution of institutional forms and of financial structure, such as the growth of mutual funds, may thus be seen as a form of adaptation and improvement in the ways these functions are fulfilled, under pressure from competitive forces. Financial evolution is seen as a form of 'innovation spiral' as innovations drive the system towards greater efficiency. Various paradigms have been proposed. Merton and Bodie (1995) focus on six functions, as follows:

(a) the provision of means for clearing and settling payments to facilitate exchange of goods, services and assets;
(b) the provision of a mechanism for pooling of funds from individual households so as to facilitate large-scale indivisible undertakings, and the subdivision of shares in enterprises to facilitate diversification;
(c) provision of means to transfer economic resources over time, across geographic regions, countries or among industries;
(d) provision of means to manage uncertainty and control risk;
(e) providing price information, thus helping to co-ordinate decentralised decision-making in various sectors of the economy;
(f) providing means to deal with incentive problems when one party to a financial transaction has information the other does not, or when one is an agent of the other, and when control and enforcement of contracts is costly.

In this context, growth of certain types of financial intermediary (or market) is partly explicable in terms of a changing comparative advantage in terms of the functions they fulfil.

To give an example of the functional approach, one may examine the role of banks and the competition they face (see also Davis, 2000, on a functional analysis of pension funds and Davis and Steil, 2001, on institutional investors). Hence in terms of clearing and settling payments, banks provide payments services but so, increasingly, do markets and money market funds. For pooling, bank loan books are in the form of diversified portfolios, but so are the asset portfolios of institutional investors. Regarding transfer of economic resources over time and space, banks are able to accomplish this via transformation in terms of maturity and via foreign and industrial lending – but so do bond markets. To manage uncertainty and control risk, we can say that banks in themselves limit risk to depositors by providing liquid deposits which are insulated by bank capital from volatility of the value of loans (liquidity insurance). In markets, the provision of such insulation may require the use of derivatives. Concerning price information, banks as noted tend to rely on private information, although their lending itself may thus offer information to others. Markets require public information. Finally banks have a comparative advantage for small and information intensive assets (such as small business loans) in overcoming incentive problems.

## 1.5 BANK-BASED VERSUS MARKET-BASED SYSTEMS

Why do we see major contrasts between financial systems in terms of the size of the banking sector relative to securities markets, in the composition of corporate balance sheets and in modes of corporate governance?

Following the discussion above, it can be seen that a financial system has two goals, to channel resources to the most productive use (allocation) and ensure returns for financiers (governance). Following from the paradigms of intermediation given in Section 1.2, and fulfilling in different ways the financial functions set out in Section 1.4, there are well-known contrasts in the behaviour of financial institutions and markets in the major OECD countries, notably as they relate to the financing, governance and monitoring of companies.

The general division is between the Anglo-Saxon systems of the United Kingdom, United States, Canada, and Australia on the one hand and the systems that have prevailed historically in Continental Europe and Japan on the other. We shall employ this paradigm to characterise financial systems throughout the book, albeit emphasising that they are benchmarks rather than accurate descriptions of financial systems in the real world (we seek to make an overall assessment in Section 11.1). We suggest that the core of the traditional distinction between the two systems is in terms of the finance and control of corporations, distinguishing between direct control via debt and market control via equity (see Davis, 1995a). This is manifested in differing balance sheet structure.

Relationship-based financial systems along the lines of the stylised German or Japanese model follow the commitment paradigm, as outlined in Section 1.2 above. This typically involves companies having exclusive financing relationships with a small number of creditors and equity holders. External finance itself is largely in the form of bank loans. Accordingly, households gain liquidity from banks and diversification indirectly via the assets held in banks' portfolios. Firms depend to a considerable extent on internal finance, which they may obtain not only via retained earnings but also by balance-sheet pension reserves. On the equity side, banks are significant shareholders in their own right and in Germany are represented on supervisory boards both as equity holders and as creditors; there is also widespread cross-shareholding among companies.[11]

Long-term relationships in this system reduce information asymmetry and agency costs. Private information becomes more important than public, which may give rise to information rents to providers of external finance. Desire by intermediaries to maintain reputation reduces risks of exploitation of such exclusive relationships. In these countries, banks exert corporate governance most decisively via their control rights as creditors. They may influence the firm by varying the maturity of debt as well as taking control when firms default or violate debt contracts.[12] They may also provide rescue finance to firms in financial difficulty, recouping the expense by charging higher spreads when the firm recovers. Besides direct equity holdings and creditor links, banks in these countries have also been able to exert control through the voting rights conferred on them by custody of bearer shares of individual investors who have surrendered their proxies.

In terms of corporate finance, bank lending dominates and securities markets and institutional investment (other than insurance) are of minor importance, with bond issues and equity issues not playing a major role in fundraising by firms. In terms of corporate governance, the influence of non-bank financial shareholders is often limited by voting restrictions, countervailing influence of corporate shareholders, and lack of detailed financial information, as well as the right of other stakeholders (such as employees, suppliers, and creditors) to representation on boards. Many firms are in any case not quoted. Implicitly, monitoring of managers is delegated to a trusted intermediary – the bank. In practice, equity holders are often discriminated against in such systems, to the advantage of the

11 However, bi-directional cross-holdings are typically means of cementing alliances or collusion rather than exerting control.

12 Hoshi *et al.* (1993b) show how profitable Japanese firms sought to avoid the costs of bank links when access to public debt issuance was liberalised.

creditors, for example in terms of dividends. Such discrimination may make minority investors unwilling to invest, leaving equity markets themselves underdeveloped.[13] The system may be vulnerable to development of securities markets and institutional investors, as well as to enhanced banking competition (Davis and Steil, 2001).

Summarising the characteristics expected of relationship banking systems (adapted from Schmidt *et al.*, 2001), they include:

- banks dominate the financial sector, while institutional investors play a minor role;
- household accumulation is mainly in the form of claims on banks and insurance companies;
- households may be credit-rationed, reflecting the precedence given to companies;
- internal finance of firms is important for finance of investment; pension reserves are an important source of internal financing for companies;
- external financing of firms depends on long-term bank loans, underpinned by close relationships;
- complementing corporate finance, pension systems are social security (pay-as-you-go) or internally financed by corporations;
- capital markets are underdeveloped;
- cross-shareholding among companies is high;
- most companies are not quoted; those that are, are held by few large shareholders;
- shareholders are joined by other stakeholders in corporate governance, such as employees; stakeholders are encouraged to make firm-specific investments;
- external control by the capital market is low.

Arm's-length or market-oriented financial systems are commonly thought to be typified by the UK and US systems (see our own assessment in Section 11.1). Liquid and thick financial markets provide the range of financial instruments that economic agents need; and liquid financial markets reduce investment risk and open up scope for diversification by investors. Monitoring is provided by specialists such as rating agencies and venture capital firms, as well as commercial and investment banks. Short-term spot

13 Note that there is also evidence that banks may be inadequate as monitors, not seeking to discipline managers as long as the firm is far from default (Harris and Raviv, 1990).

transactions rather than long-term relationships predominate, with external financing of corporations taking place by short-term bank lending and bond issuance, as well as equity issuance. Debt financiers are protected only by explicit contracts and legal enforcement; creditors may intervene only when liquidation is threatened. Public information is predominant. Institutional investors, notably pension funds, are more important than banks, with households accumulating funded pension claims with them.

In respect of governance, hostile takeover activity, which is a distinguishing mark of Anglo-Saxon systems, seeks to resolve the conflict of interest between management and shareholders; the firms that deviate most extensively from shareholders' objectives – and that consequently tend to have lower market values as shareholders dispose of their holdings – have a greater likelihood of being acquired. The threat of take-over, as much as its manifestation, acts as a constraint on managerial behaviour. Institutional shareholders, both directly and via non-executive directors, can have an important role to play in this context, both in complementing takeover pressure as a monitoring constraint on management behaviour and in evaluating takeover proposals when they arise.

Summarising the characteristics expected of arm's length financial systems (adapted from Schmidt *et al.*, 1999), they include:

- household accumulation is mainly in the form of capital market investment, directly or indirectly via institutional investors, and in particular households accumulate funded pension claims, with pay-as-you-go social security being less generous;
- institutional investors dominate the financial sector, while banks play a minor role;
- capital markets are highly developed;
- market-based financial systems offer debt more readily to households, either held on banks' books or securitised;
- external financing of firms depends heavily on capital markets, either directly (new issues of debt or equity) or indirectly (securitised loans), and institutional investors are major suppliers of it;
- bank credit to companies is short-term and at arm's length (i.e. on a transaction-by-transaction rather than a relationship basis);
- most companies are quoted and are widely held; cross-shareholdings are rare;
- corporate control is directed to shareholder value via market mechanisms (takeovers);
- external control by the capital market is high;
- relations of firms to other stakeholders such as labour are based on

explicit short-term contracts, which does not encourage firm-specific investment.

In terms of empirical studies, work on financial systems has in some cases tended to validate these stylised facts. For example, Schmidt *et al.* (2001), looking at the UK, France and Germany, found that the features in the two bulleted lists indeed characterised Germany on the one hand and the United Kingdom on the other. They suggested that both systems exhibit considerable path-dependence. France, on the other hand, was felt to be in a state of transition, with some features of one system and some of the other. For example, the capital market has become more important as a source of funds and destination for household saving, while cross-shareholdings between firms remain sizeable and pension funds have yet to develop. The controlling function of the state in corporate governance, directly or via the 'elites' has faded and has yet to be replaced.

On the other hand, Scholtens (1997) criticises the clear distinctions often put forward in the literature. He finds indeed that the relative sizes of banks and pension funds, equity in company liabilities and household assets, and characteristics of corporate governance fit in with the traditional distinction. But in terms of bank dominance in corporate finance, short-term lending, bank and market competitiveness, the scope of market finance, derivatives and firm indebtedness, less evidence was seen of the expected differences, with individual countries showing idiosyncratic patterns thought to be related to 'financial regulation, culture and tradition'. We shall make our own evaluation of the degree to which the paradigms hold in Section 11.1, and of their relative costs and benefits in Section 11.4. It will be seen that most countries do not simply fit the paradigms, although a general trend towards Anglo-Saxon modes of financing and governance is apparent.

## 1.6 FINANCIAL DEVELOPMENT AND FINANCIAL STRUCTURE

An alternative approach helping to explain differences in financial structure looks on it as an evolutionary process. This is not entirely independent of the above paradigms, as relationship banking is often seen as an earlier phase of financial development than arm's-length financing.

There is a widespread perception, backed by empirical observation, that financial systems go through stages of development. For example, Rybczinski (1997) suggests that one can distinguish a bank, market and securitised phase. Most Emerging Market Economies (EMEs) are still in the bank-oriented phase, while OECD countries are either in the market or securitised phase (where 'securitised' implies a growing importance of securities finance generally rather than just packaging of loans in the form of securities).

Underlying changes in corporate financial structure during development can be traced in terms of corporate finance theory:

(1) An entrepreneur can begin a firm by relying on his own funds and retained earnings, but rapid growth of his enterprise requires access to external finance. The simplest form of this is from his family, who will be able to monitor him closely and hence protect their own interests.
(2) Banks tend to be the first to offer external funds, as they have a comparative advantage in monitoring and control of entrepreneurs lacking a track record, for example in terms of access to information, ability to take security and to exert control via short maturities.
(3) Equity issuance becomes important when companies' bank debt becomes sizeable in relation to existing own-funds, as the high resultant level of gearing gives rise to conflicts of interest between debt and equity holders. Banks may also protect themselves by means of covenants or even the acceptance of equity stakes, which internalise the associated agency costs.
(4) Corporate bond markets are only viable when firms have a very high reputation, as this then constitutes a capital asset, which would depreciate if the firm engaged in opportunistic behaviour (Diamond, 1991). High credit quality is needed because, due to free-rider problems etc, bond market investors are likely to have less influence and control over management than equity holders or banks, even if one allows for the existence of covenants. Rating agencies help to alleviate associated information problems, but do not thereby open the bond market for firms with poor reputations or volatile profitability.

Stylised facts drawn from empirical observation suggest a somewhat more complex pattern (see Allen and Gale, 2000), although the idea of phases remains helpful. As noted, Schmidt *et al.* (2001) argue that there is path dependence, meaning that a bank-based system such as Germany will not automatically develop into a market-based system. However, they acknowledge that a financial crisis, perhaps triggered by uncoordinated, far-reaching reforms, could lead to that result, because elements such as trust, implicit contracts and mutually consistent expectations which underpin relationship banking would be very difficult to rebuild after such a crisis.

Empirically, as shown by Demirgüç-Kunt and Levine (2000), banks, non-banks and stock markets are larger, more active and more efficient in richer countries. Furthermore, stock markets become more active and efficient relative to banks in OECD countries, and there is some tendency for financial systems to become more market-oriented as the countries become richer. Meanwhile, countries with a Common Law tradition, protection of shareholders' rights, sound accounting, low corruption and no explicit deposit insurance tend to be market-based, whatever their income level. In contrast, countries with a French Civil Law tradition, weaker protection of the rights of shareholders and creditors, weaker contract enforcement and accounting standards, restrictive banking regulation, high corruption and inflation tend to have underdeveloped banks and markets. The few countries with a German law tradition, which offers strong protection for creditors, tend to have strong bank-based systems.

Rajan and Zingales (2000) show that financial development has not been monotonic. The major OECD countries were, on some measures, more financially developed in 1913 than 1980, and a significant reversal in financial development and financial integration took place between 1913 and 1950. A tightening of regulation in that period led to a decline in the size and importance of the financial sector relative to GDP. Examples in the US were the separation of commercial and investment banking, interest rate ceilings and bans on interstate banking, in the wake of the Great Depression. Meanwhile, entry conditions to financial intermediation were tightened and capital controls were imposed in most countries after the Gold Standard came to an end. For a detailed description of historical trends in financial systems see Goldsmith (1969) and Allen and Gale (2000).

This tightening of regulation resulted, in Rajan and Zingales' view, from resistance of incumbents in the financial system to openness and competition in a period when economic developments were generally unfavourable. This meant that their concerns found a sympathetic hearing from non-financial players seeking insurance via deposit insurance, despite lower compensation for their claims. The imposition of such structural regulation implied that the financial service provided to the non-financial sector was suboptimal, with for example low deposit rates and rationing of credit to households. It did, however, prevent banks from taking excessive risks in response to the guarantee provided by the safety net of deposit insurance and the lender of last resort – a factor that has come to the fore in the aftermath of more recent liberalisation (see Section 1.7). The fact that the financial systems of the G-7 were still emerging from this highly-regulated period in 1970 should be borne in mind in assessing the data.

## 1.7 FACTORS UNDERLYING RECENT FINANCIAL CHANGE

A mere description of the different stylised phases of the development of the financial system does not tell us anything about the underlying causes of the evolution. Nor does it help to explain why financial systems in different industrial countries are currently at different phases, and what kind of development we would expect to see in the future. Therefore, it is important also to assess factors which underlie these changes, which may be classified under headings such as technological development; deregulation and liberalisation (i.e. the regulatory environment); increased and transformed wealth of individuals; and globalisation. These factors are very much interrelated, and authors differ in the emphases they put on what are often interlocking or mutually reinforcing causal relations.

One of the most important underlying factors shaping the structure of the financial system is the pattern of technological development that has been seen over recent decades. This has reshaped the relative costs of different banking and financial services and facilitated the production of new types of services. The costs of collecting, processing and using information have decreased dramatically.[14] This has for example entailed more efficient production of financial information and better techniques for assessing and pricing risks, in turn reducing the cost of external finance. On balance, it has tended to favour markets rather than banks in the context of the greater reliance of the former on public rather than private information. (Information Technology allows more information to become public and for public information to be more widely and rapidly disseminated.)

Technological development has also facilitated the rapid development of new financial products. While a large proportion of innovations could not have been possible without developments achieved in the theory of finance, it is mostly technological progress that has made the wide use of these innovations possible. The independent role of financial innovations is a debated issue, whereby some commentators would see them as a major factor in themselves in generating financial change, and some as by-products or natural consequences of technological development. A general point is that innovations help shift the financial system closer to the Arrow-Debreu paradigm, where contingent markets provide forms of insurance and financial intermediaries are less needed than hitherto.

---

14 At the same time, however, some have argued that financial services have in some fields become more capital intensive, leading to clearer economies of scale and scope.

The deregulation and liberalisation process that has been an ongoing issue for some time has also permitted an increase in the overall level of competition in the financial systems.[15] This has reversed the trends to regulation which had been imposed in the interwar and early postwar period, as highlighted above (Rajan and Zingales, 2000). Several major types of deregulation can be discerned (see Edey and Hviding, 1995):

- the abolition of interest-rate controls or cartels that fixed rates;
- the abolition of direct controls on credit expansion;
- the removal of capital controls;
- the removal of regulations restricting establishment of foreign institutions;
- the development and improvement of money, bond, and equity markets;
- the removal of regulations segmenting financial markets; and
- the deregulation of fees and commissions in financial services.

Partly to offset these, there has been a tightening of prudential supervision, particularly in relation to capital adequacy and often harmonised internationally. The Basel Capital Adequacy Accord of 1988 and its successor currently under negotiation are key examples (see Danielsson *et al.*, 2001, for a critical view of the new Accord).

This last point shows that liberalisation is not a removal of all regulation, but a shift in its locus from structural to prudential regulation. This step has indeed been essential, because otherwise the financial sector would take excessive risks. This was highlighted by Keeley (1990), who showed that, when the banking system is uncompetitive, a banking licence is valuable so that there is no incentive to take risks (higher market volatility and lower capital) and jeopardise it. When there is increased competition, the value of the bank franchise falls, so the loss from bankruptcy is less. Indeed, there is an incentive to go for higher risks, increasing margins at cost of heightened volatility of profits. This paradigm is applicable without a safety net of deposit insurance and the lender of last resort, but the latter worsens moral hazard (Greenbaum and Thakor, 1995). This is because incentives for depositors to monitor banks' risk profiles is nullified, and equity holders have heightened incentive to take risks or minimise capital to maximise the option value of insurance (unless the insurance is correctly priced).

The main motivations of the authorities in deregulating have been:

---

15 However, deregulation was arguably not always a causal factor in the way that the forces of technology and growth of institutional investors are, but was often a belated response to changes already underway.

- to increase competition (and hence to reduce costs of financial services);
- to improve access to credit for the private sector;
- to improve efficiency in determining financial prices and allocating funds;
- pressures from competition authorities to remove cartels;
- a desire to maintain competitiveness of domestic markets and institutions;
- increased flexibility and responsiveness to customers;
- facilitating financial innovations;
- securing a ready market for increasing sales of government bonds; and
- as mentioned, desire to secure stability of such a system against excessive risk-taking.

Note that these are broadly in line with the desire for an improvement in the way the various functions of the financial system set out in Section 1.4 are fulfilled. Securing of stability, however, has proved difficult to achieve, as witness the resurgence of financial instability since 1970 after a rather tranquil period since the 1930s (Davis, 1995b).

It would be wrong to see deregulation purely as a proactive shift by the authorities. In many cases, it was necessitated by structural and technological shifts that had already made existing regulations redundant. In this context, the role of institutional investors may be highlighted, whether indirectly or directly (Davis and Steil, 2001). Their own growth is a function of demography, the increased funding of pensions, rising wealth and development of securities markets. Notably, it was the willingness of institutions to bypass domestic securities markets that led to deregulation of fee and commission structures that were contrary to their interests (as in the case of the Big Bang in the United Kingdom). Governments more generally have sought to improve the functioning of their domestic bond markets, so as to satisfy the liquidity needs of institutional investors, in the hope of thereby reducing their own funding costs.

Abolition of exchange controls, in countries such as the United Kingdom and Japan, can be seen in the light of a desire to ease upward pressure on the exchange rate via capital outflows, in the context of growing pressure by institutions to invest offshore. The US deregulation of secondary trading of private placements (Article 144a) showed a recognition that institutions do not require elaborate investor protection – and was a response to fear of competition for domestic securities issuance generated by offshore issues of bonds to institutional investors.

Some of the banking deregulation that occurred in the 1980s was seen as an essential step owing to the intense competition that banks faced from institutions. The abolition of the US interest rate regulations (Regulation

Q) owing to competition from money market funds is a good example; easing of reserve requirements is another (although clearly, wholesale delocalisation of banking was also an implicit threat). The fact that institutional and capital-market competition left banks with lower quality credits made the removal of controls on credit expansion, on the one hand, and capital adequacy regulation, on the other, all the more urgent. Moreover, once the process of liberalisation began, one measure quickly led to others, owing to the desire to maintain a level playing field (within countries) and competitive equality (between countries).

As noted, the wealth of individuals has increased, and a larger proportion of the population is making portfolio investments. This partly results from changing demographics, i.e. ageing of the population, which in itself has increased the average wealth of people, but also from changes in pension systems in a number of countries from a pay-as-you-go to a funded basis (Davis, 1995a). The prospect for the future is for more such change. Some political economists also claim that due to this change in wealth, the political climate has become more investor-friendly. The increased number of wealthy individuals has changed the demand for financial services. Traditional banking services or products, while maintaining a strong position in liquidity provision, are not adequate for people interested in diversification and maximisation of return subject to risk in the context of long-term investments. The associated rise in demand for securities has entailed an increased importance of brokerage, fund management and consultancy activities. While there are new providers for these services, banks could remain at centre-stage, albeit with their services more oriented towards asset management, and hence a change in their income structure.

In addition to overall increase in wealth of individuals, the type of wealth typically held has changed towards financial instead of real wealth. That is manifested in the long-term increase in the relative market value of stock exchanges. The increase in financial wealth relates closely to the shift towards a securitised phase of financial markets and also to the increased importance of institutional investors. This is because they have a comparative advantage over direct holdings of securities by individuals, owing to superior possibilities of diversification, specialisation in information collection, sharing of asset management expertise and reduction in transactions costs for large trades.

To illustrate how these trends are impacting on the analysis given above, we outline how modernisation is affecting the various theories of intermediation set out in Section 1.2. Concerning transactions costs, the more developed markets are, the better their performance relative to intermediaries, and also technology is leading to a reduction in transactions costs for market intermediation, via securitisation of loans, commercial paper, electronic trading etc. The last of these factors also facilitates trading and diversification directly by individuals. Concerning liquidity insurance, demand for deposits is itself declining as individuals utilise credit cards, ATMs and other instruments which save in transactions costs. Concerning asymmetric information, development of rating agencies, and more generally better disclosure and accounting, are making the free rider disadvantages of markets relative to intermediaries less marked. The improvements in market infrastructure make a wider range of firms able to access debt securities markets.

More generally, Allen and Santomero (1998) suggest that these financial developments imply that the traditional arguments presented in Section 1.2 are no longer sufficient to justify intermediaries' existence and continued growth. Accordingly, a sound theory of intermediation should in their view also take into account the activity of risk transfer and risk control between and by intermediaries on the one hand, and facilitation of participation in markets by individuals on the other. Scholtens and van Wensveen (1999) suggest in addition that dynamic aspects of financial innovation and adaptation of institutions to gain competitive advantage should play a central role.

Equally, the above-mentioned developments underlie recent changes in the structure of the financial system. Following the classification in Section 1.5 above, financial systems are departing from the bank-oriented phase and becoming more market-oriented or even securitised. The share of deposits in household portfolios is declining, not only owing to shifts to long-term assets related to demography but also linked to general increases in wealth and consequent changes in preferences. Meanwhile, again aided by technology as noted above, the disintermediation process on the assets side is underway in a number of countries.

# 2 The key differences between the balance sheets

In a further introductory chapter, we now go on to discuss issues in the structure of national balance sheets which are used in Chapters 4–10 to illustrate financial structures. It should be noted at the outset that a number of key aspects of financing are not shown by data from national balance sheets. In particular, no detail is provided on the maturity, terms, liquidity and negotiability of different instruments. There are inevitably some important definitional differences (such as availability of data for households as opposed to the personal sector, which also includes unincorporated businesses). These need to be taken into account in interpreting the tables. Moreover, individual national balance sheets provide much more detail than the sector and instrument breakdown proposed, and hence some key assumptions, aggregations and omissions are needed to make the data broadly comparable. However, we maintain that a fairly simple breakdown is needed to ensure comparable coverage for all countries, which can be discussed on an economic basis. For similar reasons, as discussed below, we omit detail on trade credit (credit transacted between non-financial firms), given that its statistical treatment is different between countries.

Historically, there were important differences between the balance sheet tables. Fortunately, with the advent of such national balance sheet accounting standards as SNA 93 and ESA 95, the differences have become much less important than was the case before 1995 (see for example the discussion in Davis, 1986). Pan-European comparisons are likely to be particularly accurate for recent years. It remains the case that the data for 1970, 1980 and 1990 should be viewed with greater caution than later data. Note also that for data reasons the first UK observation is generally for 1975, except for households and companies. Moreover, some differences remain, as detailed here, notably between the US and other countries. Also some data are not available, denoted 'na' in the tables. Note that besides the discussion here, some further differences between balance sheets will be brought out when we assess the individual tables.

## 2.1 SOURCES OF DATA

The sources of the data are as follows (Internet addresses are subject to change):

*United States*

- Produced by Board of Governors of the Federal Reserve System.
- Publication: Flow of funds accounts for the United States.
- Internet: http://www.federalreserve.gov/releases/Z1/ (free download).
- Data available consistently from 1952 online
- Reference: Guide to the Flow of Funds Accounts, order from http://www.federalreserve.gov/releases/Z1/ffguide.htm (fee payable for publication).
- Flow and stock data produced 9-10 weeks after the end of the reporting period (source of timeliness information for all countries, Bertrand, 2000).

*United Kingdom*

- Produced by Office of National Statistics.
- Publication: Financial Statistics, Financial Balance Sheets.
- Internet: http://www.statistics.gov.uk/statbase/tsdtimezone.asp?vlnk=fsc (free download).
- Data available from 1987 online (definitions close to ESA 95) and from 1975 on paper (national definitions), with data from 1966 for the personal, company and non-bank financial institution sectors.
- Reference: Financial Statistics Explanatory Handbook.
- Flow and stock data produced 12 weeks after the end of the reporting period.

*France*

- Produced by Banque de France.
- Publication: The national financial accounts.
- Internet: http://www.banque-france.fr/gb/stat/main.htm (Free download).
- Data available from 1995 online (ESA 95), and from 1969 on paper (national definitions).

- Reference: General Presentation, http://www.banque-france.fr/gb/stat/cptanat/7a.htm.
- Flow and stock data produced 18 weeks after the end of the reporting period.

*Italy*
- Produced by Banca d'Italia.
- Publication: Supplements to the statistical bulletin; financial accounts.
- Internet: http://www.bancaditalia.it/pubblicazioni/statistiche/supplementi/pimecf;internal&action=contenuti.action (free download).
- Data available from 1997 online (ESA 95) and from 1965 on paper (national definitions).
- Reference: Methodological Appendix in the above publication. A Financial Accounts methodology manual was published in April 2002 (see *I conti finanziari dell'Italia*, *Tematiche istituzionali*, Banca d'Italia). An English translation will follow.
- Flow and stock data produced 22 weeks after the end of the reporting period.

*Canada*
- Produced by Statistics Canada.
- Publication: National balance sheet accounts, annual estimates.
- Internet: http://www.statcan.ca/english/IPS/Data/13-214-XDB.htm (Fee payable for diskettes).
- Data available consistently from 1961 on diskette.
- Reference: A guide to the financial flow and national balance sheet accounts, see http://www.statcan.ca/english/IPS/Data/13-585-XPE.htm (fee payable).
- Flow data produced 8 weeks after the end of the reporting period, and stock data 12 weeks after the end of the reporting period.

*Germany*
- Produced by Deutsche Bundesbank.
- Publication: Financial Accounts for Germany.
- Internet: http://www.bundesbank.de/stat/stat_veroeffentlichungen.en.php (free download).
- Data available from 1991 online (ESA 95), and from 1949 on paper (national definitions).
- Reference: see publication above.
- Flow and stock data produced 25 weeks after the end of the reporting period.

*Japan*

- Produced by Bank of Japan.
- Publication: Preliminary Estimates of Flow of Funds, also available in Bank of Japan Economic Statistics Monthly.
- Internet: http://www.boj.or.jp/en/siryo/siryo_f.htm (free download)
- Data available from 1990 (1993 SNA) and from 1964–1999 (1968 SNA) online, and from 1954 on paper.
- Reference: Guide to Japan's Flow of Funds Accounts, see http://www.boj.or.jp/en/down/siryo/data/faqsj.pdf.
- Flow and stock data produced 12 weeks after the end of the reporting period.

Our own work has entailed extensive gathering of historical material on paper in order to obtain data for periods earlier than those shown above to be available online or on diskette. The reader is referred to the explanatory sources listed above for more technical detail than can be provided in this chapter, as well as Bertrand (2000) and Bank of Japan (2000), which cover important related issues, the former covering all OECD countries and the latter covering the G-5.[16]

## 2.2 SECTORAL DIFFERENCES

In terms of sector breakdown, the balance sheets provide differing splits. As shown in Table 2.1, this has necessitated various types of aggregation. Sector definitions and breakdowns have also evolved for individual countries, except for the US and Canada, which provide consistent data back to before 1970 (1952 for the US and 1961 for Canada).

For the household/personal sector, the difficulty in comparability stems largely from the varying availability of data for unincorporated business (where the personal sector equals households plus unincorporated firms). The household sector is defined separately in the US, but unincorporated businesses are added for our purposes to provide comparable data on the personal sector. For Canada, only the personal sector (including unincorporated business) is available and we accordingly work with it. In the UK, Italy, France and Japan, only the personal sector is available for all or most of the earlier years. But from 1990 in the tables (UK) and 1998 (Italy,

16 In 2000, of 29 OECD countries, 20 compiled financial transaction (flow) accounts, 19 compiled stock data and 12 produced full balance sheet tables (Bertrand, *ibid*).

Table 2.1 *Balance sheet sectors and their aggregation*

*UK*

Household/personal: Personal sector to 1980; households and non-profit institutions serving households (NPISH) from 1990

Companies: Industrial and commercial companies, public corporations to 1980; private non-financial corporations, public non-financial corporations from 1990

Government: Central government, local authorities to 1980; general government from 1990

Foreign: Overseas to 1980; rest of the world from 1990

Financial institutions: Monetary sector, other financial institutions, Bank of England to 1980; monetary financial institutions, other financial intermediaries and auxiliaries, insurance corporations and pension funds from 1990

Banks: Monetary sector, Bank of England to 1980; monetary financial institutions from 1990

Insurance and pensions: Life assurance and pension funds to 1980, insurance corporations and pension funds from 1990

Mutual funds: Unit trusts, investment trusts

*US*

Households/personal sector: Households and non-profit organisations, non-farm non-corporate business, farms

Companies: Non-farm non-financial corporate business

Government: State and local government, federal government

Foreign: Rest of the world

Financial Institutions: Commercial banking, savings institutions, credit unions, bank personal trusts and estates, life insurance companies, other insurance companies, private pension funds, state and local government employee retirement funds, money market mutual funds, mutual funds, closed-end funds, government-sponsored enterprises, federally-related mortgage pools, issuers of asset backed securities, finance companies, mortgage companies, real estate investment trusts, security brokers and dealers, funding corporations, monetary authority

Banks: Commercial banking, savings institutions, credit unions, bank personal trusts and estates, monetary authority

Insurance and pensions: Life insurance companies, other insurance companies, private pension funds, state and local government employee retirement funds

Mutual funds: Money market mutual funds, mutual funds, closed-end funds

*Germany*

Household/personal: Households, housing to 1990; households and non-profit organisations from 1998

Companies: Enterprises except housing to 1990; non-financial corporations from 1998

Table 2.1 (*Continued*)

Government: Government to 1990; general government from 1998
Foreign: Rest of the world
Financial institutions: All financial sectors to 1990; domestic financial sectors, total from 1998
Banks: Banking institutions, building and loan associations to 1990; monetary financial institutions from 1998
Insurance and pensions: Insurance enterprises
Mutual funds: Investment funds

*Japan*
Household/personal: Personal sector to 1990; households and private non-profit organisations from 1998
Companies: Corporate business, public corporations to 1990; non-financial corporations from 1998
Government: Central government, local government to 1990; general government from 1998
Foreign: na to 1990; overseas from 1998
Financial institutions: Financial institutions
Banks: Banks, Bank of Japan to 1990; central bank plus depository corporations from 1998
Insurance and pensions: Trust (excluding securities investment trusts), insurance to 1990; insurance and pension funds from 1998
Mutual funds: Securities investment trusts

*Canada*
Households/personal sector: Persons and unincorporated business
Companies Non-financial private corporations, non-financial government corporations
Government: Government, social security funds
Foreign: Non-residents
Financial Institutions: Public and private financial institutions, monetary authorities, mutual funds
Banks: Chartered banks and near banks, total quasi banks, monetary authorities
Insurance and pensions: Life insurance companies and pension funds
Mutual funds: Mutual funds

*France*
Household/personal: Ménages, entreprises individuelles (households and unincorporated businesses) to 1990; households, non-profit organisations from 1998
Companies: Societés non financières, grandes enterprises nationales (non-financial firms and large nationalised firms) to 1990; non-financial corporations from 1998

Table 2.1 (*Continued*)

Government: État, organismes diverses d'administration centrale, administrations publiques locales, administrations de securité sociale (state, other central government, local government and social security administrations) to 1990; general government from 1998
Foreign: Étranger plus DOM-TOM (foreign sector plus overseas departments and territories) to 1990; rest of the world from 1998
Financial institutions: Banque de France, banques, caisses d'épargne, CDC, societés financière et assimilées, institutions financière diverses, OPCVM, organismes d'assurance et de capitalisation, mutuelles (Banque de France, banks, savings banks, other financial institutions, mutual funds, insurance sector) to 1990; financial corporations from 1998
Banks: Banque de France, banques, caisses d'épargne, CDC, societés financière et assimilées, institutions financière diverses (Banque de France, banks, savings banks, other financial institutions) to 1990; monetary financial institutions from 1998
Insurance and pensions: Organismes d'assurance et mutuelles (insurance and mutual sector) to 1990; insurance corporations from 1998
Mutual funds: OPCVM (mutual funds)

*Italy*
Household/personal: Famiglie (personal sector) to 1990; households and non profit institutions serving households from 1998
Companies: Imprese (enterprise sector) to 1990; non-financial corporations from 1998
Government: Settore pubblico (public sector) to 1990; general government from 1998
Foreign: Estere (foreign sector) to 1990; rest of the world from 1998
Financial institutions: Istituzioni creditizie (financial sector) to 1990; financial corporations from 1998
Banks: Banca d'Italia, Aziende di credito (Bank of Italy plus banks) to 1990; monetary financial institutions from 1998
Insurance and pensions: Istituti di assicurazione (insurance institutions) to 1990; insurance corporations and pension funds from 1998
Mutual funds: na

France, Japan) we can only use the household sector (including non-profit organisations serving households and sole traders), with other types of unincorporated businesses being included in the corporate sector. For Germany, we use the household sector plus housing for the years up to 1990 as a proxy for households. The latter is included since it incorporates mortgage loans, at a cost also of including some loans to construction companies. Unincorporated business in Germany is then included in companies. The last years for Germany use the common ESA95 definition (households plus non-profit organisations serving households and sole traders).

The issues for the corporate sector are largely a mirror image of those for households/persons. In the US, Canada, and other countries up to 1990, the corporate sector excludes unincorporated business, except in Germany. For 1998 and 2000, the sector includes unincorporated firms other than sole traders, except in the US and Canada. For cross-country consistency, and also in line with ESA 95, we have consistently included public non-financial corporations with private ones. Correspondingly, the definition of the public sector is general government, including local authorities and social security funds but excluding public corporations. In the US some public non-financial companies are included in general government and cannot be divided out, while public financial companies are included in the financial sector.

The financial sector is defined to include the central bank, and all financial institutions, as detailed in Table 2.1. Corresponding to the discussion of non-financial public corporations, public financial firms other than the central bank are also included in the financial sector. In some countries, the balance sheets provide a simple sum of all financial firms' assets and liabilities, while in countries such as the US, a considerable amount of aggregation has to be undertaken. This may affect the degree of consolidation (i.e. netting out of assets and liabilities), although most countries other than the US seek in the sector and aggregate tables to present unconsolidated figures, i.e. gross assets and liabilities.

The foreign sector is relatively straightforward, being identified separately in all the contemporary balance sheets (but not in Japan before 1998). We also provide complementary information on international investment positions from IMF harmonised balance-of-payments capital account data. In principle, the results should be the same, although in practice differences in valuation and coverage make for variations.

Turning to the subsectors, we define banks to include the central bank, in line with the 'Monetary Financial Institutions' concept. For Germany, banks are defined to include Housing Loan Institutions (*Bausparkassen*) and in the US, Savings Institutions are added to commercial banks. For EU countries, we also include money market mutual funds in line with the ESCB approach. Naturally, these are also included in definitions of mutual funds (but double counting is avoided in the overall financial sector). Mutual fund data are incomplete for the UK, Italy and Germany. As regards life insurance and pension funds, there is a difficulty in earlier years in Japan with trust accounts that include pension funds and also forms of long-term deposit. Both are included in life insurance and pension funds for the years

Table 2.2 *Instruments and their aggregation*

*UK*

Deposits: Notes and coins, deposits with UK banks, national savings, other financial institutions and building societies to 1980; currency and deposits from 1990

Money market instruments: Tax instruments, treasury bills, local authority temporary debt to 1980; short-term money market instruments from 1990

Equity: Ordinary and preference shares to 1980; shares and other equity excluding mutual funds from 1990

Mutual funds: UK unit and investment trusts to 1980; mutual fund shares from 1990

Bonds: British government securities, UK debenture and loan stocks to 1980; long term bonds from 1990

Loans: Bank lending, public sector loans, other domestic loans, hire purchase and instalment debt, loans for house purchase, issue department holding of commercial bills to 1980; loans from 1990

Life and pension claims: Equity in life insurance and pension funds to 1980; insurance technical reserves from 1990

FDI: Overseas direct investment (including loans to subsidiaries) to 1980; na from 1990

Central bank reserves: na to 1980; monetary gold and SDRs from 1990

Other: Domestic trade and other credit, other domestic assets/liabilities, accruals of taxes, rates and interest to 1980; other accounts receivable, financial derivatives from 1990

*US*

Deposits: Checkable deposits and currency, time and savings deposits, net interbank transactions, US deposits in foreign countries

Money market instruments: Money market mutual fund shares, federal funds and security repurchase agreements, open market paper

Equity: Corporate equities

Mutual funds: Mutual fund shares

Bonds: Treasury securities, agency securities, municipal securities and loans, corporate and foreign bonds

Loans: Bank loans NEC, other loans and advances, mortgages, consumer credit, security credit

Life and pension claims: Life insurance and pension fund reserves, investment in bank personal trusts

FDI: US direct investment abroad/foreign direct investment in US

Central bank reserves: Gold and foreign exchange reserves, SDR certificates and treasury currency,

Other: Trade credit, taxes payable by business, proprietors' equity in non corporate business, miscellaneous financial claims, sector and instrument discrepancies

Table 2.2 (*Continued*)

*Germany*

Deposits: Funds placed with banks, funds placed with building and loan associations to 1990; currency and deposits from 1998

Money market instruments: Money market paper

Equity: Shares at market prices to 1990; shares, other equity from 1998

Mutual funds: Mutual fund shares

Bonds: Bonds at market prices to 1990; bonds from 1998

Loans: Short-term bank loans, longer-term bank loans, building and loan association loans, insurance enterprise loans to 1990; loans from 1998

Life and pension claims: Funds placed with insurance enterprises to 1990; claims on insurance corporations from 1998

FDI: na

Central bank reserves: External position of the Bundesbank to 1990; Monetary gold and special drawing rights from 1998

Other: Other claims to 1990; other claims, claims from company pension commitments, financial derivatives from 1998

*Japan*

Deposits: Currency, demand deposits, time deposits, CDs, foreign currency deposits, government deposits to 1990; currency and deposits from 1998

Money market instruments: Short-term government securities/financing bills, call money, bills purchased and sold, commercial paper, Bank of Japan loans

Equity: Stocks at market value to 1990; shares and other equities, foreign securities pro rata from 1998

Mutual funds: Securities investment trust

Bonds: Industrial bonds, government bonds, local government bonds, bank debentures, external bonds, to 1990; also structural financing instruments, mortgage securities and foreign securities pro rata from 1998

Loans: Loans by private financial institutions, loans by public financial institutions

Life and pension claims: Trust, insurance to 1990; insurance and pension reserves from 1998

FDI: na to 1990; outward direct investment from 1998

Central bank reserves: na to 1990; foreign exchange reserves from 1998

Other: Trade credit, deposits with trust fund bureau to 1990; also foreign trade credits, other foreign claims and debts, accounts receivable/payable, financial derivatives from 1998

*Canada*

Deposits: Currency and bank deposits, other deposits, foreign currency deposits

Money market instruments: Canada short-term paper, other short-term paper

Equity: Shares

Mutual funds: na

Table 2.2 (*Continued*)

Bonds: Canada bonds, provincial bonds, municipal bonds, other bonds
Loans: Consumer credit, mortgages, bank loans, other loans
Life and pension claims: Life insurance and pensions
FDI: Foreign investments
Central bank reserves: Official reserves
Other: Corporate claims, government claims, other liabilities, trade payables

*France*
Deposits: Moyens de règlement en francs, autres liquidités (notes and coins, deposits) to 1990; currency and deposits from 1998
Money market instruments: Titres de marché monétaire (money market securities) to 1990; negotiable short and medium term securities from 1998
Equity: Actions, autres participations (minus OPCVM) (shares and other participations excluding mutual funds) to 1990; shares and other equity excluding mutual fund shares from 1998
Mutual funds: Titres d' OPCVM (mutual fund shares)
Bonds: Obligations (bonds) to 1990; bonds and similar paper from 1998
Loans: Prêts a court terme minus prêts et crédits commerciaux et décalages comptables, crédits a moyen et long terme minus prêts et crédits commerciaux (short medium and long term loans excluding trade credit and accruals adjustment) to 1990; loans from 1998
Life and pension claims: Réserves techniques d'assurance (insurance technical reserves)
FDI: na
Central bank reserves: Moyens de paiement internationaux (Banque de France), or (central bank liquid assets, gold) to 1990; monetary gold and SDRs from 1998
Other: Prêts et crédits commerciaux, décalage comptable (trade credit, accruals adjustment) to 1990; other accounts receivable or payable, financial derivatives from 1998

*Italy*
Deposits: Biglietti e monete, depositi a vista, altri depositi (notes and coin, sight deposits, other deposits) to 1990; currency and transferable deposits, other deposits from 1998
Money market instruments: Titoli a breve termini (short-term securities)
Equity: Azioni e altri partecipazioni (shares and participations) to 1990; shares and other equity from 1998
Mutual funds: Quote di fondi communi (mutual fund shares)
Bonds: Titoli a medio/lungo termini (medium and long term securities) to 1990; bonds from 1998
Loans: Crediti a breve termini, crediti a medio/lungo termini (short, medium and long term loans)
Life and pension claims: Riserve techniche di assecurazioni (insurance technical

Table 2.2 (*Continued*)

| |
|---|
| reserves) |
| FDI: na |
| Central bank reserves: Oro (gold) to 1990; monetary gold and SDRs from 1998 |
| Other: Altri conti attivi e passivi (other assets and liabilities) to 1990; other accounts receivable/payable, financial derivatives from 1998 |

up to 1990, while from 1998 a more correct definition of life and pension funds is available. For countries other than Canada, general insurance is included with life business. In most of the G-7 countries, there are a significant number of financial institutions which are neither banks nor institutional investors, such as US Federally related mortgage pools and securities brokers and dealers.

## 2.3 INSTRUMENT DIFFERENCES

As for sectors, it has been necessary also for instruments to sum a number of categories to get a broadly comparable set of series. Definitions and breakdowns have also evolved for individual countries, except for the US and Canada, which as noted provide consistent data back to before 1970. The full details are shown in Table 2.2; here we present some key points.

Deposits are defined to include bank deposits (in domestic and foreign currency), notes and coin, but to exclude money market instruments such as Treasury Bills and Commercial Bills, which have their own separate category. For the US, money market mutual fund shares are included in money market instruments and excluded from mutual funds in the sector tables. Special types of deposit such as government deposits with the Trust Fund Bureau in Japan are excluded from the deposit category to ensure comparability and also avoid double counting (since the Bureau holds identified government debt as an asset and has Postal Deposits of the public as a liability).

Equity excludes mutual funds, except in Canada where the breakdown is not available. Except for the US, equity includes participations and other untraded shares, which boost the total considerably in countries such as France (see Tables 4.7–4.10 and Section 4.7). In countries other than Japan, unquoted shares are estimated on a fair value basis while in Japan they are at book value. In Japan, for the years 1970–90, some of the quoted equity values had to be estimated, since again only book values were provided in the tables on the liability side. Bonds are at market value for recent years (except for the US where they are at book value), but in earlier years are also at book value in countries such as Japan. We include government, corporate and bank bonds as well as securitisations in this total.

Loans are defined to exclude trade credit, which is incorporated in 'other assets/liabilities' owing to its different definitions across countries (foreign trade credit only in Germany, for example). We also exclude from loans the 'accounting differences' (accrual lags), which only appear in the case of France. For the household sector, we have presented the breakdown of loans in terms of housing loans versus consumer loans. In fact, for EU countries other than the UK, this breakdown is presented in terms of short versus long-term loans, which we have taken to be broadly in line with the consumer/housing split. According to Bank of Japan (2000), in Germany and Japan loans are measured net of direct and indirect write-offs, while elsewhere only direct write-offs are removed.

The definition of foreign direct investment (FDI) seeks to include only fixed investment, with any financial claims (deposits, loans, bonds, equities) being included in their respective instrument categories. In practice FDI data are only available from the flow of funds accounts of the US, Japan and Canada, with the data being omitted or included in foreign holdings of securities elsewhere. However, IMF data do give consistent estimates of FDI for all countries. In Japan, there is a difficulty because the category 'overseas securities' does not provide any breakdown between bonds and equities. We have allocated this category to the correct instrument category in line with the relative holdings of domestic bonds and equities.

Central Bank reserves are gold, foreign exchange reserves and SDRs, except for Italy where only gold can be separately identified, and the UK, where data are not available in the balance sheet. Note that for countries as a whole, gold and SDRs should be the only asset with no corresponding liability. It would appear that for most of the tables used, this is indeed the case (see also Davis, 1986), although, in some, gold is incorrectly included as a liability of the rest of the world.

In the US, company pension reserves are based on actuarial calculations of liabilities, whereas elsewhere they are based on the value of assets held by pension funds. We count bank personal trusts as long-term institutional investment as well as life and pension claims.

The 'other asset' category has been excluded from the principal tables to ensure comparability, but details are provided in two separate tables, see Appendix 2.1. For all countries, the category includes trade credit and instruments specifically named as 'other or miscellaneous assets'. For France it includes also the accruals adjustment; for the UK accruals of taxes, rates and interest; for the US it includes proprietors' equity in non-corporate business, while in Japan it includes deposits with the trust fund bureau. German data include non-financial and financial corporations' pension commitments, which are held on the balance sheet rather than being funded externally (these exist also in Japan but are not shown in the national balance sheets). Finally, we include in 'other assets' financial derivatives, data on which are available only for the EU and Japan in the last three years. Note that some of these are quite sizeable items, as discussed below, but are excluded from the standard tables as they are not incorporated generally elsewhere and/or do not fit into standard instrument categories.

## 2.4 STATISTICAL DIFFERENCES

One key difference between balance sheets generally is the aggregation of intra-sectoral claims. In the US they are often netted out, so for example the corporate sector is not shown as holding any equity as an asset, while interbank claims are netted out. This is not the case in the other countries, where intercorporate, interbank etc. claims are included on a gross basis. In practice, we resolved the difficulty with interbank claims by using gross data for interbank claims provided in banking data by the Federal Reserve Board (see 'Assets and Liabilities of Commercial Banks in the United States', H8, reference http://www.federalreserve.gov/releases/h8/).

There is a more general problem with equities in the US, in that corporate equity at market value is only included as a footnote in the assets/liabilities table, and equity for banks and other financial firms is not identified separately. In practice one can proxy bank equity by a net worth variable in the Federal Reserve Board's banking data (reference as above).

A second factor is the treatment of trade credit. In countries such as Germany only international trade credit is identified, while in Italy trade credit is not identified before 1998. For this reason, as noted, we exclude trade credit from consideration as an asset or liability of the household or corporate sector.

A third issue relates to valuations. For most countries, we have market values for all assets in recent years but this is not the case for bonds or unquoted shares in the earlier years. Foreign direct investment is also typically valued at book values.

Note also that there is typically a residual in the flow of funds arising from unrecorded claims. This is usually not of major importance, with the statisticians attempting to minimise the discrepancy. For details of residuals in balance sheet tables for the UK, US, Germany and Japan see Davis (1986).

## APPENDIX 2.1: OTHER ASSETS

Table 2.3 shows 'other assets', which, as noted above, constitute assets which are outside the standard instrument categories, and hence to ensure comparability are not included in the portfolio share tables or ratios to GDP in the main tables commented on above. We consider that the best way to illustrate the importance of these assets and liabilities is to show ratios to GDP.

For most sectors and countries, the assets are of fairly negligible size, below 10 per cent of GDP. In the UK, the only asset category exceeding this level is for the company sector, which is largely trade credit. In the US, the other assets are much more significant for a number of sectors. In the household sector, the asset concerned is largely equity in unincorporated businesses, which is not included in the data for other countries. For companies, there is again trade credit and taxes payable by business. The financial sector also has a sizeable other asset category, which is accounted for by taxes payable by business, miscellaneous financial claims, sector and instrument discrepancies. All three US discrepancies are around 50 per cent of GDP.

In Germany, the largest discrepancy on the assets side is for companies, and is largely foreign trade credits. For Japan, the General Government sector holds assets in the form of the Trust Fund Bureau (42 per cent of GDP), which are counted as liabilities of the financial sector (largely deposits with the Postal Savings system). Companies have again sizeable trade credits on the asset side (60 per cent of GDP). Furthermore, since the revision of the financial accounts, there have appeared large other assets for the financial sector, which include in particular 'other foreign claims and debts'. Most of these appear in the accounts of the banking system also. In Canada other assets are corporate claims, government claims, other liabilities and trade payables. It can be seen that these are over 50 per cent of GDP for the corporate sector and the financial sector. In France the main other asset is trade credit and accounting discrepancies for the corporate sector – around 40 per cent of GDP. Finally in Italy, other corporate assets is the only category to exceed 10 per cent of GDP – since 1998. Again, it is largely trade credit, which was not identified in earlier tables.

Turning to 'other liabilities', the pattern is for most countries comparable for the corporate sector, since trade credits, except for the US and Germany, are included in an unconsolidated manner. For Germany, an additional other liability for companies is the unfunded pension claims held on the balance sheet. Other liabilities of the US financial sector exceed those of the corresponding assets, whereas elsewhere they are comparable. In recent years, Japan has had large other liabilities of the financial sector, which are accounted for *inter alia* by the Trust Fund Bureau.

Table 2.3 *Other assets (per cent of GDP)*

| | | UK | US | Germany | Japan | Canada | France | Italy |
|---|---|---|---|---|---|---|---|---|
| Households | 1970 | 15.4 | 66.1 | 4.8 | 1.1 | 9.4 | 15.4 | 7.2 |
| | 1980 | 8.8 | 81.0 | 7.0 | 1.4 | 13.6 | 6.8 | 2.2 |
| | 1990 | 9.6 | 65.8 | 9.9 | 2.8 | 11.2 | 3.3 | 7.5 |
| | 1998 | 8.2 | 60.9 | 11.1 | 9.2 | 6.4 | 4.2 | 1.9 |
| | 2000 | 8.4 | 60.2 | 11.5 | 10.6 | 3.4 | 8.3 | 2.6 |
| General government | 1970 | 17.3 | 1.4 | 6.5 | 10.9 | 34.4 | 25.7 | 0.0 |
| | 1980 | 12.2 | 2.0 | 5.3 | 20.9 | 26.9 | 12.3 | 0.0 |
| | 1990 | 6.8 | 3.2 | 9.5 | 30.9 | 27.2 | 11.8 | 1.5 |
| | 1998 | 5.3 | 2.1 | 0.2 | 45.1 | 25.6 | 11.2 | 6.2 |
| | 2000 | 5.8 | 2.3 | 0.2 | 42.4 | 28.4 | 10.1 | 7.0 |
| Companies | 1970 | 24.8 | 20.2 | 8.6 | 70.3 | 40.1 | 49.0 | 0.6 |
| | 1980 | 18.7 | 28.1 | 11.9 | 86.6 | 41.6 | 38.2 | 0.8 |
| | 1990 | 16.6 | 43.3 | 20.5 | 70.6 | 49.8 | 45.1 | 0.8 |
| | 1998 | 10.9 | 51.5 | 14.1 | 60.4 | 67.2 | 39.8 | 26.9 |
| | 2000 | 12.4 | 55.7 | 17.9 | 64.0 | 72.4 | 43.9 | 27.2 |
| Foreign | 1970 | 1.0 | 0.4 | 11.2 | 0.0 | 35.7 | 3.9 | 0.0 |
| | 1980 | 0.5 | 1.6 | 13.9 | 0.0 | 28.4 | 5.1 | 0.1 |
| | 1990 | 1.0 | 2.2 | 15.8 | 0.0 | 25.9 | 1.8 | 0.8 |
| | 1998 | 1.9 | 4.9 | 5.3 | 5.5 | 38.5 | 10.3 | 4.4 |
| | 2000 | 1.8 | 5.0 | 6.4 | 4.2 | 38.6 | 14.1 | 5.0 |
| Financial | 1970 | 0.2 | 6.6 | 0.0 | 0.0 | 14.4 | 18.7 | 0.0 |
| | 1980 | 2.9 | 12.8 | 0.0 | 0.0 | 19.6 | 11.6 | 1.9 |
| | 1990 | 3.5 | 25.5 | 0.1 | 3.3 | 37.5 | 14.0 | 3.9 |
| | 1998 | 4.2 | 38.8 | 7.1 | 85.0 | 81.6 | 26.5 | 3.6 |
| | 2000 | 4.3 | 41.3 | 10.4 | 77.3 | 91.3 | 33.6 | 5.6 |
| Banking | 1970 | 0.0 | 3.5 | 0.0 | 1.4 | 2.5 | 15.5 | 0.6 |
| | 1980 | 1.2 | 7.3 | 0.0 | 0.8 | 8.6 | 9.4 | 0.1 |
| | 1990 | 1.2 | 10.6 | 0.0 | 0.8 | 9.1 | 9.7 | 2.2 |
| | 1998 | 0.7 | 13.7 | 4.9 | 69.6 | 19.9 | 16.8 | 3.4 |
| | 2000 | 0.5 | 13.4 | 7.9 | 66.9 | 17.4 | 27.3 | 4.9 |
| Mutual funds | 1970 | 0.1 | 0.0 | na | 0.0 | 1.2 | 0.1 | na |
| | 1980 | 0.1 | 0.0 | na | 0.0 | 0.3 | 0.0 | na |
| | 1990 | 0.1 | 0.2 | 0.1 | 2.3 | 1.0 | 0.6 | na |
| | 1998 | 0.6 | 0.8 | 0.0 | 0.0 | 9.0 | 1.8 | na |
| | 2000 | na | 1.0 | na | 0.0 | 12.1 | na | na |
| Insurance and pensions | 1970 | 0.0 | 2.4 | 0.0 | 0.0 | 1.3 | 1.2 | 0.0 |
| | 1980 | 9.6 | 4.3 | 0.0 | 1.1 | 1.8 | 1.6 | 0.1 |
| | 1990 | 1.6 | 10.3 | 0.0 | 13.4 | 4.7 | 2.5 | 0.1 |
| | 1998 | 2.3 | 9.9 | 2.2 | 6.2 | 12.1 | 1.7 | 0.0 |
| | 2000 | 2.4 | 9.4 | 2.5 | 8.5 | 13.6 | 2.1 | 0.1 |

Note: for general government, foreign, financial and banking sectors, the first observation for the UK is 1975 and not 1970.

Table 2.4 *Other liabilities (per cent of GDP)*

| | | UK | US | Germany | Japan | Canada | France | Italy |
|---|---|---|---|---|---|---|---|---|
| Households | 1970 | 14.3 | 10.9 | 3.9 | 14.2 | 8.8 | 24.6 | 0.0 |
| | 1980 | 11.3 | 16.0 | 2.3 | 15.0 | 7.3 | 14.6 | 0.0 |
| | 1990 | 12.8 | 16.3 | 1.3 | 15.0 | 8.5 | 19.8 | 1.4 |
| | 1998 | 6.5 | 18.3 | 0.6 | 12.5 | 8.4 | 8.6 | 6.0 |
| | 2000 | 6.5 | 18.8 | 0.7 | 12.4 | 8.8 | 9.2 | 7.4 |
| General government | 1970 | 1.0 | 8.9 | 0.1 | 0.1 | 41.4 | 23.4 | 5.4 |
| | 1980 | 0.5 | 9.7 | 2.2 | 0.0 | 41.5 | 10.8 | 3.0 |
| | 1990 | 2.6 | 13.9 | 1.9 | 0.0 | 47.5 | 3.9 | 0.0 |
| | 1998 | 2.3 | 14.8 | 0.0 | 3.6 | 52.2 | 7.3 | 5.8 |
| | 2000 | 4.5 | 14.3 | 0.0 | 3.6 | 50.9 | 8.1 | 5.6 |
| Companies | 1970 | 25.7 | 15.9 | 17.8 | 55.9 | 50.0 | 37.1 | 0.0 |
| | 1980 | 22.1 | 34.1 | 20.9 | 68.2 | 52.4 | 35.3 | 0.3 |
| | 1990 | 20.8 | 29.1 | 29.0 | 50.9 | 44.8 | 29.9 | 8.6 |
| | 1998 | 15.2 | 29.6 | 17.1 | 52.6 | 53.5 | 38.3 | 28.4 |
| | 2000 | 14.9 | 26.9 | 20.6 | 56.8 | 55.2 | 45.3 | 29.2 |
| Foreign | 1970 | 8.9 | –0.4 | 8.6 | 0.0 | 9.8 | 6.3 | 4.5 |
| | 1980 | 2.9 | 0.9 | 11.7 | 0.0 | 18.5 | 8.6 | 2.3 |
| | 1990 | 2.7 | 1.9 | 22.7 | 0.0 | 21.2 | 7.0 | 0.8 |
| | 1998 | 2.0 | 2.4 | 6.0 | 15.9 | 41.0 | 11.1 | 6.2 |
| | 2000 | 1.8 | 6.4 | 7.6 | 15.5 | 39.3 | 16.4 | 8.1 |
| Financial | 1970 | 1.3 | 27.8 | 0.0 | 12.5 | 23.9 | 11.3 | 5.9 |
| | 1980 | 1.9 | 29.3 | 0.0 | 23.7 | 22.2 | 8.6 | 11.4 |
| | 1990 | 2.6 | 58.2 | 1.1 | 26.5 | 28.0 | 11.0 | 3.0 |
| | 1998 | 2.6 | 104.2 | 12.1 | 132.4 | 52.2 | 20.2 | 3.6 |
| | 2000 | 3.3 | 112.2 | 13.5 | 120.4 | 51.2 | 30.7 | 3.1 |
| Banking | 1970 | 0.0 | 16.6 | 0.0 | 1.0 | 10.0 | 7.7 | 5.7 |
| | 1980 | 0.0 | 14.9 | 0.0 | 2.7 | 11.5 | 7.9 | 11.4 |
| | 1990 | 1.4 | 19.4 | 0.7 | 7.7 | 17.9 | 9.6 | 2.6 |
| | 1998 | 0.5 | 25.1 | 8.8 | 17.2 | 34.5 | 30.0 | 5.6 |
| | 2000 | 0.5 | 24.0 | 10.0 | 14.4 | 31.6 | 41.3 | 5.4 |
| Mutual funds | 1970 | 11.3 | 4.4 | na | 1.8 | 3.0 | 1.6 | na |
| | 1980 | 6.2 | 4.7 | na | 3.0 | 1.5 | 2.6 | na |
| | 1990 | 9.1 | 18.8 | 9.8 | 13.8 | 5.3 | 31.1 | na |
| | 1998 | 21.6 | 55.0 | 30.2 | 8.6 | 33.4 | 44.8 | na |
| | 2000 | na | 62.0 | na | 10.7 | 36.1 | na | na |
| Insurance and pensions | 1970 | 0.0 | 5.5 | 0.0 | 0.7 | 0.9 | 1.0 | 0.0 |
| | 1980 | 46.1 | 6.4 | 0.0 | 1.1 | 1.2 | 0.8 | 0.0 |
| | 1990 | 1.0 | 12.9 | 0.4 | 0.0 | 1.5 | 1.1 | 0.0 |
| | 1998 | 2.0 | 14.0 | 3.3 | 4.5 | 1.9 | 0.5 | 0.1 |
| | 2000 | 2.7 | 13.4 | 3.5 | 4.3 | 2.7 | 0.6 | 0.1 |

Note: for general government, foreign, financial and banking sectors, the first observation for the UK is 1975 and not 1970.

# 3 Aspects of the macroeconomic history of the G-7

## INTRODUCTION

In Chapter 1 we provided background to the developments in balance sheets by reference to the theory of finance and developments in financial structure and regulation. Chapter 2 complemented this by providing an outline of the data sources and the main statistical differences between them. In this third chapter we provide further background in terms of some of the key macroeconomic developments that have been experienced by the G-7 during the past three decades, as well as over the longer term. These have themselves influenced and conditioned the accumulation and financing behaviour of the key sectors, independently of the overall orientation of the financial system to bank domination or market orientation. For example, we observe different degrees of willingness to hold fixed rate bonds in countries which have experienced high and volatile inflation from those where price stability has been broadly maintained. A rapid ageing of the population in the absence of a generous social security system prompts pension saving.

Besides being relevant background, the macroeconomic data presented in this chapter also enable us to approach the issue of whether the differences in balance sheets make a difference to economic performance. This is a topic to which we return in Chapter 11.

## 3.1 A LONG-TERM VIEW

Tables 3.1–3.3 from Davis and Madsen (2001) give growth, inflation, total factor productivity, equity and bond yields for successively shorter

Table 3.1 *Secular averages for macroeconomic and financial indicators (1870–1999), per cent*

| | US | UK | Canada | Germany | France | Italy | Japan |
|---|---|---|---|---|---|---|---|
| Growth | 3.5 | 2.0 | 3.8 | 3.1 | 2.4 | 2.5 | 4.0 |
| Inflation | 2.1 | 3.1 | 2.3 | 92.7 | | 7.6 | |
| Total factor productivity | 1.7 | 0.7 | 1.3 | 1.6 | na | 1.6 | na |
| Real equity returns | 8.7 | | | −79.8 | | | |
| Real bond yields | 2.4 | 2.2 | 2.2 | −87.2 | | −2.8 | |

Table 3.2 *Long-term averages for macroeconomic and financial indicators (1920–99), per cent*

| | US | UK | Canada | Germany | France | Italy | Japan |
|---|---|---|---|---|---|---|---|
| Growth | 3.2 | 2.1 | 3.8 | 3.8 | 3.3 | 3.0 | 4.6 |
| Inflation | 3.0 | 4.0 | 3.0 | 147.0 | 9.3 | 10.2 | 12.9 |
| Total factor productivity | 1.6 | 1.1 | 1.5 | 2.5 | 2.3 | 1.8 | 2.4 |
| Real equity returns | 9.8 | 9.1 | 7.5 | −129.0 | 6.9 | 7.1 | 2.6 |
| Real bond yields | 2.2 | 2.7 | 3.2 | −140.7 | −2.8 | −2.9 | −7.0 |

periods up to 1999. Table 3.1, which is incomplete, shows extant data back to 1870. It can be seen that economic growth has been relatively low in the UK, which in 1870 was the most developed country, and much higher in the US, Canada and Japan, with France, Germany and Italy intermediate. That said, these average growth rates were themselves unprecedented in history when 1.5 per cent or less has been the rule.

Total factor productivity, underlying growth, is broadly in line with the growth differences (the rest of growth being accounted for by increases in factor inputs of labour and capital). The long-term inflation performance in Germany, shown in Tables 3.1 and 3.2, as well as corresponding real asset returns, is marked by the hyperinflation of the early 1920s, when prices rose by thousands of percent in a single year. This experience underlies the caution of German savers and investors as well as the orientation to price stability of the monetary authorities in that country. In the Anglo-American countries inflation was around 2–3 per cent over this long period. Total returns on equity (including dividends) are only available for the US, at an average of 8.7 per cent in real terms. Bond yields in the Anglo-Saxon countries are around 2 per cent but are negative in Italy.

Table 3.3 *Postwar averages for macroeconomic and financial indicators (1950–99), per cent*

| | US | UK | Canada | Germany | France | Italy | Japan |
|---|---|---|---|---|---|---|---|
| Growth | 3.3 | 2.5 | 4.1 | 4.1 | 3.7 | 3.8 | 6.1 |
| Inflation | 3.4 | 4.9 | 3.4 | 2.4 | 9.2 | 12.5 | 15.2 |
| Total factor productivity | 1.4 | 1.1 | 1.4 | 2.7 | 2.5 | 2.4 | 3.3 |
| Real equity returns | 10.2 | 11.2 | 7.8 | 12.8 | 8.5 | 8.4 | 12.9 |
| Real bond yields | 2.4 | 2.6 | 3.3 | 4.3 | 2.1 | 2.4 | 2.1 |

Looking at Table 3.2, since 1920, the data are comprehensive. Growth evidently was higher than in the previous 50 years (given average growth is higher) except in the US. France, Italy and Japan are all shown to have been prone to inflation, as well as Germany. This was also reflected in negative real bond yields on average. Equity returns are high despite inflation in France and Italy, as well as in the Anglo-Saxon countries, but not in Japan.

Finally, Table 3.3 illustrates the postwar era, perhaps the most relevant background to the balance sheet tables. In this period, bank-dominated Japan and Germany recorded very high growth and real equity returns (averaging 13 per cent) linking to postwar reconstruction. Total factor productivity growth is estimated to be much higher in Continental Europe and Japan than in the market-oriented Anglo-Saxon countries, partly no doubt reflecting catch-up of living standards and technologies. Inflation in France, Italy and Japan remained very high on average, in marked contrast to Germany, which had the lowest inflation of the G-7. This reflects the tight counterinflationary policy of the Bundesbank. Partly as a consequence, real bond yields have been far higher in Germany than elsewhere.

## 3.2 DEMOGRAPHIC ASPECTS

Further background is provided by demographic developments. Its relevance is in terms of the impact of demographics on saving (see Chapters 1 and 5) as well as, more tentatively, on economic performance (a young labour force may be more dynamic). Recent years have seen dramatic changes in life expectancy, which as shown in Table 3.4 are strongly correlated across G-7 countries. Japanese average longevity is somewhat greater, but all of the countries are at most four years apart in this respect.

Table 3.4 *Life expectancy at birth*

| Years | 1970–1975 | 1980–1985 | 1990–1995 | 2000 |
|---|---|---|---|---|
| United Kingdom | 72 | 74 | 76 | 78 |
| United States | 73 | 75 | 77 | 77 |
| Germany | 71 | 73 | 76 | 77 |
| Japan | 74 | 77 | 79 | 81 |
| Canada | 73 | 76 | 78 | 79 |
| France | 72 | 75 | 78 | 79 |
| Italy | 72 | 75 | 78 | 79 |

Source: World Bank (1996), US Department of the Census.

Table 3.5 *Fertility rates*

| No. of children per female | 1970–1975 | 1980–1985 | 1990–1995 | 2000 |
|---|---|---|---|---|
| United Kingdom | 1.8 | 1.8 | 1.8 | 1.7 |
| United States | 1.8 | 1.8 | 2.0 | 2.1 |
| Germany | 1.5 | 1.4 | 1.2 | 1.4 |
| Japan | 1.9 | 1.8 | 1.5 | 1.4 |
| Canada | 1.8 | 1.7 | 1.9 | 1.6 |
| France | 1.9 | 1.8 | 1.7 | 1.7 |
| Italy | 2.2 | 1.4 | 1.3 | 1.2 |

Source: World Bank (1996), US Department of the Census.

Table 3.6 *Projections of elderly dependency ratio*

| Population 65 & over as per cent of population aged 20–64 | 2000 | 2035 | 2050 |
|---|---|---|---|
| United Kingdom | 27 | 45 | 45 |
| United States | 22 | 38 | 38 |
| Germany | 27 | 54 | 53 |
| Japan | 28 | 54 | 65 |
| Canada | 20 | 42 | 46 |
| France | 27 | 48 | 51 |
| Italy | 29 | 57 | 67 |

Source: Dang *et al.* (2001).

Table 3.5 shows the somewhat greater differences in fertility. Most countries again show a common trend, of a decline in fertility since the 1970s, but the current level is much higher in the US than elsewhere. Rates in Italy, Japan and Germany, at below 1.5, are well below replacement, implying a future decline in the overall population unless there is major influx of immigrants. Reflecting fertility and longevity (as well as immigration), the share of elderly people in the population of all the G-7 has already increased over 1960–90 and is projected to be boosted strongly in the coming decades (Table 3.6). This indicates a major future strain on pension systems, with risks also for the wider economy and financial system (Davis, 2002d).

## 3.3 THE LAST THREE DECADES

A sharper impression of the recent performance of the economies of the G-7, which is relevant to financial asset and liability holdings, is provided by a focus on recent decades. Table 3.7 indicates that in terms of economic growth, the overall pattern was one of rapid growth in the 1950s and 1960s, followed by a major slump in the 1970s and 1980s, with a recovery in the 1990s in the US and Germany. The slowdown, which also affected productivity, is widely discussed – underlying factors clearly include the oil price shock.

Inflation soared in the 1970s and 1980s before falling back to earlier levels in the 1990s. Germany showed the lowest inflation up to 1980. Share returns were high in the 1950s, 1980s and 1990s, with a major slump in the 1970s. Finally, real bond yields fell to zero in the 1970s before recovering in the 1980s and 1990s to historically high levels in all the G-7.

The patterns of public, foreign and private sector deficits and surpluses are shown in Tables 3.8–3.10. These aggregates – representing the difference between income and expenditure of these three sectors – add to zero by identity (the private sector is estimated by residual). They represent the net acquisition of financial assets for the sectors and hence underlie the net wealth that has been accumulated (assets less liabilities), abstracting from capital gains and losses. They also give clues as to the types of asset accumulation for other sectors – for example a country with a large public sector deficit and a private sector surplus would be likely to have significant holdings of government bonds by the household sector. Note that financial intermediaries do not have significant surpluses and deficits, running as they do a balanced financial position in normal times. Hence the private sector position is the sum of the household sector position (usually in surplus) and corporations (often in deficit).

Table 3.7 *Decade–by–decade macroeconomic data*

| | Canada | US | Japan | France | Germany | Italy | UK | G–7 |
|---|---|---|---|---|---|---|---|---|
| Growth | | | | | | | | |
| 1950–59 | 5.4 | 4.0 | 8.6 | 5.1 | 8.5 | 5.6 | 2.6 | 5.7 |
| 1960–69 | 5.2 | 4.1 | 10.8 | 5.7 | 4.9 | 5.8 | 3.1 | 5.6 |
| 1970–79 | 4.7 | 2.8 | 5.2 | 3.7 | 3.1 | 3.9 | 2.5 | 3.7 |
| 1980–89 | 3.1 | 2.5 | 3.9 | 2.3 | 1.8 | 2.5 | 2.4 | 2.7 |
| 1990–99 | 2.2 | 3.0 | 2.1 | 1.7 | 2.2 | 1.3 | 1.9 | 2.0 |
| Inflation | | | | | | | | |
| 1950–59 | 2.4 | 2.1 | 3.1 | 6.2 | 1.1 | 3.2 | 1.9 | 2.8 |
| 1960–69 | 2.5 | 2.3 | 5.4 | 3.9 | 2.4 | 3.5 | 3.5 | 3.4 |
| 1970–79 | 7.4 | 7.1 | 9.1 | 8.9 | 4.9 | 12.5 | 12.6 | 8.9 |
| 1980–89 | 6.5 | 5.6 | 2.5 | 7.4 | 2.9 | 11.4 | 7.4 | 6.2 |
| 1990–99 | 2.2 | 3.0 | 1.2 | 1.9 | 2.3 | 4.1 | 3.7 | 2.6 |
| Real share returns | | | | | | | | |
| 1950–59 | 11.9 | 17.7 | 32.7 | 20.0 | 30.4 | 20.2 | 15.8 | 21.2 |
| 1960–69 | 7.9 | 6.1 | 11.2 | 1.5 | 5.3 | 1.4 | 5.8 | 5.6 |
| 1970–79 | 4.4 | 0.3 | 7.5 | 2.0 | –0.7 | –12.6 | 7.3 | 1.2 |
| 1980–89 | 6.0 | 11.9 | 18.5 | 19.6 | 17.7 | 21.5 | 15.8 | 15.9 |
| 1990–99 | 9.0 | 15.5 | –5.2 | 14.5 | 11.6 | 11.2 | 11.3 | 9.7 |
| Real bond yields | | | | | | | | |
| 1950–59 | 1.2 | 0.9 | 3.6 | –0.5 | 5.5 | 3.0 | 2.5 | 2.3 |
| 1960–69 | 3.2 | 2.3 | 2.2 | 1.6 | 4.2 | 2.8 | 3.1 | 2.8 |
| 1970–79 | 1.1 | 0.4 | –1.4 | 0.0 | 3.1 | –1.5 | –0.7 | 0.1 |
| 1980–89 | 5.2 | 5.1 | 4.0 | 4.4 | 4.6 | 3.1 | 3.8 | 4.3 |
| 1990–99 | 5.8 | 3.7 | 2.3 | 5.2 | 4.2 | 4.5 | 4.3 | 4.3 |

Beginning with the external account (Table 3.8), the United States has shown a marked evolution in its behaviour, with a balanced position up to the late 1970s, after which it ran a deficit on average over 5-yearly periods. This was particularly large in the late 1980s and late 1990s, and has impacted on the foreign asset/liability position (see Chapter 6). A broadly similar pattern is apparent in the UK, although there, deficits were already apparent in the 1970s. Germany and Japan, by contrast, have run persistent surpluses, which reached a peak in the late 1980s. Hit by reunification, Germany has not recovered this position and has been in balance or deficit in the 1990s, while Japan, although suffering from stagnation, continued in surplus throughout the 1990s. Canada contrasts in having run a deficit throughout the 35-year period shown, except in the late 1990s. France and Italy have had the most diverse experience, with four quinquennia of

Table 3.8 *External balance/GDP, per cent*

| | US | UK | Germany | France | Japan | Italy | Canada |
|---|---|---|---|---|---|---|---|
| 1965–69 | 0.3 | 0.0 | 1.1 | −0.3 | 0.8 | 2.7 | −2.3 |
| 1970–74 | 0.1 | −0.4 | 1.1 | −0.1 | 0.9 | −0.5 | −1.4 |
| 1975–79 | 0.0 | −0.6 | 0.7 | 0.4 | 0.6 | 0.6 | −3.8 |
| 1980–84 | −0.7 | 0.7 | 0.2 | −0.9 | 0.9 | −1.5 | −1.4 |
| 1985–89 | −2.7 | −2.4 | 4.2 | −0.2 | 3.2 | −0.7 | −2.9 |
| 1990–94 | −1.0 | −2.2 | 0.0 | 0.0 | 2.4 | −0.8 | −3.4 |
| 1995–00 | −2.5 | −1.2 | −0.6 | 1.9 | 2.3 | 1.7 | 0.0 |

Table 3.9 *General government balance/GDP, per cent*

| | US | UK | Germany | France | Japan | Italy | Canada |
|---|---|---|---|---|---|---|---|
| 1965–69 | −0.9 | −0.7 | −0.4 | 0.8 | 0.4 | −3.5 | −0.1 |
| 1970–74 | −1.5 | −0.9 | −0.1 | 1.5 | 0.5 | −6.6 | −0.1 |
| 1975–79 | −2.5 | −4.0 | −3.3 | −0.6 | −3.0 | −10.1 | −3.7 |
| 1980–84 | −4.0 | −3.4 | −2.9 | −2.2 | −2.6 | −10.5 | −6.0 |
| 1985–89 | −4.2 | −1.2 | −1.3 | −2.5 | 0.4 | −11.0 | −6.0 |
| 1990–94 | −4.7 | −5.1 | −2.6 | −4.0 | −0.1 | −10.7 | −7.7 |
| 1995–00 | −0.5 | −1.5 | −2.0 | −3.0 | −5.3 | −3.8 | −0.4 |

deficits and three of surpluses. France's external position kept below 1 per cent of GDP in absolute terms, except for the surplus of the late 1990s. Italy has witnessed periods of marked deficit (such as the early 1980s) as well as surplus (late 1960s and late 1990s).

Turning to general government flow positions (Table 3.9), the US ran a persistent deficit on average throughout, but it was much more sizeable in 1980–95 than at other times – no less than 4 per cent of GDP. Over this period the US had a 'twin deficit' with the public deficit having an external counterpart. More generally, it has been rare for any G-7 country to run a balanced or surplus position over 5-year periods. Only France and Japan managed to do so, in the period up to 1975. Italy has seen the most severe and sustained deficits, of over 10 per cent of GDP from 1975 to 1995, corresponding to rising government debt, while periods with deficits of over 5 per cent of GDP have been seen in Canada, the UK and most recently in Japan. For EU countries, the late 1990s have in all cases seen a reduction in deficits, partly reflecting economic conditions but also the fiscal consolidation mandated by the Maastricht treaty (EMI, 1998). There are of course strong links with public bond issuance as well as the net financial wealth

Table 3.10 *Estimated private sector balance/GDP*

| | US | UK | Germany | France | Japan | Italy | Canada |
|---|---|---|---|---|---|---|---|
| 1965–69 | 1.2 | 0.7 | 1.5 | −1.1 | 0.4 | 6.2 | −2.2 |
| 1970–74 | 1.5 | 0.5 | 1.2 | −1.6 | 0.3 | 6.0 | −1.3 |
| 1975–79 | 2.5 | 3.4 | 3.9 | 1.0 | 3.6 | 10.7 | −0.1 |
| 1980–84 | 3.4 | 4.1 | 3.1 | 1.2 | 3.4 | 9.1 | 4.6 |
| 1985–89 | 1.5 | −1.3 | 5.5 | 2.2 | 2.9 | 10.3 | 3.1 |
| 1990–94 | 3.7 | 3.0 | 2.6 | 4.1 | 2.6 | 10.0 | 4.4 |
| 1995–00 | −2.0 | 0.4 | 1.4 | 4.9 | 7.6 | 5.4 | 0.4 |

of the public sector more generally (see Chapter 6).

Finally, the private sector situation is shown in Table 3.10. Note that these data are estimated from figures for the external and general government position. In most periods the net position has been a surplus, with the household sector accumulating at a rate in excess of corporate sector net financing requirements. The most important exception has been the United States since 1995, when both sectors have been in deficit, a pattern mirrored to a lesser degree in the UK in 1985–9. Large surpluses have been seen in Canada and latterly in Japan. In Davis (1995c), it is shown that private sector deficits tend to be highly unstable, shifting at times rapidly to surplus – and destabilising the macroeconomy, when financial instability occurs.

# 4 Corporate finance

We now move from the general discussion of financial systems and balance sheets to the individual sectors that comprise them. Given the sharp focus of the bulk of the general theory outlined in Chapter 1 on financing of the corporate sector, we will analyse first the corporate sector, beginning with an economic overview, before looking at the balance sheet tables.

## 4.1 CORPORATE FINANCE AND BALANCE SHEET STRUCTURE – THEORETICAL BACKGROUND

As outlined in Davis (1995b), at a basic level, firms in financing investment may either draw on their income (retained earnings) or call for external finance. They have a choice of external financing methods between debt and equity. Equity is more risky to stockholders because creditors are paid first. Also dividends are not fixed (distribution is optional), thus exposing shareholders to agency costs. Hence equity is costlier, as well as being discriminated against by most tax systems (see Brealey and Myers, 2002; Tanzi and King, 1995).[17] Meanwhile, debt may increase the risk to the firm of bankruptcy. Rising debt is generally considered to increase financial risks, hence the cost or availability of finance offered by the market, particularly when adverse conditions arise.

On the other hand, Modigliani and Miller (MM) (1958) proved that under certain rather strict conditions, the debt/equity ratio is irrelevant to

17 Brealey and Myers (2002) discuss the effects of tax on corporate financial decisions. See also Miller (1977), who emphasised the importance of personal as well as corporate tax in determining the net tax gain from borrowing.

the cost of capital and, implicitly, to the lenders' assessment of risk. A corollary is that the cost of external funds is identical to that of internal financing via retentions. Irrelevance occurs when financing decisions cannot affect investment/consumption opportunities, and hence perceived pay-offs to claimants on the firm. In order for this to be the case, it is necessary for the firm to be unable to alter the income stream produced, and also to be unable to repackage the stream by changing the nature of claims held against it. The first is ensured by the independence of real decisions, whereby perceptions of investment decisions and the resulting stream of income are given independent of financing. Second, the firm is unable to repackage the stream of income if monopoly power over it is ruled out. This is ensured by the ability of individuals to offset changes introduced by the firm by means of shifts in their own portfolios (which requires borrowing and lending freely at the market rate).

An example clarifies this concept (see Davis, 1995b). Suppose there is uncertainty, but two firms have the same mean and variance of return. One is levered, the other is not, and initially the value of equity is the same in each firm; the geared firm has a higher total value (debt plus equity). Then (given the lower legal priority of the claims of shareholders than those of bondholders to the income of the geared firm) there is an incentive for shareholders in the levered firm to increase their income by selling their shares or borrowing at a given interest rate, and buying shares in the unlevered firm. The process depresses share prices in the levered firm and raises them in the unlevered until returns to the shareholders in each firm, net of interest payments, are equal. At this point the valuation of the firms is the same and so, therefore, is the cost of capital (expected profit divided by valuation), which is equal to that of an equity-financed firm of the same risk class. The equity yield of the levered firm is of course higher, reflecting the larger proportion of debt in the capital structure. 'Home-made leverage' thus offers a shareholder the advantages that the levered firm seeks, and the cost of capital is the same for all firms with the same mean and variance of return.

It should be noted that the analysis concerns firms in the same risk class. MM allow firms in different risk classes to have different costs of capital. Hence, even if the theorem applied, increased debt might raise the cost of capital should the distribution of debt issue shift to riskier firms. However, the main problems with the theorem are that MM's analysis excludes the possibility of costly bankruptcy and taxation, and assumes perfect capital markets and symmetry of information, and/or complete contracts, between borrowers and lenders.

Costs of bankruptcy imply that the transfer of ownership of assets when a firm defaults is neither smooth nor costless. Costs of bankruptcy in turn mean market interest rates will rise with debt-to-equity ratios. Note that these costs arise partly from conflicts of interest among claimholders, as for example secured creditors prefer earlier liquidation than unsecured creditors or equity holders. Equity finance will obviate such difficulties, albeit at a cost as indicated by the sizeable premium typical of the cost of equity relative to debt finance (Table 1.1). Meanwhile simple debt structures and relationship banks, as discussed in Section 1.5 above, may decrease such costs by enhancing scope for workouts or renegotiations rather than formal bankruptcy. Hence financial structure itself may affect the incidence of costs of bankruptcy. Wider costs of bankruptcy include externalities on other creditors and the economy as a whole. They reflect *inter alia* the overall level of leverage in the corporate sector, as indicated by the debt–equity ratio.

This is offset by tax deductibility of interest payments as is typical of G-7 countries, which, as noted above, gives a spur to debt issue, since it means higher leverage entails a reduction in the cost of capital. Gordon and Malkiel (1981) concluded that observed corporate financial structures comprising both debt and equity arise from a balance between these offsetting forces. Gertler and Hubbard (1989) make the further distinction between individual and business-cycle (or unsystematic and systematic) risk[18] and suggest that tax deductibility induces firms to absorb more of the latter than they otherwise would, thus increasing default risk. This arises from the tax subsidy noted here, as well as the restrictions on indexation of interest payments to the cycle. It also results from costs of renegotiation (see the discussion below), that ensure that debt cannot take on the equity features needed to respond to business-cycle risk.

Further objections to MM relate to imperfections or asymmetries in capital markets. For example, individual investors may not be able to borrow at the same interest rate as firms in order to adjust their portfolios in an offsetting manner, either because their credit rating is lower than firms, owing to differences in perceived default risk, or because of disequilibrium credit rationing (arising e.g. from government controls) they may not be able to borrow at all. There may be legal limits on the distribution of their portfolios (e.g. life insurers, which in some countries are unable to hold significant amounts of equity).[19] In these cases 'home-made leverage' may

---

18 Individual risk includes internal and business risk, while business-cycle risks are non-diversifiable risks affecting the aggregate economy.

19 See Davis (2002c).

not be possible. In addition, transactions costs are likely to prevent fully offsetting financial moves by investors.

## 4.2 AGENCY COSTS AND CYCLICAL EFFECTS

Another problem with the 'irrelevance' of corporate financing is asymmetric information between corporations and their financiers and consequent adverse selection and moral hazard in the context of incomplete contracts, as discussed in Section 1.2 in the context of financial intermediation. Owing to related difficulties, borrowers cannot credibly commit themselves to repay lenders in all circumstances, while lenders are limited in their ability to screen and monitor borrowers. This brings in the basic problems of the debt contract: the ability of borrowers to commit themselves credibly to remunerating lenders – and the ability of lenders to screen and monitor borrowers – sets a limit to feasible transfers of funds. Given asymmetric and costly information, the choice of project is not independent of finance; a more highly levered firm may choose riskier investments – a problem of 'agency costs', in this case costs arising from the conflict of interest between a firm's owners and creditors (see Jensen and Meckling, 1976; Myers, 1977). These imply *inter alia* that external financing is costlier than internal, while there is generally rationing of credit. This may be rationing by price (for firms where information is freely available) or by quantity (where asymmetric information is severe).

The availability of internal financing may thus impact on real decisions (Fazzari, Hubbard and Petersen, 1988) as firms prefer to – or are constrained to – finance themselves by internal funds owing to higher costs of external finance. These effects may vary over time, giving rise to cyclical changes in credit supply in equilibrium (as suggested by the theoretical models of Holmstrom and Tirole, 1997, and Repullo and Suarez, 2000).

In more detail, Mishkin (1991) suggests that variations in agency costs affecting credit supply may occur via a number of channels, prompting potentially sharp changes in the availability of corporate finance (the channels may be compounded to the extent that they also affect financial intermediaries during periods of systemic risk). All are likely to be more severe for firms with high debt–equity ratios (i.e. low net worth), a higher mean and variance of returns and where asymmetric information is severe. First, if interest rates rise due to monetary tightening or merely to balance the credit market, adverse selection may increase sharply, giving rise to a substantial decline in credit availability. Second, heightened uncertainty, such that lenders find it harder to screen borrowers, increases adverse-selection problems, potentially reducing credit supply. Collateral is a means whereby asymmetric information problems may be reduced (as the lender is then confident of recovering his loan even if the borrower proves to be of low quality). But this means that a decrease in the valuation of assets (e.g. a stock market decline provoked by a change in future profit expectations), by lowering collateral values, sharply increases adverse selection for lenders. Reductions in credit supply will impinge more on low-quality borrowers for whom there is asymmetric information.

A parallel mechanism operates via the link of net worth to moral hazard. Given asymmetric information and incomplete contracts, borrowers have incentives to engage in activities that may be to their advantage, but which harm the lender by increasing risk of default. They hence limit credit availability, or subject the borrower to costly monitoring. The agency problem is greater when borrowers have low net worth, as they have less to lose from default. Besides being due to stock-market declines, net worth could decline due to an unanticipated disinflation or deflation that redistributes wealth from debtors to creditors. Such effects are plausibly greater for low-quality firms that have low net worth before such crises occur and which may be confined to banking markets.

Such patterns are said to give rise to a 'financial accelerator' (Bernanke, Gertler and Gilchrist, 1996) as changes in cash flow or asset prices over the cycle give rise to pro-cyclical feedback effects of agency costs on the cost of external finance and hence on real corporate expenditures. This will operate particularly via borrowers whose net worth is most heavily affected during a recession, and for borrowers whose activities are riskier or harder to monitor. Small firms are examples in each case. Small firms may be assigned a higher credit risk rating, without regard to the state of the business cycle, since it is more difficult for potential lenders to assess the risk of default by small firms due to the problems of asymmetric information. The owner of a small firm has in general much better information on his firm's performance than the bank and more control of the outcome. In contrast, the performance of larger firms will be reflected in their corporate bond spread and share price listed on equity markets, and the state of the firm's balance sheet will be under continual scrutiny by investment analysts in the market.

As detailed in Ashworth and Davis (2001), during an expansion when monetary policy is relaxed, all firms can initially finance themselves with retained earnings while balance sheets are strong. In these periods the demand for external finance is likely to be low. Demand for external finance picks up late in the cycle as investment demand outstrips retentions. In a downturn, revenue typically falls faster than expenditure, leading both large and small firms to redouble their demand for external finance, but from different sources. Smaller firms are more likely to be solely reliant for their external finance on banks, which normally require that assets be provided as collateral for loans and charge high spreads. Larger firms should find it easier to borrow through the corporate bond markets or use their credit standing to obtain unsecured lending at lower spreads from banks.

A dynamic process of intensifying price and quantity rationing of credit may overlay this pattern. The recession itself reduces asset values and net worth, thus raising the incidence of credit rationing, notably for small firms. An increase in interest rates for monetary policy purposes, if it triggers or accompanies the recession, will result in lower asset prices and higher interest repayments. These will, again, cause a deterioration in balance sheets and increase the risk of default on any outstanding loans and may increase the spread further, compounding effects on income gearing of the initial rise in interest rates. This may make it harder for firms to secure future borrowing at any price and lead to an increase in bankruptcies and business failures.

To summarise so far, external finance availability can be expected to vary over the cycle, in line with variation in agency costs. This means that balance sheet composition affects real activity. We have already noted that this gives rise to the financial accelerator, which applies to debt finance generally. There is also thought to be a 'credit channel' which focuses on the availability of bank credit for firms unable, owing to asymmetric information, to access market finance. Most work has looked at the special issue of small firms confined to banks and probably lacking external funds, in the US market which is typically not characterised by strong commitment of banks to borrowers and where a multibank system operates.

There are monetary policy implications since tightening *per se* will tend to raise the cost of credit for the small firm sector to a disproportionate extent (Kashyap *et al.*, 1994; Christiano *et al.*, 1996). Thus monetary policy will have a composition-of-output effect independent of its effect on the aggregate level of output. This effect will be particularly marked where the substitute channel of credit – from large firms via trade credit – is poorly developed or (as in the UK) tends to be replaced by large firms taking credit from small. If small firms are of particular importance to the growth of employment and to innovation, overall economic performance could be adversely affected. Meanwhile, independent of monetary policy, any effort by banks to raise profitability in the wake of loan losses will bear disproportionately on this sector.

The phenomena identified in Sections 4.1 and 4.2 are thought to give rise to a number of features of corporate finance, such as distribution of dividends despite tax disadvantages,[20] dependence of firms on retained earnings for investment, and also preference for debt rather than equity as a source of external finance.[21] The balance between these factors gives rise to the types of typical financial structure observed empirically, with positive debt and equity.

Again as noted in Section 1.3, agency costs are not confined to debt finance, and may indeed be more acute for equity finance. The conflict of interest between managers and shareholders, linked to the optional nature of dividend payments as well as asymmetric information, often makes new issues prohibitively expensive (owing to the greater need for monitoring than for debt) despite equity's superiority in terms of risk sharing (Myers and Majluf, 1984). In effect, debt has a superior form of incentive compatibility (Gale and Hellwig, 1985) since it allows the borrower to retain residual income while, in the case of default, control switches to the lender. Equity rationing is likely to be particularly severe in recessions, with similar mechanisms to those identified above applying.

## 4.3 FINANCIAL STRUCTURE AND INDUSTRIAL DEVELOPMENT

An emerging strand of the literature traces the symbiotic relationship between financial structure and the pattern of industrial development in the light of the theories of intermediation. This offers further clues as to factors underlying patterns of corporate financing.

At a sectoral level, the insider (relationship banking) model discussed in Section 1.5, with its emphasis on private information and on stakeholder relationships rather than public disclosure and liquidity, may be superior at implementing policies that need consensus among stakeholders. Such consensus policies may in turn encourage high levels of fixed investment by the firm and of the employees in firm-specific skills, in the context of long-lived corporations. On the other hand, the outsider (arm's-length) models in which institutional investors play a greater role may be better at responding to change and building up new firms. As Allen and Gale (1997) argued, capital market financing could therefore be economically benefi-

---

20 According to signalling models (Bhattacharya, 1979), dividends tend to reduce asymmetries of information between managers and investors by conveying information about firms' prospects and quality.

21 The intuition is that equity issues are particularly prone to exploitation of mispricing by well-informed insiders (Myers and Majluf, 1984).

cial in emerging industries with high financial and economic risks and in which knowledge about industry is uncertain (e.g., IT, biotechnology) where banks cannot be expected to have 'superior understanding' of management. Stock markets deal well with diversity of opinion. In contrast, relationship banking may have a comparative advantage in industries in which markets are mature and innovation and uncertainty are low, as banks can then accurately monitor and diversify risk among companies.

Carlin and Mayer (1999) note that financial systems of market-based OECD countries, whose industries focus on such R&D, are well suited to its financing. Bhattacharya and Chiesa (1995) on the other hand argue that firms involved in R&D may prefer bank finance to avoid disclosure of proprietary information to competitors. An aspect of financial systems characterised by 'commitment', as defined in Section 1.2, is that shareholding is typically not distributed but held by large blockholders. Large blockholders of shares cannot anonymously withdraw from past commitments (Franks and Mayer, 1994), such concentrated ownership being suited to activities involving investment by other stakeholders (such as willingness of workers to develop firm-specific skills).

Dewatripont and Maskin (1995) suggest that decentralised financial systems with many small banks (and markets) may impose tighter budget constraints than centralised systems with large banks (and no market alternative), as small banks do not have resources to recapitalise firms. They may thus more readily foreclose, as well as ration credit more tightly, notably for longer-term projects. Alternatively, according to Huang and Xu (1998), multibank systems may have tighter budget constraints because information sharing needed for refinancing does not occur, given conflicts of interest between banks. On the other hand, the multibank system may be superior at financing higher-risk, R&D-style projects where uncertainty is high and the option to foreclose is valuable. A corollary is that soft budget constraints in bank-based systems may lead to overlending in order to recoup monitoring costs. This may be the case particularly when funds are abundant, as in East Asia prior to the 1997 crisis (Rajan and Zingales, 1998b; Davis, 1999a), with Japan also being a cautionary example (Hoshi and Kashyap, 1999; Hutchinson and McDill, 1999).

Empirically, Rajan and Zingales (1998a) sought to test the link from financial development to growth of certain industries by assessing development of industries in relation to the product of a measure of their dependence on external finance and development of financial systems (notably in respect of accounting standards). They found that industries which (in the US) are most dependent on external finance grow more rapidly when financial systems are developed in this sense.

## 4.4 EMPIRICAL EVIDENCE ON CORPORATE FINANCING PATTERNS

Most work on the balance sheets of the corporate sector focuses on liability composition. Extant work has indicated that there are indeed systematic differences between Anglo Saxon and Continental countries, with higher debt in the latter (thought to reflect relationship banking) and more equity in the former. Corporate debt in the former is also more likely to be in the form of securities, with loans predominating almost entirely in the latter. For examples of such comparisons, see Davis (1986, 1995b). Comparing Germany and France, Deutsche Bundesbank (1999) shows that the balance sheets of individual small firms remained bank-dependent in Germany, while large firms were becoming less so between 1987 and 1995 – and all sizes of French corporations became less bank-dependent over the same period. Meanwhile Mayer (1996) showed that equity holdings in Continental Europe and Japan tended to be more concentrated in few owners than in the UK and US. Financial institutions tend to be the main owners in the latter and individuals and other companies in the former, see also Table 4.7. This is consistent with weaker corporate governance, as discussed in Section 1.3, and consequent need for large shareholders.

Greater contrasts are apparent in looking at studies of the flow of funds for the corporate sector. For example, Corbett and Jenkinson (1997), looking at net flow data for Germany, Japan, the UK and US, found internal finance to be the most important source of finance in all countries, consistent with high relative costs of external finance, but more so in the UK and US than in Germany and Japan. Bank finance was found to be most important in three of the four countries, with the exception being the US (where bank and bond finance were co-equal). External finance via equity was found to be low in all cases, and negative in the UK and US (due to takeovers and equity retirements).

On the other hand, Schmidt *et al.* (2001) suggest that the results of the Corbett/Jenkinson paper, and other similar exercises such as Mayer (1988), are due to misspecification. The earlier papers assume that all external financing is used first to pay off debt or equity incurred to finance investment in earlier periods, and only the remainder used for investment now, and not to repay external finance. Only internal financing is assumed to have no such offset. The upshot is that the contribution of external finance is biased downwards. The Schmidt *et al.* method is to construct gross finance data. The results suggest that, from 1970–96, German and Japanese banks consistently provided more than three quarters of external finance for their corporate sectors, in line with relationship banking, while in the US, banks' share fell from 50 per cent to 36 per cent over the same period, with non-banks making a growing contribution (and that of households fell from 12 per cent to 6 per cent). Hence it was reconfirmed that securities markets are shown to be a distinctive feature of the US, also on the flow side.

An interesting paradox has emerged in the empirical literature that focuses on flows of financing to the corporate sector, and their division between internal and external funds in countries at different stages of development (Allen and Gale, 2000). In OECD countries, internal financing tends to be larger than external financing, with the majority of the latter being in the form of bank debt (for a recent view, see Corbett and Jenkinson, 1997). This is of course consistent with the agency costs and asymmetric information points made above and in Sections 1.2–1.3, although it may also reflect a high proportion of large established firms, which generate considerable cash flow.

Singh (1995), in contrast, suggests that the proportion of corporate financing accounted for by external funds is large in EMEs and dominates internal finance, with equity financing also being larger than debt. This may of course reflect a shortage of funds, as well as heightened agency costs for debt when legal and financial systems are poorly developed and there is a preponderance of small, young firms. The pattern of dependence on external finance, if sustained, would also imply a heightened vulnerability of EME corporate sectors to financial turbulence, independent of the structural features of the financial system,[22] although the predominance of equity offers a partial offset. Meanwhile Davis (2001b) notes the potential benefits for firms' stability if they can access both bank and bond finance. But on the other hand, Davis and Ioannidis (2002) empirically show the limitations of this even in the US, where bank finance appears to be needed first in order for bond finance to be feasible. This confirms the predictions of the theoretical work of Holmstrom and Tirole (1997).

As regards corporate governance, a cross-country study of the UK, Germany and France by Schmidt *et al.* (2001) suggests that the UK and Germany showed stable patterns consistent with the paradigms outlined in Section 1.3 above, but France showed a sort of vacuum, with the former control by the state and other corporations via cross-holding being withdrawn but not yet replaced by the capital market or internal control. Banks are widely involved in financing, also tending to control asset managers, but are not powerful in terms of corporate control.

---

22 Consistent with this, Fauver *et al.* (1999) show that conglomerates which generate diversified cashflows perform better than specialised firms in EMEs, which is opposite to the result for OECD countries.

Davis (2002a) explored the relationship between the growth of institutional investor holdings of corporate equity as a share of the total outstanding and corporate sector performance at an economy-wide level in the G-7. Results were consistent with effects which differ between Anglo-Saxon and relationship-banking countries. For example, institutions appear to restrain investment and boost dividends and productivity growth in the former. Generally, institutional shareholding is consistent with shifts in corporate performance towards shareholder-value maximising approaches. Davis also summarised the legion of articles on corporate performance and institutional holdings at a micro level, which on balance also favour a positive influence of institutional investors on corporate governance, and hence on performance in terms of equity returns.

Turning to evidence for cyclical effects (see the summary in Ashworth and Davis, 2001), important empirical tests of the 'financial accelerator' hypothesis for the US include Bernanke *et al.* (1996), who show that, after a monetary tightening, the relationship between internal funds and investment becomes stronger for smaller firms than larger firms. Additionally, small firms experience much more pro-cyclical variation in economic activity than do large firms. Oliner and Rudebusch (1996) found similar results. Hu (1999), using individual firm data, showed that monetary contractions reduce investment more for highly leveraged firms than for less leveraged ones. Using flow of funds data, Christiano *et al.* (1996) showed that following a monetary policy shock, borrowing of large corporate firms rises for some time, before falling off in the subsequent recession (perhaps because cash flows fall before expenditures can be adjusted). In contrast, the borrowing of small non-corporate firms (whose net worth may be hit by the monetary policy action) is much weaker.

Less work has been done on studying the impacts of these effects in countries other than the US. Vermuelen (2000) has applied the approach to Germany, France, Italy and Spain using micro data and shows that weak balance sheets are more important in explaining investment during downturns than strong balance sheets during upturns, while effects of the accelerator are greatest for small firms. Looking at the UK, Guaraglia (1999) finds a significant link from financial variables to inventory investment, which is stronger for firms with weak balance sheets, during periods of recession and when there is tight monetary policy. See Lund and Wright (1998) for an investigation into the sources of external funds for small firms in the UK.

A corollary of the financial accelerator is that financial systems that cope better with agency costs will offer more external financing, *ceteris paribus*. Indeed, studies such as Hoshi *et al.* (1993a) suggest that close bank relationships of firms in the Japanese industrial groups eases such constraints considerably (or did, before that country's financial crisis). But work such as Horiuchi and Okazaki (1994) finds the opposite result for Japan, and for Germany Edwards and Fischer (1994) and Gorton and Schmidt (1996) also find little evidence of a positive effect. Note also that new and small firms typically have greater external financing needs than large established ones (cash cows), even abstracting from possible greater information asymmetries for such firms. They will hence be more vulnerable to any decline in availability of external finance.

Concerning the credit channel, Gertler and Gilchrist (1994) found a larger role for bank credit in explaining inventory fluctuations for small firms than large ones, as well as a larger and speedier impact of monetary policy on small firms' expenditure and borrowing. They attributed these patterns to the credit channel, interacting with the high costs small firms face in switching sources of credit; lower value put on relationships with small firms by banks, and financial weakness of small firms. These mean small firms are the first to be credit rationed. Gertler and Gilchrist (1992) observed a perverse increase in loans for large companies following a monetary tightening, while there is an immediate reduction for small firms. They attribute this to large firms meeting cash flow shortages by both running down buffer stock deposits and increasing loans. As small firms face high costs of access to credit, such distress borrowing is not possible. See Saidenberg and Strahan (1999) for a recent look at the importance of banks as a source of funds for large businesses in the US.

Complementing these results, Kashyap *et al.* (1994) show that bank-dependent firms lacking bond ratings and with low liquidity are most likely to cut inventories in periods of monetary tightness.[23] Morgan (1994) found sizeable increases in loans made under commitment – likely to be held by larger and stronger borrowers – during periods of tight money. Research quoted in Bernanke (1993) shows that loans made at sizeable spreads relative to US prime rate, to small and risky firms, shrink as a proportion of total loans as monetary policy becomes restrictive. Finally in Japan, Hoshi *et al.* (1993a) show liquidity is more important for the investment by firms that do not have a main bank link during periods of tight money, and find the credit mix is a significant determinant of investment and inventories.

On the asset side, most studies of corporate sector balance sheet behaviour have looked at the determinants of liquidity holdings (see for example

23 Similarly, Bernanke, Gertler and Gilchrist (1996) found using panel data that both small and bank-dependent firms had more procyclical inventories than other firms, a pattern they attributed to agency costs.

Bruinshoofd and Kool, 2001; Kim *et al.*, 1998; and Opler *et al.*, 1999) rather than financial assets including equity. An explanation has to be sought as to why firms hold low-yielding liquid assets when they could use the resources to invest in high-yielding but illiquid capital. Empirical work tends to support a long-run target for corporate liquidity, based on transactions and opportunity cost motives. Also important are asymmetric information problems and consequent limits to external finance, which contribute to a precautionary demand for liquidity. In the short run, the so-called buffer-stock approach and the pecking-order theory in finance suggest liquidity may passively accommodate shocks to the firm's financial position.

Other areas of corporate finance on which empirical work has been undertaken include the role of trade credit, foreign direct investment and pension liabilities. These are, however, not generally treated directly in the context of the overall corporate balance sheet.

## 4.5 COMPANY SECTOR BALANCE SHEETS

We now go on to examine the assets and liabilities of the corporate sectors in the G-7 in Tables 4.1–4.4 in the light of the survey above. On the asset side, for European countries, the largest proportion is in equity holdings, while, in Japan and Canada, deposits predominate (see Table 4.1). Whilst Japan also has an important role for equities, Canadian companies also have a large percentage of loans, which have declined somewhat recently. There may be a slight definitional issue for the US, which has a high level of foreign direct investment and no equity holdings indicated as they are netted out. FDI is only shown for a subset of countries, and the statistical basis differs, as witness 53 per cent of financial assets in the US and only 0.2 per cent in Canada. A more harmonised estimate is provided in the IMF data shown in Tables 7.5–7.7. The limitation of work on assets focused on liquidity only is apparent from these points.

One of the most substantial changes in corporate asset portfolios over the last thirty years is the behaviour of broad money demand. Italian firms previously had quite a substantial demand at 62 per cent of financial assets but this has declined to 13 per cent due to a switch to equity holding. Assets have grown much faster than liquidity. Declines in broad money in Germany and France (where deposits were never particularly important) have also coincided with a move to equity. Underlying forces may include financial liberalisation (increasing real returns) but also declining requirements for compensating balances by banks[24] and (in countries such as the US and France) an increase in the attractiveness and availability of money

Table 4.1 *Company sector financial assets (per cent of total)*

| | | UK | US | Germany | Japan | Canada | France | Italy |
|---|---|---|---|---|---|---|---|---|
| Deposits notes coin | 1970 | 17.2 | 29.5 | 60.1 | 80.2 | 36.9 | 16.9 | 62.4 |
| | 1980 | 23.4 | 21.8 | 63.1 | 71.9 | 57.3 | 32.2 | 31.6 |
| | 1990 | 37.2 | 24.2 | 52.8 | 57.6 | 48.5 | 10.2 | 17.0 |
| | 1998 | 32.1 | 20.5 | 22.8 | 48.5 | 66.3 | 6.8 | 19.4 |
| | 2000 | 23.3 | 22.7 | 17.3 | 44.1 | 66.0 | 5.5 | 13.1 |
| Money market inst | 1970 | 3.6 | 0.1 | 0.1 | 0.0 | 6.0 | 0.2 | 0.0 |
| | 1980 | 2.3 | 1.7 | 0.1 | 0.0 | 7.5 | 0.0 | 1.6 |
| | 1990 | 2.9 | 2.7 | 1.2 | 1.5 | 20.5 | 3.1 | 0.8 |
| | 1998 | 2.5 | 7.8 | 1.0 | 1.1 | 9.1 | 2.7 | 0.5 |
| | 2000 | 2.3 | 9.8 | 1.1 | 2.2 | 9.9 | 4.3 | 0.2 |
| Loans | 1970 | 3.9 | 8.6 | 0.0 | 0.0 | 27.4 | 0.0 | 6.9 |
| | 1980 | 3.4 | 9.1 | 0.0 | 0.0 | 22.5 | 0.0 | 5.2 |
| | 1990 | 17.6 | 11.5 | 0.0 | 0.0 | 17.6 | 0.2 | 11.1 |
| | 1998 | 17.0 | 7.4 | 6.0 | 8.8 | 14.4 | 13.6 | 4.7 |
| | 2000 | 15.1 | 5.7 | 7.2 | 8.3 | 14.5 | 10.8 | 6.0 |
| Bonds | 1970 | 2.7 | 11.2 | 3.9 | 3.8 | 13.1 | 1.4 | 1.1 |
| | 1980 | 3.4 | 5.5 | 6.9 | 5.7 | 3.5 | 3.1 | 0.6 |
| | 1990 | 1.7 | 7.6 | 5.3 | 3.4 | 5.4 | 1.3 | 10.8 |
| | 1998 | 2.2 | 5.2 | 4.4 | 6.2 | 4.7 | 2.1 | 8.2 |
| | 2000 | 1.6 | 4.7 | 8.3 | 4.6 | 4.4 | 1.1 | 7.3 |
| Equity | 1970 | 20.8 | na | 35.9 | 15.9 | 12.9 | 81.4 | 29.5 |
| | 1980 | 15.2 | na | 30.0 | 22.4 | 7.1 | 64.3 | 61.1 |
| | 1990 | 40.5 | na | 38.4 | 36.0 | 5.5 | 81.0 | 60.3 |
| | 1998 | 46.2 | na | 60.2 | 29.0 | 5.1 | 68.3 | 63.6 |
| | 2000 | 57.7 | na | 60.8 | 35.1 | 4.9 | 73.1 | 71.3 |
| Mutual funds | 1970 | 0.0 | 0.4 | 0.0 | 0.1 | na | 0.0 | 0.0 |
| | 1980 | 0.0 | 0.2 | 0.0 | 0.1 | na | 0.3 | 0.0 |
| | 1990 | 0.1 | 0.9 | 2.3 | 1.5 | na | 4.1 | 0.0 |
| | 1998 | 0.1 | 4.7 | 5.6 | 0.6 | na | 6.5 | 3.6 |
| | 2000 | 0.0 | 4.1 | 5.3 | 0.9 | na | 5.2 | 2.1 |
| FDI | 1970 | 51.8 | 50.2 | na | na | 3.7 | na | na |
| | 1980 | 52.2 | 61.6 | na | na | 2.0 | na | na |
| | 1990 | na | 53.1 | na | na | 2.3 | na | na |
| | 1998 | na | 54.4 | na | 5.9 | 0.3 | na | na |
| | 2000 | na | 53.0 | na | 4.9 | 0.2 | na | na |

24 Compensating balances are deposits that banks require from borrowers in return for provision of loan finance. Usually, banks lend more than the required amount and demand that the excess be held on deposit with them.

Table 4.2 *Company sector financial assets (per cent of GDP)*

| | | UK | US | Germany | Japan | Canada | France | Italy |
|---|---|---|---|---|---|---|---|---|
| Deposits | 1970 | 6.5 | 4.8 | 17.1 | 33.0 | 4.5 | 8.4 | 28.0 |
| | 1980 | 7.9 | 4.7 | 19.9 | 40.7 | 8.1 | 11.3 | 21.3 |
| | 1990 | 21.2 | 4.3 | 24.2 | 50.8 | 8.8 | 12.2 | 7.5 |
| | 1998 | 23.3 | 4.4 | 15.2 | 35.7 | 14.4 | 9.6 | 8.1 |
| | 2000 | 27.4 | 5.4 | 14.5 | 35.1 | 14.4 | 10.6 | 9.2 |
| Money market inst | 1970 | 1.3 | 0.0 | 0.0 | 0.0 | 0.7 | 0.1 | 0.0 |
| | 1980 | 0.8 | 0.4 | 0.0 | 0.0 | 1.1 | 0.0 | 1.1 |
| | 1990 | 1.6 | 0.5 | 0.5 | 1.3 | 3.7 | 3.7 | 0.4 |
| | 1998 | 1.8 | 1.7 | 0.7 | 0.8 | 2.0 | 3.8 | 0.2 |
| | 2000 | 2.7 | 2.3 | 0.9 | 1.7 | 2.2 | 8.3 | 0.2 |
| Loans | 1970 | 1.5 | 1.4 | 0.0 | 0.0 | 3.3 | 0.0 | 3.1 |
| | 1980 | 1.2 | 1.9 | 0.0 | 0.0 | 3.2 | 0.0 | 3.5 |
| | 1990 | 10.0 | 2.1 | 0.0 | 0.0 | 3.2 | 0.3 | 4.9 |
| | 1998 | 12.3 | 1.6 | 4.0 | 6.5 | 3.1 | 19.1 | 1.9 |
| | 2000 | 17.7 | 1.4 | 6.0 | 6.6 | 3.2 | 20.9 | 4.2 |
| Bonds | 1970 | 1.0 | 1.8 | 1.1 | 1.6 | 1.6 | 0.7 | 0.5 |
| | 1980 | 1.2 | 1.2 | 2.2 | 3.2 | 0.5 | 1.1 | 0.4 |
| | 1990 | 1.0 | 1.4 | 2.5 | 3.0 | 1.0 | 1.5 | 4.7 |
| | 1998 | 1.6 | 1.1 | 3.0 | 4.6 | 1.0 | 2.9 | 3.4 |
| | 2000 | 1.9 | 1.1 | 7.0 | 3.7 | 1.0 | 2.2 | 5.1 |
| Equity | 1970 | 7.8 | na | 10.2 | 6.5 | 1.6 | 40.2 | 13.2 |
| | 1980 | 5.2 | na | 9.5 | 12.7 | 1.0 | 22.6 | 41.2 |
| | 1990 | 23.1 | na | 17.6 | 31.7 | 1.0 | 96.7 | 26.5 |
| | 1998 | 33.6 | na | 40.1 | 21.4 | 1.1 | 96.1 | 26.4 |
| | 2000 | 67.9 | na | 51.0 | 27.9 | 1.1 | 142.1 | 50.2 |
| Mutual funds | 1970 | 0.0 | 0.1 | 0.0 | 0.0 | na | 0.0 | 0.0 |
| | 1980 | 0.0 | 0.1 | 0.0 | 0.0 | na | 0.1 | 0.0 |
| | 1990 | 0.0 | 0.2 | 1.0 | 1.3 | na | 4.9 | 0.0 |
| | 1998 | 0.1 | 1.0 | 3.7 | 0.4 | na | 9.2 | 1.5 |
| | 1999 | 0.1 | 1.2 | 4.0 | 1.3 | na | 9.5 | 1.6 |
| | 2000 | 0.1 | 1.0 | 4.5 | 0.7 | na | 10.2 | 1.5 |
| FDI | 1970 | 19.4 | 8.1 | na | na | 0.4 | na | na |
| | 1990 | na | 9.5 | na | na | 0.4 | na | na |
| | 1998 | na | 11.7 | na | 4.3 | 0.1 | na | na |
| | 1999 | na | 12.1 | na | 3.3 | 0.1 | na | na |
| | 2000 | na | 12.6 | na | 3.9 | 0.1 | na | na |
| Total assets | 1970 | 37.5 | 16.1 | 28.4 | 41.2 | 12.2 | 49.4 | 44.9 |
| | 1980 | 33.9 | 21.4 | 31.6 | 56.7 | 14.1 | 35.2 | 67.5 |
| | 1990 | 56.9 | 17.9 | 45.9 | 88.2 | 18.2 | 119.4 | 43.9 |
| | 1998 | 72.7 | 21.5 | 66.7 | 73.8 | 21.7 | 140.7 | 41.5 |
| | 2000 | 117.6 | 23.8 | 83.8 | 79.6 | 21.8 | 194.3 | 70.5 |

Table 4.2 (*Continued*)

| | | UK | US | Germany | Japan | Canada | France | Italy |
|---|---|---|---|---|---|---|---|---|
| Memo: | 1970 | 8.8 | 6.6 | 18.2 | 34.6 | 6.8 | 9.2 | 28.5 |
| liquidity/ | 1980 | 9.9 | 6.2 | 22.1 | 43.9 | 9.7 | 12.5 | 22.8 |
| GDP | 1990 | 23.8 | 6.2 | 27.2 | 55.1 | 13.6 | 17.5 | 12.5 |
| | 1998 | 26.7 | 7.2 | 18.8 | 41.1 | 17.4 | 16.3 | 11.7 |
| | 2000 | 31.9 | 8.9 | 22.4 | 40.5 | 17.5 | 21.1 | 14.6 |

market instruments. Some perspective, supporting the concept of target liquidity, is, however, given by ratios to GDP (Table 4.2) which show a rise in deposits in the UK and Canada and roughly constant ratios elsewhere, except for Italy.

Looking at the importance of each of the countries' company sector financial assets as a proportion of GDP (see Table 4.2), we can see that they are now very large for the UK, at 118 per cent, and especially for France, with 194 per cent. Both these countries have seen substantial increases in the last thirty years: more than threefold in each case, mainly in the form of direct equity holdings.

Corporate liquidity is usually defined as deposits and other short-term assets plus bonds. This total was highly variable across countries in 2000, at around 32 per cent of GDP for the UK, 9 per cent for the US, 22 per cent for Germany, 40 per cent for Japan, 17 per cent for Canada, 22 per cent for France and 15 per cent for Italy. The robustness of the corporate sectors is accordingly variable (bearing in mind that borrowing capacity and short-term liabilities outstanding are also important factors). Note that there is no marked pattern of lower liquidity in market oriented countries as might have been expected from the precautionary motive set out above (if agency costs of external finance are higher). Relatively high liquidity in Japan may reflect poor investment opportunities and conversely, the positive outlook in the US in 2000 may have restrained liquidity. In addition, short-term money market liabilities such as commercial paper, which substitute for liquidity, are readily issued in the US. The UK does not follow the US in respect of low liquidity, however. We note that UK banks are often accused of credit rationing unduly, especially to small firms, and this may help explain high liquidity.

Liabilities for the corporate sector, as expected, come mainly in the form of equity; see Table 4.3. France, the US and UK have the largest proportion of equities for our sample of countries (around 70 per cent for these countries in 1998 and 2000). The average over these recent years in Italy,

Table 4.3 *Company sector liabilities (per cent of total)*

| | | UK | US | Germany | Japan | Canada | France | Italy |
|---|---|---|---|---|---|---|---|---|
| Money market Inst | 1970 | 0.0 | 0.7 | 0.8 | 0.0 | 1.3 | 0.0 | 0.0 |
| | 1980 | 0.3 | 1.2 | 0.4 | 0.0 | 2.1 | 0.0 | 0.3 |
| | 1990 | 0.6 | 1.9 | 0.1 | 2.6 | 6.6 | 1.3 | 0.1 |
| | 1998 | 0.9 | 1.2 | 0.1 | 1.3 | 5.1 | 1.1 | 0.3 |
| | 2000 | 0.9 | 1.5 | 0.4 | 1.4 | 5.3 | 1.4 | 0.1 |
| Loans | 1970 | 18.8 | 17.3 | 58.8 | 74.3 | 19.4 | 36.2 | 59.6 |
| | 1980 | 26.5 | 19.8 | 68.5 | 71.9 | 29.1 | 44.6 | 43.8 |
| | 1990 | 35.7 | 21.3 | 67.4 | 80.4 | 28.5 | 25.8 | 44.0 |
| | 1998 | 22.3 | 9.8 | 41.5 | 57.3 | 24.1 | 20.9 | 41.0 |
| | 2000 | 22.5 | 11.1 | 42.8 | 50.9 | 23.2 | 16.1 | 36.4 |
| Bonds | 1970 | 8.0 | 15.4 | 4.2 | 3.8 | 22.9 | 4.4 | 8.7 |
| | 1980 | 2.3 | 17.4 | 2.8 | 3.8 | 19.0 | 5.2 | 3.5 |
| | 1990 | 5.4 | 18.7 | 3.0 | 6.4 | 17.4 | 4.1 | 3.5 |
| | 1998 | 5.6 | 12.3 | 1.8 | 11.8 | 19.0 | 4.1 | 1.8 |
| | 2000 | 6.5 | 13.2 | 1.3 | 10.9 | 16.8 | 3.4 | 0.7 |
| Equity | 1970 | 59.9 | 65.7 | 36.2 | 21.9 | 56.4 | 59.5 | 31.7 |
| | 1980 | 48.4 | 57.0 | 28.3 | 24.3 | 49.8 | 50.2 | 52.4 |
| | 1990 | 58.4 | 49.5 | 29.6 | 10.6 | 47.5 | 68.8 | 52.4 |
| | 1998 | 71.1 | 71.6 | 56.6 | 29.6 | 51.8 | 73.9 | 56.9 |
| | 2000 | 70.2 | 67.5 | 55.4 | 36.8 | 54.7 | 79.0 | 62.7 |
| FDI | 1970 | 13.3 | 1.0 | na | na | na | na | na |
| | 1980 | 22.6 | 4.7 | na | na | na | na | na |
| | 1990 | na | 8.6 | na | na | na | na | na |
| | 1998 | na | 5.1 | na | na | na | na | na |
| | 2000 | na | 6.7 | na | na | na | na | na |

Canada and Germany was 55–60 per cent, while in Japan it was around 30 per cent. Bear in mind, however, that growth in equity proportions largely reflects valuations rather than issuance – data on flows in 1995–2000 are shown in Tables 4.5–4.6. The implied debt–equity ratios, which as noted in Section 4.2 may be crucial to the availability of external finance, are thus generally higher in bank-based systems. This may offset any benefits these systems offer in terms of credit availability relative to market-based systems, and may entail heightened fragility of the corporate sector as and when the corporate sector evolves towards the Anglo-Saxon model. It may also, as discussed in Section 4.3, reflect industrial structure.

In terms of debt finance, in most of the G-7, loans are generally the most important component, with 51 per cent of liabilities in this form for Japan

Table 4.4 *Company sector liabilities (per cent of GDP)*

| | | UK | US | Germany | Japan | Canada | France | Italy |
|---|---|---|---|---|---|---|---|---|
| Money Market Inst | 1970 | 0.0 | 0.7 | 0.5 | 0.0 | 1.5 | 0.0 | 0.0 |
| | 1980 | 0.2 | 1.0 | 0.3 | 0.0 | 2.5 | 0.0 | 0.3 |
| | 1990 | 1.0 | 2.0 | 0.0 | 4.1 | 7.9 | 2.4 | 0.1 |
| | 1998 | 2.2 | 2.1 | 0.2 | 2.7 | 6.5 | 3.0 | 0.4 |
| | 2000 | 2.5 | 2.8 | 0.7 | 3.0 | 6.8 | 5.3 | 0.2 |
| Loans | 1970 | 21.1 | 17.8 | 39.7 | 80.8 | 22.1 | 45.1 | 55.0 |
| | 1980 | 18.8 | 16.0 | 43.6 | 97.5 | 33.9 | 42.0 | 44.7 |
| | 1990 | 58.9 | 21.8 | 59.8 | 128.8 | 34.5 | 48.3 | 47.0 |
| | 1998 | 52.5 | 17.6 | 52.6 | 120.0 | 31.0 | 56.3 | 47.9 |
| | 2000 | 65.8 | 19.9 | 63.1 | 110.6 | 29.6 | 60.0 | 54.1 |
| Bonds | 1970 | 8.9 | 15.8 | 2.8 | 4.2 | 26.1 | 5.5 | 8.0 |
| | 1980 | 1.6 | 14.1 | 1.8 | 5.2 | 22.2 | 4.9 | 3.6 |
| | 1990 | 8.8 | 19.2 | 2.6 | 10.3 | 21.0 | 7.7 | 3.8 |
| | 1998 | 13.3 | 22.0 | 2.2 | 24.7 | 24.5 | 11.0 | 2.1 |
| | 2000 | 19.1 | 23.6 | 1.9 | 23.7 | 21.4 | 12.7 | 1.1 |
| Equity | 1970 | 67.1 | 67.6 | 24.4 | 23.8 | 64.2 | 74.3 | 29.3 |
| | 1980 | 34.4 | 46.1 | 18.0 | 33.0 | 58.1 | 47.2 | 53.6 |
| | 1990 | 96.3 | 50.7 | 26.2 | 16.9 | 57.5 | 128.7 | 56.0 |
| | 1998 | 167.1 | 128.4 | 71.6 | 62.0 | 66.5 | 199.1 | 66.4 |
| | 2000 | 205.3 | 120.6 | 81.6 | 79.9 | 69.8 | 293.4 | 93.2 |
| FDI | 1970 | 14.9 | 1.1 | na | na | na | na | na |
| | 1980 | 16.1 | 3.8 | na | na | na | na | na |
| | 1990 | na | 8.8 | na | na | na | na | na |
| | 1998 | na | 9.2 | na | na | na | na | na |
| | 2000 | na | 11.9 | na | na | na | na | na |
| Total liabilities | 1970 | 112.0 | 102.9 | 67.4 | 108.8 | 113.9 | 124.9 | 92.3 |
| | 1980 | 71.2 | 81.0 | 63.7 | 135.6 | 116.7 | 94.1 | 102.2 |
| | 1990 | 165.1 | 102.5 | 88.7 | 160.2 | 120.9 | 187.1 | 106.9 |
| | 1998 | 235.1 | 179.4 | 126.5 | 209.4 | 128.5 | 269.5 | 116.8 |
| | 2000 | 292.7 | 178.8 | 147.3 | 217.2 | 127.7 | 371.4 | 148.6 |
| Memo: Debt/GDP | 1970 | 30.0 | 34.3 | 43.0 | 85.0 | 49.7 | 50.6 | 63.0 |
| | 1980 | 20.7 | 31.1 | 45.7 | 102.6 | 58.6 | 46.9 | 48.6 |
| | 1990 | 68.8 | 43.0 | 62.5 | 143.2 | 63.5 | 58.4 | 50.9 |
| | 1998 | 68.0 | 41.8 | 55.0 | 147.4 | 62.0 | 70.3 | 50.4 |
| | 2000 | 87.4 | 46.3 | 65.7 | 137.2 | 57.9 | 78.0 | 55.4 |

and 43 per cent in Germany – the archetypal relationship-banking countries – and 36 per cent for Italy. France and the predominantly English speaking countries use debt in the form of loans the least for company finance, with the shares of liabilities being 16–23 per cent in 2000. A sizeable proportion of liabilities are in the form of corporate debt securities for the two North American countries. Canada has 17 per cent of liabilities in bonds (and also 5.3 per cent in money market instruments) whilst the US has 13 per cent in bonds and only 1.5 per cent in MMIs. Companies in Japan also use bonds with almost 11 per cent of liabilities in that form. Elsewhere – including the UK – debt security instruments are still relatively unimportant as a means of financing, indicating a lack of diversified funding mechanisms in terms of debt finance (Davis, 2001b). This lack of 'multiple channels of intermediation' leaves corporations vulnerable to shocks affecting banks via the credit channel and may also help to explain higher precautionary levels of corporate liquidity outside the US and Canada.

As regards trends, all countries have seen a decline in bank lending as a share of liabilities in the 1990s, partly reflecting the financial crises faced by companies in the early 1990s due to overindebtedness (Davis, 1995c), as well as the rise in equities. The move in Japan has been particularly sharp, from 80 per cent to just over 50 per cent. Germany has also seen a sizeable shift away from loans in the 1990s: from 67 per cent of total liabilities in 1990 to 43 per cent in 2000. The sharpest change in the ratio of loans to bonds has been in Japan where, as noted by Hoshi *et al.* (1993b), this has entailed a marked change in financial structure generally. Smaller changes, usually entailing a rise in the ratio of bonds to loans, are also apparent elsewhere.

As a proportion of GDP, corporate liabilities are substantial and amount to more than the total of GDP of each of the G-7 countries (Figure 1.1 and Table 4.4). The French corporate sector had the largest liabilities at 371 per cent of national income in 2000. Also with substantial liabilities was the United Kingdom (293 per cent) and Japan (217 per cent). Germany, Italy and Canada had the lowest corporate liabilities as a proportion of GDP. For most countries, the level of liabilities in 2000 was greater than both the levels in 1970 and 1990.

Of course, the nature of liabilities differs sharply between debt and equity, in terms of the implications for default risk, as well as the sensitivity of investment to the cycle. The debt/GDP ratio (including money market instruments, loans and bonds) may be more informative concerning credit risk and financial fragility. Indeed, Davis (1995b) showed a strong effect of the debt/GDP ratio on credit spreads and defaults in the G-7, albeit with levels which differ between bank and market related countries. The table shows that in 2000 this aggregate stood highest in Japan at 137 per cent of GDP, followed by the UK and France at around 80 per cent. The other countries had comparable levels of around 50 per cent. This high gross debt forms a partial offset to high levels of liquidity in countries such as the UK and Japan, although their net debt/GDP ratio remains high, being 65 per cent in the UK and 97 per cent in Japan, compared with 57 per cent in France and below 45 per cent elsewhere.

## 4.6 FLOW DATA FOR THE CORPORATE SECTOR

The main focus of this work is on stock data for assets and liabilities. However, we acknowledge that additional information on financing may be provided by the flow counterparts of these balance sheets. In particular, flow data allow us to discern whether rising equity corresponds to a rise in valuations alone or whether it corresponds to a flow of financing, as well as assessing external finance constraints. It also provides an additional means of gauging differences in financial structure, as discussed in Sections 4.4 and 11.1. We accordingly present data over the years 1995–2000 (average and year-by-year) in Figures 4.1–4.2 and Tables 4.5–4.6. Given the variability of flows, it may be best to focus on the average data. Note that there is often a sizeable unidentified item between the sum of identified instruments and the total.

There is quite a range of experiences for our countries in terms of company asset flows over the six-year period, with the UK and Canada at the upper end of asset accumulation as a percentage of GDP, averaging no less than 15–22 per cent of GDP. We can see this in Figure 4.1 and Table 4.5. For the UK, this has mainly been of the form of increased flows to equity (due to international takeover activity) and for Canada mainly bonds and loans as well as unidentified items. France has also seen relatively high inflows to assets, with these being concentrated in equity holdings.

Flows to liabilities (Figure 4.2 and Table 4.6) were again high for the UK and Canada, with flows of 16–26 per cent of GDP on average. Liability flows in France, the US, Germany and Italy were 5–10 per cent of GDP, while the Japanese incurrence was zero. This seems likely to be cyclical, given the relative weakness of Japanese activity and the Japanese banking crisis. Concerning composition, identified flows for Canada were again mainly of equity, and in the UK both equity and loan flows were sizeable. High levels of equity issuance are not consistent with suggestions of rationing due to adverse selection highlighted in Section 1.3. But this was a buoyant period in terms of the cycle and equity prices, so generalisations may not be valid.

The flow pattern in Table 4.6 is not consistent with the view of a simple divide between Continental/Japanese loan-based systems and others. The

Table 4.5 *Company sector acquisition of financial assets (per cent of GDP)*

| | | UK | US | Germany | Japan | Canada | France | Italy |
|---|---|---|---|---|---|---|---|---|
| Deposits notes coin | 1995 | 1.4 | 0.1 | 0.6 | 1.5 | 1.5 | 0.6 | 0.0 |
| | 1996 | 2.7 | 0.6 | 1.5 | −0.8 | 4.0 | 0.7 | 0.0 |
| | 1997 | 2.8 | 0.2 | −0.8 | −0.6 | 3.1 | 0.8 | 0.7 |
| | 1998 | 0.5 | 0.2 | 0.6 | 0.5 | 0.3 | −0.1 | −0.1 |
| | 1999 | 3.1 | 0.8 | −0.2 | 1.7 | 3.1 | 0.3 | 0.6 |
| | 2000 | 5.3 | 0.3 | 0.1 | −0.2 | −0.1 | 1.4 | 1.2 |
| Money market inst | 1995 | 0.1 | 0.3 | 0.1 | −0.1 | 0.8 | 0.8 | 0.1 |
| | 1996 | 0.2 | 0.3 | −0.2 | 0.1 | 1.0 | −1.3 | −0.3 |
| | 1997 | −0.2 | 0.3 | 0.0 | −0.1 | 0.4 | 0.0 | −0.1 |
| | 1998 | 0.0 | 0.3 | 0.0 | 0.4 | 0.9 | 0.8 | 0.0 |
| | 1999 | −0.1 | 0.3 | −0.3 | 0.1 | 2.2 | 2.7 | −0.2 |
| | 2000 | −0.2 | 0.4 | 0.5 | 0.6 | 0.1 | 2.2 | 0.0 |
| Loans | 1995 | 1.2 | 0.0 | 0.8 | −0.2 | 3.4 | 0.9 | 0.9 |
| | 1996 | −0.1 | −0.1 | 0.5 | 0.1 | 3.9 | 2.2 | 0.3 |
| | 1997 | 1.5 | 0.3 | 0.4 | −0.3 | 6.2 | 1.3 | 0.3 |
| | 1998 | 2.2 | −0.2 | 1.2 | −0.1 | 6.5 | 2.0 | 0.5 |
| | 1999 | 2.6 | 0.0 | 1.5 | 0.5 | 5.0 | 2.0 | 0.6 |
| | 2000 | 4.9 | 0.0 | 1.8 | 0.0 | 5.3 | 0.9 | 0.4 |
| Bonds | 1995 | 0.4 | −0.1 | −0.5 | 0.0 | 2.9 | 0.4 | 0.5 |
| | 1996 | −0.2 | −0.1 | −0.4 | 0.5 | 3.8 | 1.4 | 0.4 |
| | 1997 | −0.3 | −0.5 | −0.3 | 0.8 | 4.2 | −0.4 | −0.4 |
| | 1998 | 0.3 | 0.0 | 0.4 | −0.2 | 4.2 | −1.5 | 0.1 |
| | 1999 | −0.3 | −0.1 | 2.2 | 0.0 | 2.3 | 0.3 | 0.4 |
| | 2000 | 0.6 | 0.1 | 2.0 | 0.0 | 4.3 | −0.6 | 0.2 |
| Equity | 1995 | 4.4 | na | 0.7 | 0.0 | 2.1 | 1.2 | 0.7 |
| | 1996 | 5.2 | na | 0.6 | 0.1 | 3.2 | 1.4 | 0.4 |
| | 1997 | 6.4 | na | 0.8 | 0.1 | 2.9 | 2.1 | 0.6 |
| | 1998 | 7.8 | na | 3.2 | −0.2 | 2.5 | 3.2 | 0.2 |
| | 1999 | 14.1 | na | 3.4 | 0.2 | 1.5 | 5.2 | 2.2 |
| | 2000 | 21.8 | na | 5.1 | 0.3 | −2.3 | 9.2 | 1.6 |
| Mutual funds | 1995 | 0.0 | 0.1 | 0.2 | −0.8 | na | 0.1 | 0.0 |
| | 1996 | 0.0 | 0.0 | 0.3 | 0.0 | na | 0.9 | 0.0 |
| | 1997 | 0.0 | −0.1 | 0.5 | −0.3 | na | −0.3 | 0.2 |
| | 1998 | 0.0 | 0.1 | 0.4 | 0.3 | na | 0.5 | 0.4 |
| | 1999 | 0.0 | 0.0 | 0.4 | 1.0 | na | 0.0 | 1.0 |
| | 2000 | 0.0 | 0.0 | −0.1 | −0.4 | na | 1.2 | 0.0 |
| Total assets | 1995 | 7.6 | 5.7 | 2.8 | 4.2 | 19.1 | 5.6 | 2.4 |
| | 1996 | 7.7 | 5.2 | 3.8 | 2.7 | 29.6 | 5.3 | 1.2 |
| | 1997 | 10.4 | 1.8 | 2.3 | −7.1 | 30.5 | 4.3 | 1.5 |
| | 1998 | 10.9 | 6.5 | 6.1 | −3.0 | 28.6 | 5.5 | 1.0 |

Table 4.5 (*Continued*)

| | UK | US | Germany | Japan | Canada | France | Italy |
|---|---|---|---|---|---|---|---|
| 1999 | 19.0 | 6.9 | 6.1 | 7.1 | 24.0 | 13.0 | 6.0 |
| 2000 | 35.0 | 5.8 | 9.3 | 1.1 | 29.5 | 17.8 | 3.9 |
| **1995–2000 average** | | | | | | | |
| Deposits | 2.6 | 0.4 | 0.3 | 0.3 | 2.0 | 0.6 | 0.4 |
| MMI | 0.0 | 0.3 | 0.0 | 0.2 | 0.9 | 0.9 | –0.1 |
| Loans | 2.0 | 0.0 | 1.0 | 0.0 | 5.1 | 1.5 | 0.5 |
| Bonds | 0.1 | –0.1 | 0.6 | 0.2 | 3.6 | –0.1 | 0.2 |
| Equities | 9.9 | 0.0 | 2.3 | 0.1 | 1.6 | 3.7 | 0.9 |
| Mutual funds | 0.0 | 0.0 | 0.3 | 0.0 | 0.0 | 0.4 | 0.3 |
| *Total assets* | *15.1* | *5.3* | *5.1* | *0.9* | *26.9* | *8.6* | *2.6* |

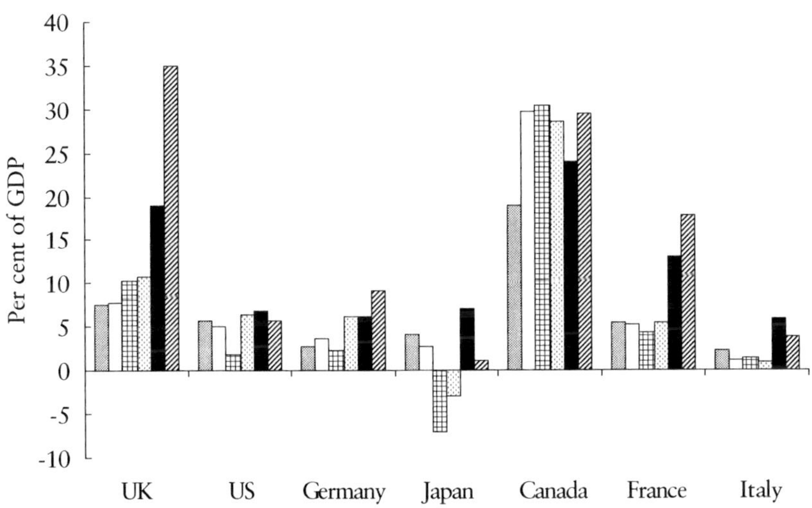


Figure 4.1 *Corporate acquisition of financial assets 1995–2000*
Note: For each country each group of bars represents (from left to right) 1995, 1996, 1997, 1998, 1999, 2000.

UK shows the highest bank borrowing, while in Japan bank borrowing is negative. US equity issuance is shown to be negative, but unlike elsewhere this nets across both asset and liability acquisition. US corporations were retiring equity (via takeovers and buybacks) or purchasing equity as an asset, faster than new issues even at the height of the 1990s bull

Table 4.6 *Company sector acquisition of liabilities (per cent of GDP)*

| | | UK | US | Germany | Japan | Canada | France | Italy |
|---|---|---|---|---|---|---|---|---|
| Money market inst | 1995 | 0.2 | 0.2 | 0.0 | −0.1 | 0.7 | −0.2 | 0.0 |
| | 1996 | 0.2 | 0.0 | 0.0 | 0.2 | 1.5 | 0.7 | 0.0 |
| | 1997 | 0.2 | 0.3 | 0.0 | −0.1 | 0.4 | 0.0 | 0.0 |
| | 1998 | 0.4 | 0.3 | 0.0 | 0.0 | 3.4 | 0.2 | 0.2 |
| | 1999 | 0.3 | 0.4 | 0.2 | 0.1 | 1.8 | 0.8 | −0.1 |
| | 2000 | 0.0 | 0.5 | 0.3 | 0.7 | 2.3 | 1.7 | 0.0 |
| Loans | 1995 | 3.1 | 1.5 | 1.5 | 2.9 | 0.5 | 2.8 | 3.0 |
| | 1996 | 3.5 | 0.8 | 3.6 | 2.3 | 0.1 | 1.6 | 0.7 |
| | 1997 | 5.2 | 0.3 | 0.0 | −0.1 | 0.4 | 0.0 | 0.6 |
| | 1998 | 4.1 | 1.7 | 4.8 | −4.0 | 2.2 | 1.5 | 1.9 |
| | 1999 | 5.0 | 1.9 | 6.4 | −2.0 | 1.7 | 3.0 | 4.0 |
| | 2000 | 9.9 | 2.1 | 8.4 | −3.2 | 1.9 | 4.3 | 6.8 |
| Bonds | 1995 | 1.7 | 1.3 | −4.6 | 0.4 | 2.1 | 0.1 | −0.2 |
| | 1996 | 0.6 | 1.5 | −0.3 | 0.3 | 0.8 | 0.3 | 0.0 |
| | 1997 | 1.7 | 0.3 | 0.0 | −0.1 | 0.4 | 0.0 | −0.1 |
| | 1998 | 2.0 | 2.6 | −0.2 | −1.6 | 3.7 | 0.8 | −0.1 |
| | 1999 | 4.4 | 2.5 | −0.2 | −0.3 | 2.4 | 1.5 | −0.2 |
| | 2000 | 4.4 | 1.8 | 0.2 | −0.9 | 1.7 | 1.3 | −0.2 |
| Equity | 1995 | 2.7 | −0.8 | 0.7 | 1.2 | 3.4 | 2.8 | 1.3 |
| | 1996 | 3.5 | −0.9 | 1.1 | 1.3 | 8.8 | 3.7 | 1.5 |
| | 1997 | 3.7 | 0.3 | 0.0 | −0.1 | 0.4 | 0.0 | 1.2 |
| | 1998 | 6.2 | −3.0 | 2.8 | 1.0 | 10.3 | 4.0 | 1.0 |
| | 1999 | 10.6 | −1.5 | 1.7 | 2.0 | 6.8 | 5.5 | 2.1 |
| | 2000 | 21.3 | −1.7 | 5.6 | 1.5 | 14.0 | 8.1 | 0.4 |
| FDI | 1995 | na | 0.7 | na | na | na | na | na |
| | 1996 | na | 0.9 | na | na | na | na | na |
| | 1997 | na | 0.3 | na | na | na | na | na |
| | 1998 | na | 1.6 | na | na | na | na | na |
| | 1999 | na | 2.8 | na | na | na | na | na |
| | 2000 | na | 1.8 | na | na | na | na | na |
| Total liabilities | 1995 | 7.8 | 5.3 | −1.6 | 5.6 | 17.0 | 8.0 | 5.7 |
| | 1996 | 7.7 | 5.1 | 4.8 | 5.6 | 27.1 | 7.0 | 3.2 |
| | 1997 | 11.0 | 3.4 | 4.0 | −4.3 | 31.0 | 6.1 | 2.4 |
| | 1998 | 12.9 | 7.1 | 8.4 | −8.4 | 29.3 | 1.4 | 3.2 |
| | 1999 | 21.3 | 7.8 | 9.3 | 1.7 | 24.4 | 13.7 | 7.6 |
| | 2000 | 36.1 | 7.0 | 15.2 | −0.9 | 29.6 | 20.0 | 8.4 |
| **1995–2000 average** | | | | | | | | |
| MMI | | 0.2 | 0.3 | 0.1 | 0.1 | 1.7 | 0.5 | 0.0 |
| Loans | | 5.1 | 1.4 | 4.1 | −0.7 | 1.1 | 2.2 | 2.8 |
| Bonds | | 2.5 | 1.7 | −0.8 | −0.4 | 1.8 | 0.7 | −0.1 |
| Equities | | 8.0 | −1.3 | 2.0 | 1.2 | 7.3 | 4.0 | 1.2 |
| FDI | | 0.0 | 1.4 | 0.0 | 0.0 | 0.1 | 0.0 | 0.0 |
| *Total liabilities* | | *16.1* | *5.9* | *6.7* | *−0.1* | *26.4* | *9.4* | *5.1* |

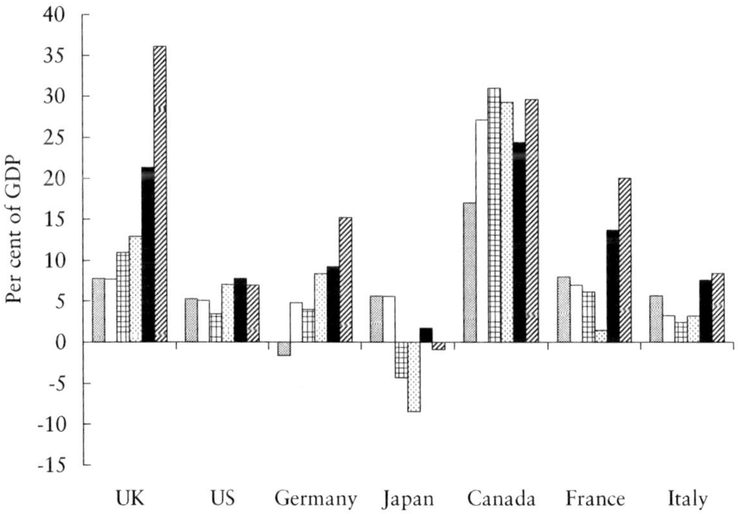


Figure 4.2 *Corporate acquisition of liabilities 1995–2000*
Note: As Figure 4.1.

market. Elsewhere, net equity flows were also negative in the UK and Germany.

## 4.7 OWNERSHIP OF EQUITIES

Holdings of corporate equities are, as noted in Section 1.3, important for corporate governance. Unfortunately we can only obtain holdings of domestic shares, which are most relevant, in the UK, France and Italy. Elsewhere foreign shares are also included. Data are for all shares (including unquoted) except in Canada where we only show quoted shares. Subject to these caveats, table 4.7 shows that, in the UK and US, institutional investors hold around 40 per cent of equities, and in Germany, Japan and Canada institutional investors also hold around 20 per cent. Only in France and Italy are holdings by the domestic institutional investor sector a trivial share of equities. As noted, Davis (2002a) provides some evidence that institutions may exert a positive influence on corporate performance as their share of equity holdings increases.

Banks hold around 10 per cent of equities in Germany, Japan and France. Foreign sector holdings (including those of foreign institutional investors

Table 4.7 *Corporate equity holders by sector end–2000 (per cent of total)*

| | UK | US | Germany | Japan | Canada | France | Italy |
|---|---|---|---|---|---|---|---|
| Households | 20 | 41 | 17 | 19 | 41 | 25 | 35 |
| Companies | 4 | na | 31 | 21 | 25 | 25 | 28 |
| Public sector | 0 | 1 | 3 | 14 | 3 | 2 | 6 |
| Foreign | 37 | 10 | 16 | 15 | 6 | 27 | 14 |
| Financial | 39 | 48 | 33 | 31 | 25 | 20 | 17 |
| Banks | 2 | 2 | 12 | 10 | 3 | 9 | 8 |
| Life/pension | 27 | 26 | 8 | 13 | 12 | 4 | 4 |
| Mutual funds | 9 | 19 | 13 | 2 | 8 | 4 | 6 |
| Total | 100 | 100 | 100 | 100 | 100 | 100 | 100 |

Note: 'Other financial intermediaries' used for mutual funds in Germany.

and foreign corporations) are very high for UK equities (at 35–40 per cent), with the next largest share of foreigners being in France (27 per cent). In Germany, Italy and Japan foreign holdings are 15–20 per cent, and 10 per cent or less in the US and Canada. Households account for 20 per cent or less of equity holdings in most of the countries analysed, with the main exceptions being the US, Canada and Italy. They have implicitly delegated responsibility for such holdings to financial institutions and non-financial corporations.

Corporate cross-holdings are low in the UK but much higher elsewhere. Most attention tends to be devoted to such cross-holdings in Germany and Japan in the context of the 'bank dominated financial system', but the largest intersectoral holdings are actually in France (25 per cent) and Canada (25 per cent). Note that such cross-holdings are typically held to cement relations and not to exert corporate governance directly. Indeed, they may shield friendly firms from takeover threats.

We disaggregate further behind the equity data for 2000, which is possible for all countries except the US, into quoted and unquoted shares. This exercise shows that the proportion of unquoted shares in the total identified in France and Italy is far above that elsewhere, either for all issuers (Table 4.8) or non-financial firms (Table 4.9). In these tables it is shown that nearly 70 per cent of the equity for France is unquoted and the share for Italy is 50 per cent; elsewhere it is below 30 per cent. Nevertheless, the stock of equity for French quoted companies is still over 100 per cent of GDP, above that in Germany, Japan and Italy, albeit well below that in the UK and Canada. Note that in Canada we proxy 'unquoted shares' by the aggregate 'corporate claims'. A similar pattern emerges at a lower level for non-financial issuers.

Table 4.8 *Domestic quoted and unquoted shares 2000*

| | Value (local currency) | | | Per cent of total | | Per cent of GDP | | |
|---|---|---|---|---|---|---|---|---|
| | Total | Quoted | Un-quoted | Quoted | Un-quoted | Total | Quoted | Un-quoted |
| UK | 2474 | 1756 | 718 | 71 | 29 | 265 | 188 | 77 |
| US | 15282 | na | na | na | na | 151 | na | na |
| Germany | 4685 | 3537 | 1148 | 75 | 25 | 118 | 89 | 29 |
| Japan | 4804 | 3753 | 1006 | 78 | 21 | 97 | 76 | 20 |
| Canada | 1802106 | 1429708 | 372398 | 79 | 21 | 173 | 138 | 36 |
| France | 4301220 | 1427342 | 2873878 | 33 | 67 | 308 | 102 | 206 |
| Italy | 3141376 | 1530190 | 1611186 | 49 | 51 | 139 | 68 | 71 |

Table 4.9 *Domestic non-financial corporate sector quoted and unquoted shares 2000*

| | Value (local currency) | | | Per cent of total | | Per cent of GDP | | |
|---|---|---|---|---|---|---|---|---|
| | Total | Quoted | Un-quoted | Quoted | Un-quoted | Total | Quoted | Un-quoted |
| UK | 1903 | 1375 | 528 | 72 | 28 | 204 | 147 | 57 |
| US | 12243 | na | na | na | na | 121 | na | na |
| Germany | 3246 | 2362 | 884 | 73 | 27 | 82 | 59 | 22 |
| Japan | 3959 | 3176 | 783 | 80 | 20 | 80 | 64 | 16 |
| Canada | 931296 | 725259 | 206037 | 78 | 22 | 90 | 70 | 20 |
| France | 3933515 | 1244300 | 2689215 | 32 | 68 | 282 | 89 | 193 |
| Italy | 2103335 | 1024552 | 1078783 | 49 | 51 | 93 | 45 | 48 |

Table 4.10 *Holders of quoted and unquoted shares (per cent of total)*

| | | House-holds | Comp-anies | Public sector | Foreign | Finan-cial | Banks | LIPF | MFs |
|---|---|---|---|---|---|---|---|---|---|
| UK | Quoted | 15 | 2 | 0 | 36 | 47 | 1 | 38 | 8 |
| | Unquoted | 32 | 9 | 0 | 40 | 19 | 7 | 1 | 12 |
| Germany | Quoted | 17 | 31 | 1 | 14 | 37 | 13 | 9 | 15 |
| | Unquoted | 17 | 32 | 10 | 22 | 19 | 10 | 3 | 6 |
| Japan | Quoted | 18 | 24 | 2 | 18 | 38 | 12 | 17 | 3 |
| | Unquoted | 22 | 13 | 52 | 3 | 10 | 3 | 0 | 0 |
| France | Quoted | 7 | 21 | 6 | 37 | 28 | 7 | 7 | 12 |
| | Unquoted | 34 | 28 | 0 | 22 | 16 | 9 | 2 | 0 |

Note: LIPF: life insurance and pension funds; MFs: mutual funds.

In Table 4.10, the data for 2000 are shown for the holders of quoted and unquoted shares. Data are for domestic shares for the UK and France and total (domestic plus foreign) in Germany and Japan. It is apparent that French quoted shares are held to a considerable extent by foreign investors – 37 per cent – while foreign holdings of unquoted shares is only 22 per cent. Domestic households and companies hold the bulk of unquoted shares, while financial institutions hold 28 per cent of quoted but only 16 per cent of unquoted. These figures are most closely comparable to the UK, except that foreigners hold 40 per cent of unquoted shares as well as 36 per cent of quoted. UK companies are less important holders of either type of share than in France, and financial institutions more so. In Germany and Japan, companies and financial institutions hold most quoted shares and for unquoted shares it is companies (Germany) and the public sector (Japan).

The implications of these patterns for corporate governance are discussed further in Section 11.3.

# 5 The household sector

## 5.1 THE HOUSEHOLD SECTOR – THEORETICAL BACKGROUND

From a theoretical perspective, the most influential economic model of aggregate wealth holding for households is the life-cycle hypothesis (LCH). This can be traced to Ando and Modigliani (1963) and has similar predictions to Friedman's (1957) permanent income hypothesis.[25] Abstracting from uncertainty, the suggested motives for divergence between consumption and income in different periods, that is to say saving, are to smooth expenditure streams and to enjoy income on assets. The optimal plan is not to consume all of one's lifetime resources in one single period, but to have an approximately constant level of consumption across one's lifetime, since the benefit from an extra unit of consumption in any single period declines with consumption. This theoretical approach is predicated on the assumption of a diminishing marginal utility of consumption in any particular time period. A constant level of consumption (or, with income growth, a trend) is maintained by saving a proportion of income in various financial assets. Apart from planning for retirement (the life-cycle motive) and smoothing consumption (precautionary motive), assets are also held for bequests and accumulated to purchase 'big ticket' items like a car or residential housing.

25 Terminology quickly becomes unhelpful in this field (Browning and Lusardi, 1996). For some, the Life-Cycle Model refers specifically to a Modigliani model with no bequests and fairly simple environment. For others it refers to a more general model where agents solve forward-looking intertemporal consumption problems, which may or may not allow for bequests, habits, and liquidity constraints.

More formally, in the LCH, planned aggregate consumption $(C_t^*)$ is a function of total resources. Total resources are the sum of human wealth $(H_t)$ and net financial wealth $(W_{t-1})$. Therefore planned consumption can be expressed as

$$C_t^* = m(H_t + W_{t-1}) \tag{5.1}$$

where $m$ is the marginal propensity to consume out of total resources. There are two difficulties with empirical implementations of equation (5.1). First, planned consumption does not always equal actual consumption owing *inter alia* to lags in adjustment. Secondly, human wealth is unobservable and typically proxied by some function of current labour income (i.e. $\tilde{H}_t = kY_t$), where also the labour-leisure choice is already assumed to be resolved. Consequently, we can derive the following, where $C_t$ is actual consumption and $\tilde{C}_t$ is target consumption (equivalent to planned consumption but based on a specification using the human wealth proxy, $\tilde{H}_t$):

$$C_t = \tilde{C}_t + \varepsilon_t \tag{5.2}$$

$$C_t = m(\tilde{H}_t + W_{t-1}) + \varepsilon_t \tag{5.3}$$

$$C_t = aY_t + bW_{t-1} + \varepsilon_t \tag{5.4}$$

A similar long-run specification is employed in Byrne and Davis (2001). Underlying this theory, in a perfect capital market, the consumer carries out 'intertemporal optimisation' by borrowing freely against the security of his human wealth (i.e. future wage income) or non-human wealth. Given a normal income profile, i.e. rising over time, with heavy expenditure on household formation in young adulthood, this is likely to mean heavy borrowing early in the life cycle and corresponding repayments later.

But as outlined in Davis (1995b) the life cycle may not be the whole story. In the real world, the consumer is likely to face several additional constraints on lifetime optimisation. In particular, capital markets are not perfect – this is especially due to the difficulty of pledging the present value of the return on human wealth (i.e. future wage earnings) as a security on loans.[26] Therefore, in general, households may not borrow freely and on an unsecured basis at the market rate of interest. Moreover, many consumers have often faced direct limits on borrowing, or penal rates of interest going beyond this, e.g. limiting borrowing against non-human wealth. Such

26 We concentrate initially on unsecured consumer borrowing, i.e. we assume the loan is not used to purchase an asset which itself forms adequate collateral.

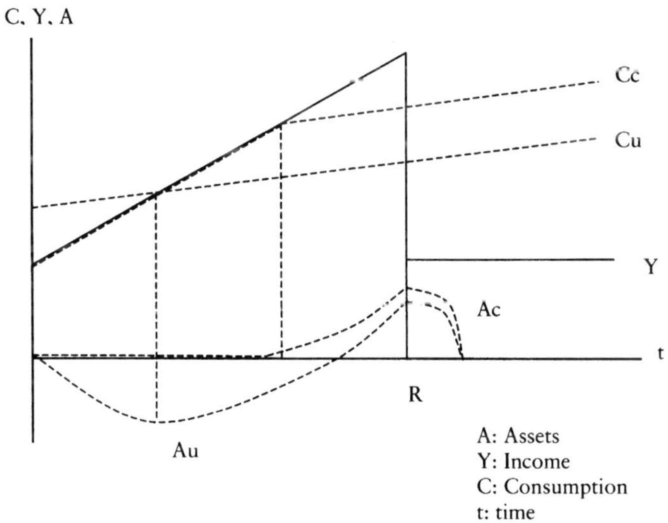


Figure 5.1 *The life cycle and liquidity constraints*
Source: Davis (1995b).

consumers are liquidity constrained[27] and their consumption will be closely tied to receipts of income, though current non-human wealth (especially that which is most liquid) will also be available to decumulate for consumption. In many cases, liquidity constraints imply that consumers cannot consume at the level defined by their lifetime consumption plan, at the points where heavy borrowing would be required early in the life span.

The contrast between liquidity constraints and the life-cycle pattern is illustrated in Figure 5.1, from Davis (1995b). The common life-cycle earnings path of the constrained and unconstrained is Y. The unconstrained (denoted u) are able to borrow, making their net assets Au negative early in the life cycle and hence their consumption Cu can be above their income. After Cu=Y the borrowing is paid back and net assets are built up to maintain consumption after retirement at R. The constrained (denoted c) are forced to consume Cc at a level equal to their income, until the point at which income exceeds their modified optimal consumption path, after which they enjoy more consumption than the unconstrained later in the life cycle. To this point, net assets Ac are 0, i.e. greater than Au. After this point, saving is required, such as to give a higher level of net assets at retirement than the unconstrained, in order to continue the higher desired

27 See Tobin (1972) and Hayashi (1985).

level of consumption. This analysis assumes no bequests and zero interest rates.

Liquidity constraints imply that welfare losses are incurred by constrained consumers, even though consumption can be made up later in the life cycle, owing to forced intertemporal rearrangement of consumption; hence the release of liquidity constraints offers welfare gains. Constraints may apply even to consumers with substantial assets if these are illiquid, i.e. either costly to encash or unacceptable as collateral for short-term loans. Pension rights, used consumer durables, houses, equities, and bonds fall, or have historically fallen, into at least one of these categories in many countries. Liquid assets will be most important for the determination of consumption. This has a major implication for the indebtedness of consumers. To the extent that liquidity constraints were once binding – and there is strong evidence for this – then a loosening of these constraints following financial liberalisation will be marked by a sharply rising debt/income and (to a lesser degree) debt/wealth ratio, and falling saving, as seen in the data below. It would also imply a lower marginal propensity to consume out of income and a swing towards total (financial) wealth as a determinant of consumption. This result is indeed found in the empirical work on the consumption function in the G-7 by Byrne and Davis (2001).

Generally, the life-cycle model, together with the existence of liquidity constraints, suggests that one should view the household sector as containing different groups. While some households are relatively unconstrained, others will be liquidity-constrained, and households will differ in age, and hence borrowing needs, as well as income and assets (see Section 3.2). Changes in the weights of these groups will affect sectoral debt and asset holdings.

The discussion of debt so far relates largely to consumer credit, because it has been assumed that no suitable collateral is available other than human wealth. Whether the arguments relating to liquidity constraints apply as strongly to credits for personal-sector investment, i.e. house purchase, is less clear. Collateral for house purchase is immediately available in the form of the title-deeds to the property – and collateral tends to reduce the credit-market problems arising from information asymmetry and incomplete contracts. Additionally, loans are often tax subsidised, and in many countries only housing loans are thus deductible (hence income gearing net of the subsidy may be relatively low).[28] In some countries, such as the UK, the social welfare system will pay interest during periods of unemployment.

---

28 See Tanzi and King (1995). Tax benefits are widely being phased out, as for example in the UK.

Compared with consumer credit, the risk to the lender relates to the risk that, owing to regional or national depression, the value of the collateral will have fallen below the outstanding principal of the loan, in which case the borrower may have an incentive to default.[29] There are obviously also transactions costs to foreclosure. However, despite this lower level of risk, certain non-price constraints on such lending have often been operative and thus the earlier insights regarding liquidity constraints are not invalidated.

## 5.2 THE HOUSEHOLD SECTOR – EMPIRICAL BACKGROUND

As discussed in Section 1.1, at the level of individual instruments, the main difference between assets is in terms of liquidity and risk. Liquid assets do not often provide a substantial rate of return but can be easily converted into expenditure items, whilst illiquid assets will generally provide a higher rate of return. There are a number of factors that determine which financial assets are used to smooth consumption. According to portfolio theory, we would expect households to adopt a diversified portfolio, but this is not always the case.

Indeed, in many countries most households hold only a simple bank account (in the UK, see Banks and Tanner, 2001). Financial liberalisation due to changes in technology is responsible for a move away from direct holdings of notes and coins. More people make use of bank accounts for money holdings, with wages increasingly paid directly into their accounts, less cash is required with easier access to Automatic Teller Machines and greater use of credit cards as a means of payment. Indeed, Bertaut and Starr-McCluer (2001), examining data from the Survey of Consumer Finance (SCF), suggest for the US that, although the share of liquid accounts in total assets has edged down in the 1990s, the number of people with simple accounts has remained high.

When they do hold a wider range of assets, it can be expected that households will trade-off risk and return when making decisions on which assets to concentrate portfolio holdings (Markowitz, 1952), with risk aversion important in portfolio selection (Tobin, 1958) as discussed in Section 1.1. See Davis (1986) for an exercise in portfolio modelling for households of

29 As long as the collateral exceeds principal ('positive equity'), the borrower can always sell the property to cover any arrears of interest. Of course, for fixed-rate loans, the lender may face risks independent of borrower default, relating to its own maturity mismatch (see the discussion of US thrifts in Davis, 2000).

the UK, US, Germany and Japan in the light of these theories. There are generally substantially higher returns to saving in shares than other forms of asset holdings (Table 1.1) but risk aversion and the need for liquid assets for precautionary and transactions purposes ensures that these holdings never dominate entirely. Theoretical portfolio models often predict a level of risk aversion which is much lower than that necessary to explain the level of share holdings (for recent evidence see Haliassos and Michaelides, 2001). In particular the equity premium puzzle suggests that stocks were historically not sufficiently riskier than bonds to explain the spread in their returns, the so-called equity premium (see Mehra and Prescott, 1985). Some recent evidence suggests that the risk premium has declined or disappeared, possibly due to the institutionalisation of portfolios (Blanchard, 1993; Shiller, 2000), although there may also have been a cyclical element in the recent equity bull market.

A diversified portfolio may be substantially dependent on information on which products are available. According to Guiso and Jappelli (2001), households in Italy and Germany appear to be particularly disadvantaged in terms of information on financial products available on the market. They hence focus investment on liquidity and bonds. Japan should probably also come into this category. Recently, however, Italy has seen a reduction in the proportion of financial assets in deposits, notes and coins (66 per cent in 1980 to 25 per cent in 2000) and has the same approximate proportion as France and the UK, although Japan lags behind the other countries somewhat (58 per cent of total in 2000).

Portfolio models typically refer to the allocation of resources between a risky asset and riskless asset. They have not until recently discussed the ratio of, say, stocks to bonds. For example, according to the mutual fund separation theorem, risk averse investors should hold much of their portfolios in riskless assets. As uncertainty, and risk aversion, increases, investors should reallocate more of their wealth to money and the ratio of bonds to stocks should stay the same in their portfolio. Canner, Mankiw and Weil (1997) suggest that the information provided by financial advisors is typically much more complex: for example, with increased risk aversion advisors will as a rule encourage greater bond holding. The authors fail to explain the 'asset-allocation puzzle' within a rational model, suggesting that investors have a preference for time invariant portfolio allocation and money illusion.

Some recent studies investigating portfolio allocation between stocks and bonds have been conducted by Brandt (1999) and Campbell and Viceira (2001). According to Brandt, portfolio choices depend upon the forcing variables of time-varying investment opportunities. He finds that the decision to allocate resources between the NYSE and 30-day Treasury bills depends upon the dividend yield, default premium, term premium and lagged excess returns. This approach is predicated on the 'overwhelming' evidence of time varying risk premium and volatility (see Fama and Schwert, 1977; Black, 1976).

Campbell and Viceira (2001) concentrate on demand for long-term bonds but also consider the situation where equities are also available for the investor. They find that the ratio of long-run bonds to equities in the optimal portfolio increases with the level of risk aversion. This is consistent with the study by Canner *et al.* on professional portfolio advice but inconsistent with the mutual fund separation theorem. It is similarly to be expected that bond holdings increase prior to retirement, in line with risk aversion and also a shorter period before assets need to be encashed. As noted by Davis (2002e), moving to bonds before retirement also protects against the impact of shifting bond yields on the income from an annuity that can be purchased.

Next we document some of the forces creating a move towards an equity culture for household wealth holders. Privatisation in the UK has been influential: for example, the heavily advertised flotation of public utilities for British Telecom (in 1984) and British Gas (in 1986), which can also be viewed as an attempt to teach the public of the merits of private wealth holdings. Germany has been a more recent beneficiary of public utility privatisation with the offering of Deutsche Telekom in 1996. Guiso (2001) suggests that there was an attempt to encourage public holdings of Italian treasury bonds, similar to the UK privatisation programme, and this may account for their relative importance in Italian household portfolio. Haliassos and Bertaut (1995) argue that lack of information is responsible for low levels of direct equity ownership in the US, given the size of potential returns. Banks and Tanner (2001) are somewhat pessimistic in their assessment of the final effect of the privatisation programme on the UK, suggesting that most households that invested in public flotation own shares only in one company.

Also increasing the equity culture has been the substantial increases in the stock exchange witnessed especially in the US in the late 1990s. Ludvigson and Steindel (1999) highlight that the aggregate value of household sector equity holdings (including those held by financial intermediaries) in the US doubled approximately in the three years after 1994. This is borne out by the comparison of stock and flow data discussed in Section 5.4, where increases in assets holdings are due to changes in valuation and less of an effect arises from net acquisition in a flow sense. To a lesser extent, increases in stock prices have also been experienced in most other industrialised countries. For example stock market capitalisation as a share of income more than doubled in Canada, France, Germany, the UK and the US between December 1994 and March 2000 (see Edison and Sløk, 2001). After March 2000 market capitalisation consistently declined and has apparently led to falls in direct stock holdings. Effects of recent declines on household sentiment will have been further exacerbated by increased uncertainty in stock returns and the correlation of returns across markets.

We have witnessed in recent years a substantial increase in the number of firms offering stocks to employees, see Thompson and Yurkuat (1999). They give evidence of a more general trend to increased use of incentive pay (whether this be in stock options or other pay instruments related to performance) which is not merely restricted to North America. In the United States in 1998, incentive pay amounted to 19 per cent of base pay, up 4 per cent from two years earlier. In France there has been a comparable increase from 9 per cent in 1996 to 14 per cent in 1998.[30] Thompson and Yurkuat suggest that incentives are becoming an expected part of total compensation for major European countries. From a household diversification perspective this does not make much sense, since employees' income will consequently be correlated with wealth holdings, as the recent Enron and Railtrack bankruptcies showed. It can make sense from the perspective of the employer to encourage firm share ownership, since it increases productivity, but not if it leads the main beneficiaries to falsify accounts, as in the scandals of Enron and WorldCom uncovered in 2002.

There have also been increases in indirect stock holding or investment through financial intermediaries, in mutual funds and retirement accounts (Davis and Steil, 2001). For example, in the US the number of mutual funds have risen from 564 in 1980 to 6,778 in 1998 (Investment Company Institute, 1998). Mutual fund growth has also been substantial in Germany, although this growth is slightly overstated by the fact that before 1985 bond-based mutual fund holdings still figured as bonds in the household balance sheet (see Börsch-Supan and Eymann, 2001). German mutual funds are still predominantly in bonds. Italy and the UK have also witnessed a substantial growth in mutual funds in the 1990s. This kind of financial holding has much lower informational and participation costs, since operational responsibility is not with the investor but with a professional fund manager.

More generally, as set out in Davis (1999b), institutionalisation of household saving can be attributed to the following factors:

---

30 Although this may not be classified as definitive evidence of a trend.

- difficulties of retirement income provision in the context of future demographic changes;
- positive effects of population-ageing on saving, and hence on development of institutional investors, abstracting from pension reform (Miles and Patel 1996). This implies a continued high rate of institutional saving;
- wealth accumulation, whereby as wealth increases, households typically wish for an increasing share of their assets to be held in the form of long-term and higher-return and higher-risk instruments such as institutional investments. This is because their liquidity needs can be catered for by a relatively small proportion of the portfolio;
- wider diffusion of knowledge among retail investors regarding institutions' comparative advantage over direct securities holdings in terms of reductions of transactions costs in the context of well-diversified portfolios;
- deregulation of the activities of institutions, e.g. in the context of the UCITS, Investment Services and Life Insurance Directives, that enhance cross-border competition in the EU;
- ongoing technological advances in communications technology and information processing, which enable institutional assets to be managed at lower cost;
- enhanced competition in asset management, linked in particular to the deregulation of the activities of banks and securities firms, on the one hand, and to banks' interest in fee income-generating activities which economise on the use of capital, on the other.

Taxation issues may be important for household portfolio selection. Notably, deferred taxation and the exemption of asset returns from taxes are an important aspect of the growth of occupational pension funds (Davis 1995a). Also, in the US, UK and Canada we have witnessed the introduction of tax-deferred individual retirement accounts. For example, US Individual Retirement Accounts (IRAs) allowed households to make tax-deductible contributions towards retirement income from 1983 to 1986. Even though general deductibility was truncated in 1986, IRAs, combined with tax privileged 401(k) accounts and self-employed contributions (see Bertaut and Starr-McCluer, 2001) have meant individual retirement balances have continued to grow.

We noted above that the age distribution of the population may affect asset holding. As regards empirical evidence of changes in asset and liability demand over the life cycle, surveyed in Davis and Li (2002), Bergantino (1998) found young households under 40 usually draw credit from the financial markets by taking out mortgages for buying houses, consistent with the life cycle of investment. This is supported by Mankiw and Weil (1989) who found housing demand is high for those aged 20–30. Thus, their borrowings tend to exceed their purchases of financial assets. Households aged 40–60 tend to provide credit to financial markets, via employer and personal pension accounts. Those households over the age of 60 tend to draw from the financial markets as a result of using accumulated assets to fund consumption at retirement. Although such findings are consistent with the life-cycle hypothesis on average, a study by Poterba (1998) suggests the life-cycle hypothesis does not accurately describe average asset accumulation profiles. Average figures are distorted by the wealthiest 10 per cent of households who hold approximately 70 per cent of financial assets. If equities are included, this will raise the number to 90 per cent.[31] Also, individuals often do not decumulate due to a desire to give bequests or uncertainty about life expectancy (Bernheim 1991).

On an individual household level, Yoo (1994) found demand for risky assets, bonds and equities in the US increases with age and decreases after individuals retire. This is supported by Bergantino (1998), who shows that US household heads under the age of 35 generally have near zero ownership of bonds and stocks. However, he finds a divergence in stock and bond profiles of older households. Ownership of stocks for those over 55 tends to decrease more rapidly than for bonds. He attributes this to possible cohort effects and risk aversion. It is also noteworthy that financial assets make up only 37 per cent of household's total assets, of which 15 per cent are held directly in stocks. Thus total assets are mostly non-financial assets, e.g. primary residences and vehicles.

Concerning debt *per se*, as noted above and in Chapter 1, households have traditionally been subject to credit rationing and a lower priority in credit allocation than companies. Substantial progress has been made towards financial liberalisation through changes in government policy, as discussed in Section 1.7, and this has often had important implications for the household sector. Changes in financial structure have loosened the constraints on households obtaining consumer credit and housing loans. With the development of money market mutual funds and consequent removal

31 See Poterba and Samwick (1997). Supporting evidence by Ameriks and Zeldes (2000) suggest half of Americans do not hold any wealth in the stock market. Whilst on a microeconomic level, Bergantino (1998) found in his data sample stocks only make up 22 per cent of US households' total financial assets. Although there is variation in the data samples given, they do suggest a small amount of household wealth is held in stock markets.

of interest rate ceilings on bank deposits, liberalisation began earlier in the United States than in most other industrial countries.

There are substantial contrasts between countries in the mortgage lending market. Besides the US, there has also been considerable deregulation in this sector in the UK, as retail banks, in addition to building societies, were able to provide mortgage finance. Elsewhere, constraints to credit continued to operate for some time. These included down-payment restrictions, with Italian households required to have 50 per cent of the value of a house before they are granted a mortgage loan from a bank, and 20 per cent in Germany. This may be largely responsible for the low relative levels of Italian household debt. Contrast this with the situation in the US where often only 5 per cent is required of the house value. Chiuri and Jappelli (2000) are of the view that in Canada, the US and the UK the mortgage market is well developed, the down-payment is relatively low and mortgage maturity normally exceeds twenty years. In Italy and Germany the market is much thinner and down-payments relatively high. These authors rule out interest rate spreads as an important supply side factor limiting the growth of mortgage lending and concentrate on down-payments being a direct indicator of credit rationing. This is consequently reflected in the small size of these countries' mortgage markets. On the other hand, down-payments have typically declined recently for G-7 countries and this is due to reduced regulation and greater competition between intermediaries (the exception is the US, unsurprisingly given the stylised fact that the US already had a much more developed financial structure).

Some apparent restrictive practices on lending appear to remain throughout the G-7. There are substantial interest rate wedges between interest rate costs on credit cards and those provided by savings accounts. This differential makes the popularity of credit cards somewhat puzzling (see Bertaut and Starr-McCluer, 2001). Nevertheless, overall, reductions in credit constraints have removed some of the impediments to borrow and may have reduced the effect of current income on consumption. This could also be true of the need for precautionary wealth holding as better access to loans may allow one to reduce liquidity levels.

It may be useful to consider the objective in accumulating wealth (for recent empirical analyses see Blake and Orszag, 1999, and Solomou and Weale, 1997, for the UK, and Börsch-Supan and Eymann, 2001, for Germany). Is it for retirement, lifetime consumption or consumption by heirs? The life-cycle model implies a need to save for purchase of housing and consumer durables. As mentioned above, there is also some evidence of a bequest motive (Bernheim, 1991). Most work focuses on the retirement motive (i.e. maintenance of lifetime consumption).

Concerning private saving, there is some evidence for the US and in an international cross-section (Feldstein, 1974, 1977, 1995) that unfunded social security pensions reduce private saving. This can be justified theoretically by a life-cycle framework, whereby a guarantee of income to maintain consumption after retirement gives rise to a form of implicit wealth accumulation, and the need to save during the working life is lessened.[32] Underlying this approach is a view that workers see contributions as a form of saving and not as a tax, and that confidence is maintained in the promises of pay-as-you-go. As the population ages and the size of unfunded liabilities increases, the negative effect on private saving could increase sharply (unless the effect is offset by increasing uncertainty over whether pension promises will be kept). Feldstein's results have been disputed (for a review, see Munnell, 1987), and other evidence suggests that the effect, even if negative, may be small; for example because social security induces early retirement, which gives incentives to save more to cover the longer retirement period, or because changes in intra-family transfers (e.g. bequests) may have offset the increase in public-sector transfers, thus leaving the need for old-age saving identical (Barro, 1974, and the discussion in Chapter 6).

Some of the literature considers the impact of an increase in pension asset holding on household wealth. For example, in a simple life-cycle model, workers save only for retirement. Hence changing employer compensation to pension benefits, instead of wages, has no effect on consumption and increases in pensions are completely offset by reductions in other kinds of wealth. However there are a number of caveats to this simple approach. Even if households only save for retirement, increasing pensions may reduce the length of working life, which may raise saving amongst workers (Feldstein, 1974). Pensions are typically illiquid assets and where individuals face binding borrowing constraints which prevent them from increasing debt in response to an increase in retirement income, pensions will increase saving. Indeed even if they are unconstrained, if households save for other reasons than retirement, increasing pension wealth will not be fully offset by reductions in other wealth. A counter argument is that pensions provide insurance against an uncertain life span, this should consequently reduce overall saving (Hubbard, 1987).

Empirical research in this area also provides a range of answers to the question whether private pensions affect saving (see the survey in Davis and

---

32 A further mechanism inducing lower saving under pay-as-you-go social security is that those who are myopic and would otherwise have continued working till they die are now able to retire.

Steil, 2001). Much of the literature[33] on private pensions and savings, such as Pesando (1992), which is focused on US defined benefit funds, suggest an increase in personal saving of around 0.35–0.5 per cent results from every 1 per cent increase in pension fund assets, though the cost to the public sector of the tax incentives to pension funds reduces the overall benefit to national savings to around 0.2 per cent. Hubbard (1986) suggests a larger effect on personal saving of 0.84 per cent; effects would be plausibly less marked for defined contribution funds, in which the worker is more likely to be able to borrow against pension wealth and in which participation is generally optional. On the other hand, Poterba, Venti and Wise (1993, 1996) suggest that 401(k) accounts in the United States have added to aggregate saving. Tax incentives are one important reason, but employer matching of contributions, payroll deduction schemes, and information seminars may also be relevant factors in encouraging net saving by this route. Similarly, Joines and Manegold (1995) find that IRAs have also raised saving in the United States (by around 0.25–0.3 per cent), while Attanasio and De Liere (1994) found that 40 per cent of contributions to IRAs are by new contributors and IRAs raise private saving by 0.2 per cent. Venti and Wise (1994) found that RRSPs (a kind of personal defined contribution pension) raises saving in Canada. These results do not extend to shorter-maturity non-pension saving instruments, even if they are tax privileged. Banks *et al.* (1994) found that tax privileged equity accounts (PEPs) as well as tax free deposits (TESSAs) had no effect on personal saving in the United Kingdom but only generated portfolio substitution.

Gale (1998) reviews the evidence and suggests that these studies may contain an econometric bias which understates the offset between pension and other saving. Correcting for this bias yields offsets that are larger than most previous estimates, and hence suggests effects of pension accumulation on saving are around 0.5 per cent at maximum. In this context, one should bear in mind that there is a move towards private pension funds and moves away from government provision (in the UK this included the removal of the link between earnings and social security pensions). This in itself may have implications for other kinds of wealth holding. Disney (2000) offers some evidence that reform of public pension systems may have the effect of boosting private saving, and highlights a study of Italy (Attanasio and Brugiavini, 1999) which shows strong results in support of this hypothesis. Even in the absence of reform, one positive effect on private saving that may accompany pay-as-you-go, where confidence in future benefits is weak, is a high level of precautionary household saving.

33 For important earlier studies, see Feldstein (1978) and Munnell (1986).

Analysts suggest that this has already been typical of Japan (see Nakagawa, 1999), where surveys suggest that the recovery in the savings propensity in the 1990s partly reflected an increase in uncertainty[34] about pension systems among young households while the old households felt anxiety about nursing care and hence sought to save more than any other age groups even in the last stages of their life cycle.[35]

## 5.3 HOUSEHOLD/PERSONAL SECTOR BALANCE SHEETS

We now assess household portfolios in the light of the above. Table 5.1 shows the household sector's portfolio of financial assets in the G-7 as a percentage of total financial assets. Deposits, equities and life insurance and pension funds are shown to be the major assets held in all cases. However, deposits remain much higher in bank-dominated Germany and Japan than in the other countries. Lowest of all is the US with only 14 per cent of financial assets held in this form, reflecting a high level of financial development and low liquidity constraints. The offset has been rising life and pension funds and mutual funds. Again, levels differ, with a distinction between the UK, US and Canada where life and pension holdings are 40 per cent or more, and the other countries where the corresponding figure is below 30 per cent. Meanwhile, direct equity holdings are highest in France (40 per cent of assets), with the US, Canada and Italy at 25 per cent and the UK, Germany and Japan below 20 per cent. Note that these figures in particular are not consistent with a sharp divide between the Anglo Saxon countries on the one hand, and Continental Europe and Japan on the other.

As regards trends, for all the G-7 we observe a broad decline between the years 1970 and 2000 in holdings of deposits, notes and coins as a com-

---

34 The issue of uncertainty is verified in the Nakagawa results by survey responses. Oyama and Yoshida (1999) find a similar result – albeit for different kinds of uncertainty – including the error from a GARCH model of income in the consumption function.

35 The rise in saving was not seen as solely age related. The middle-aged and elderly low income households felt anxiety about employment conditions given the economic situation (Nakagawa 1999), and in particular the downward revision to growth after the collapse of the financial bubble of the 1980s. Of course, the view that the pension system is unsustainable may also have strengthened as economic growth fell in the 1990s.

Table 5.1 *Household sector financial assets (per cent of total)*

| | | UK | US | Germany | Japan | Canada | France | Italy |
|---|---|---|---|---|---|---|---|---|
| Deposits notes coin | 1970 | 37.4 | 29.8 | 63.8 | 62.6 | 32.4 | 56.0 | 58.8 |
| | 1980 | 42.8 | 35.3 | 64.2 | 64.3 | 39.4 | 66.7 | 65.9 |
| | 1990 | 31.9 | 26.6 | 52.1 | 53.9 | 35.1 | 40.3 | 37.1 |
| | 1998 | 21.6 | 13.7 | 40.8 | 59.2 | 27.4 | 31.0 | 28.8 |
| | 2000 | 22.1 | 13.8 | 36.2 | 58.2 | 26.4 | 26.4 | 24.9 |
| Money market inst | 1970 | 0.3 | 0.7 | 0.0 | 0.0 | 0.1 | 0.0 | 0.0 |
| | 1980 | 0.1 | 2.3 | 0.2 | 0.0 | 1.3 | 0.0 | 9.5 |
| | 1990 | 0.1 | 3.8 | 0.4 | 0.0 | 3.6 | 2.1 | 12.7 |
| | 1998 | 0.1 | 3.1 | 0.1 | 0.0 | 0.3 | 0.5 | 2.3 |
| | 2000 | 0.1 | 3.8 | 0.0 | 0.0 | 1.2 | 0.4 | 1.0 |
| Bonds | 1970 | 7.7 | 8.3 | 9.0 | 5.7 | 14.8 | 6.6 | 20.5 |
| | 1980 | 5.4 | 7.0 | 12.7 | 7.6 | 8.0 | 10.2 | 8.2 |
| | 1990 | 1.2 | 12.0 | 15.2 | 4.9 | 6.0 | 4.0 | 18.9 |
| | 1998 | 1.2 | 7.3 | 11.6 | 3.3 | 4.1 | 2.6 | 21.0 |
| | 2000 | 1.0 | 7.2 | 10.8 | 3.3 | 4.0 | 1.9 | 17.9 |
| Equity | 1970 | 28.2 | 30.9 | 11.0 | 11.8 | 25.1 | 30.7 | 11.6 |
| | 1980 | 13.7 | 20.4 | 4.8 | 7.4 | 23.9 | 13.3 | 10.3 |
| | 1990 | 17.5 | 15.7 | 6.0 | 9.0 | 20.7 | 26.8 | 20.6 |
| | 1998 | 16.4 | 27.9 | 15.3 | 6.3 | 27.5 | 33.0 | 19.5 |
| | 2000 | 17.8 | 25.1 | 16.7 | 7.1 | 27.7 | 38.4 | 26.0 |
| Mutual funds | 1970 | 1.5 | 2.2 | 0.0 | 1.7 | na | 0.0 | 0.0 |
| | 1980 | 1.1 | 1.1 | 0.0 | 1.5 | na | 2.5 | 0.0 |
| | 1990 | 0.6 | 4.0 | 4.5 | 4.2 | na | 14.0 | 2.2 |
| | 1998 | 4.0 | 9.2 | 9.4 | 2.3 | na | 9.4 | 17.1 |
| | 2000 | 6.1 | 11.0 | 12.1 | 2.7 | na | 9.0 | 17.6 |
| Life and pensions | 1970 | 24.9 | 28.2 | 16.2 | 18.2 | 27.7 | 6.7 | 9.1 |
| | 1980 | 36.8 | 33.9 | 18.1 | 19.2 | 27.4 | 7.3 | 6.1 |
| | 1990 | 48.7 | 38.0 | 21.8 | 28.0 | 34.6 | 12.8 | 8.5 |
| | 1998 | 56.8 | 38.6 | 22.8 | 28.8 | 40.7 | 23.6 | 11.4 |
| | 2000 | 52.9 | 39.2 | 24.2 | 28.7 | 40.7 | 23.9 | 12.7 |

ponent of household sector financial wealth. This may represent a broadening and deepening of the financial systems of the major industrialised economies of the world. It has occurred despite higher returns on deposits due to financial liberalisation. Traditionally, asset holders would concentrate resources on basic methods of storing wealth in liquid form and would not hold more complex financial instruments.

One reason for the trend may be falling demand for narrow money as a medium of exchange owing to innovations such as credit card penetration

Table 5.2 *Household sector financial assets (per cent of GDP)*

| | | UK | US | Germany | Japan | Canada | France | Italy |
|---|---|---|---|---|---|---|---|---|
| Deposits notes coin | 1970 | 61.0 | 52.4 | 45.8 | 61.3 | 45.8 | 54.1 | 50.8 |
| | 1980 | 50.2 | 52.0 | 60.1 | 112.3 | 59.0 | 63.2 | 55.8 |
| | 1990 | 62.5 | 51.7 | 63.5 | 130.8 | 62.7 | 55.3 | 61.7 |
| | 1998 | 64.1 | 39.3 | 65.5 | 150.9 | 59.3 | 61.3 | 58.7 |
| | 2000 | 65.0 | 37.9 | 60.8 | 158.6 | 55.3 | 60.6 | 56.1 |
| Money market inst | 1970 | 0.5 | 1.2 | 0.0 | 0.0 | 0.1 | 0.0 | 0.0 |
| | 1980 | 0.1 | 3.4 | 0.2 | 0.0 | 2.0 | 0.0 | 8.1 |
| | 1990 | 0.2 | 7.4 | 0.4 | 0.0 | 6.4 | 2.8 | 21.2 |
| | 1998 | 0.3 | 9.0 | 0.1 | 0.0 | 0.6 | 0.9 | 4.7 |
| | 2000 | 0.4 | 10.5 | 0.1 | 0.0 | 2.5 | 0.9 | 2.2 |
| Bonds | 1970 | 12.5 | 14.7 | 6.5 | 5.6 | 20.9 | 6.4 | 17.7 |
| | 1980 | 6.4 | 10.4 | 11.9 | 13.2 | 11.9 | 9.7 | 6.9 |
| | 1990 | 2.4 | 23.3 | 18.6 | 12.0 | 10.8 | 5.5 | 31.4 |
| | 1998 | 3.5 | 21.0 | 18.7 | 8.4 | 8.9 | 5.2 | 42.8 |
| | 2000 | 2.9 | 19.7 | 18.2 | 9.0 | 8.4 | 4.4 | 40.2 |
| Equity | 1970 | 45.9 | 54.3 | 7.9 | 11.6 | 35.5 | 29.7 | 10.0 |
| | 1980 | 16.1 | 30.0 | 4.5 | 12.9 | 35.8 | 12.6 | 8.7 |
| | 1990 | 34.3 | 30.5 | 7.3 | 21.7 | 37.0 | 36.8 | 34.3 |
| | 1998 | 48.8 | 80.0 | 24.6 | 16.1 | 59.5 | 65.4 | 39.8 |
| | 2000 | 52.3 | 69.2 | 28.0 | 19.2 | 58.1 | 88.1 | 58.4 |
| Mutual funds | 1970 | 2.5 | 3.8 | 0.0 | 1.7 | na | 0.0 | 0.0 |
| | 1980 | 1.3 | 1.6 | 0.0 | 2.6 | na | 2.3 | 0.0 |
| | 1990 | 1.2 | 7.8 | 5.5 | 10.2 | na | 19.3 | 3.6 |
| | 1998 | 11.8 | 26.5 | 15.1 | 5.9 | na | 18.5 | 34.9 |
| | 2000 | 18.0 | 30.2 | 20.2 | 7.5 | na | 20.8 | 39.5 |
| Life and pensions | 1970 | 40.5 | 49.6 | 11.6 | 17.8 | 39.2 | 6.4 | 7.8 |
| | 1980 | 43.2 | 49.9 | 17.0 | 33.4 | 40.9 | 7.0 | 5.2 |
| | 1990 | 95.3 | 73.9 | 26.5 | 67.9 | 61.8 | 17.6 | 14.0 |
| | 1998 | 168.8 | 110.5 | 36.7 | 73.4 | 88.0 | 46.7 | 23.2 |
| | 2000 | 155.8 | 107.9 | 40.5 | 78.4 | 85.4 | 54.8 | 28.5 |
| Total assets | 1970 | 162.9 | 175.9 | 71.8 | 98.0 | 141.5 | 96.6 | 86.4 |
| | 1980 | 117.3 | 147.2 | 93.7 | 174.4 | 149.6 | 94.8 | 84.8 |
| | 1990 | 195.8 | 194.5 | 121.7 | 242.6 | 178.6 | 137.3 | 166.2 |
| | 1998 | 297.3 | 286.1 | 160.7 | 254.7 | 216.4 | 198.1 | 204.1 |
| | 2000 | 294.4 | 275.6 | 167.7 | 272.7 | 209.7 | 229.6 | 225.1 |

as a means of payment, ATMs reducing average real narrow money balances and workers' wages paid directly into their bank account. Additionally we have seen an adoption of alternative financial instruments, such as life and pension funds and mutual funds as a store of value (Davis and Steil, 2001), possibly also reflecting low risk aversion and higher saving by certain cohorts as the population ages (see also Section 3.2). Moreover, as the overall level of financial wealth has increased, the level of liquidity required as a percentage of total wealth has decreased. This process has been particularly marked in the US, France and Italy where holdings of deposits, notes and coins has more than halved as a proportion of wealth in the 30 years to 2000. It stands despite the micro evidence that a large proportion of the population only hold these forms of asset, suggesting diversification is largely undertaken by wealthier echelons.

The trend in equity holdings has seen them fall in the 1970s during the bear market of low returns and high revealed risks, but thereafter recover somewhat, reflecting *inter alia* privatisations, a growing equity culture and rising share prices. There has been a marked and consistent rise in life insurance and pension holdings, particularly so in France and the UK where holdings have more than doubled between 1970 and 2000. As noted, this is due to changing demographic trends (Section 3.2) and a reduction in government provision of social security pensions, as well as a rising trend in wealth more generally and high returns on such assets, while individuals have also become more conscious of the benefits of institutional investment.

In terms of the other forms of wealth holdings, the US, Italy and Germany has a large component of bonds and mutual fund holdings, with both instruments being over 10 per cent in 2000, and nearly 20 per cent each in Italy. High mutual fund holding seems to go against the idea of low information availability for Italian households expressed in Section 5.2. France has also seen a growing role for bond and mutual fund holdings over the past 30 years. In 2000, France had large relative holdings of mutual funds (9 per cent) to bonds (1.9 per cent), the latter having declined from 10 per cent in 1980. Low holdings of bonds in the UK link to poor real returns, notably in the 1970s when inflation rose sharply; in this it contrasts with Germany, where low inflation (Section 3.3) has ensured bonds remain a popular investment instrument.

In making cross-country comparisons, it is also useful to consider levels as a percentage of GDP. Comparing the ratio of total assets to income for the G-7 countries in Table 5.2 and in Figure 1.2, financial asset holdings are more than twice as large as income for all countries excluding Germany (which in 2000 was 170 per cent). Ratios in 2000 were somewhat higher in the UK, US and Japan than elsewhere. There has been a distinct upward trend since the 1970s, tempered somewhat between 1998 and 2000 by world-wide declines in the stock market, which cut 35 percentage points each off US and UK wealth/GDP ratios in 2000 compared to 1999, and which have fallen further at the time of writing. We note that declines also occurred in the 1970s, due to the equity market collapse and inflation eroding the real value of monetary financial assets, but the overall upward trend in the last 30 years remains.

With respect to deposits in Table 5.2, the household sector in all of the G-7 countries holds liquidity of 60–65 per cent of national income in 2000, apart from the US and Japan. This suggests a possible floor for liquidity holdings despite financial liberalisation and demographic trends favouring a shift away from deposits. On the other hand, in the US, deposits are only equivalent to 38 per cent of GDP and overall liquidity is 50 per cent, which, given its high level of financial development, could be a forerunner of trends elsewhere. The other outlier is Japan, with deposits of over 150 per cent of GDP in 2000, reflecting developments in the Japanese business cycle, with very low nominal rates of return on securities, and probably risk aversion by Japanese households. From a comparison of Tables 5.1 and 5.2, we can see that, although holdings of deposits, notes and coins may have declined as a percentage of total wealth holdings, they have increased since 1970 as a percentage of GDP for all G7 countries, apart from the US.

The figures for household equity holdings as a ratio to GDP are very large for France at around 90 per cent in 2000, having increased from 30 per cent in 1970. This is far higher than any other country shown (the current figure for the US is 70 per cent). This trend in the importance of equity holdings for France is much clearer when expressed as a ratio to GDP than as a percentage of total wealth. As noted in Section 4.7 above, the trend and comparatively high level in France reflects larger holdings of unquoted shares than in other countries.

The life and pension holdings for the UK stand out, at 156 per cent of GDP in 2000, with the next largest sector in the US at 108 per cent. These are countries with less generous social security pension systems, as well as generous tax incentives to pension saving, thus putting a premium on saving for retirement. As regards mutual funds, the largest holding relative to GDP is in Italy – almost 40 per cent. Italian households have shifted strongly to indirect securities holdings in recent years, mainly in bond-based mutual funds. US household mutual funds are relatively smaller at 30 per cent of GDP.

The data for household sector liabilities are presented in Table 5.3. We have two categories, namely consumer credit and housing loans. For all countries, household sector liabilities are mainly in the form of housing loans, and in most countries this dominance has increased over time. When we express liabilities as a percentage of GDP as in Table 5.4, we see that

Table 5.3 *Household sector liabilities (per cent of total)*

| | | UK | US | Germany | Japan | Canada | France | Italy |
|---|---|---|---|---|---|---|---|---|
| Consumer credit | 1970 | 10.5 | 25.0 | 12.2 | na | 31.8 | 14.7 | 28.2 |
| | 1980 | 18.3 | 21.2 | 18.2 | na | 29.7 | 10.8 | 34.3 |
| | 1990 | 15.2 | 18.9 | 20.5 | na | 26.4 | 13.5 | 41.9 |
| | 1998 | 17.8 | 20.1 | 8.0 | 11.0 | 26.2 | 6.9 | 22.9 |
| | 2000 | 19.4 | 19.9 | 7.5 | 10.9 | 27.0 | 7.0 | 20.4 |
| Housing loans | 1970 | 89.5 | 75.0 | 87.8 | na | 68.2 | 85.3 | 71.8 |
| | 1980 | 81.7 | 78.8 | 81.8 | na | 70.3 | 89.2 | 65.7 |
| | 1990 | 84.8 | 81.1 | 79.5 | na | 73.6 | 86.5 | 58.1 |
| | 1998 | 82.2 | 79.9 | 91.1 | 48.6 | 73.8 | 93.1 | 77.1 |
| | 2000 | 80.6 | 80.1 | 91.6 | 51.7 | 73.0 | 93.0 | 79.6 |

Table 5.4 *Household sector liabilities (per cent of GDP)*

| | | UK | US | Germany | Japan | Canada | France | Italy |
|---|---|---|---|---|---|---|---|---|
| Consumer credit | 1970 | 2.5 | 12.7 | 4.7 | na | 13.1 | 2.6 | 2.2 |
| | 1980 | 5.1 | 12.2 | 9.3 | na | 14.5 | 3.2 | 2.2 |
| | 1990 | 9.5 | 13.8 | 11.3 | na | 14.5 | 5.0 | 7.4 |
| | 1998 | 12.0 | 14.8 | 5.7 | 7.9 | 15.9 | 2.5 | 4.5 |
| | 2000 | 14.2 | 15.5 | 5.5 | 7.8 | 15.8 | 2.6 | 4.5 |
| Housing loans | 1970 | 21.6 | 38.0 | 33.9 | na | 28.0 | 14.9 | 5.6 |
| | 1980 | 22.8 | 45.1 | 41.7 | na | 34.3 | 26.1 | 4.3 |
| | 1990 | 52.8 | 59.2 | 43.8 | na | 40.4 | 32.2 | 10.2 |
| | 1998 | 55.3 | 59.0 | 64.8 | 34.8 | 44.9 | 33.3 | 15.2 |
| | 2000 | 59.0 | 62.2 | 67.6 | 37.1 | 42.6 | 34.6 | 17.7 |
| Total liabilities | 1970 | 24.1 | 50.6 | 38.6 | 23.9 | 41.0 | 17.5 | 7.7 |
| | 1980 | 27.9 | 57.3 | 50.9 | 50.2 | 48.8 | 29.2 | 6.5 |
| | 1990 | 62.3 | 73.0 | 55.1 | 71.1 | 54.9 | 37.2 | 17.6 |
| | 1998 | 67.3 | 73.8 | 71.1 | 71.6 | 60.9 | 35.8 | 19.7 |
| | 2000 | 73.1 | 77.7 | 73.8 | 71.8 | 58.4 | 37.2 | 22.2 |

household liabilities have been increasing, and this can be explained by the greater availability of credit to households following financial liberalisation. Liabilities have doubled in the UK and Italy (although the percentage is quite low in the latter), with substantial increases in Japan and Germany. France and the US have witnessed a small increase in liabilities as a percentage of GDP between 1970 and 2000, although the level of US indebtedness was already substantial in the 1970s, reflecting earlier finan-

Table 5.5 *Household sector financial assets (per cent of total) allowing for underlying instruments in institutional investors' portfolios*

| | | UK | US | Germany | Japan | Canada | France | Italy |
|---|---|---|---|---|---|---|---|---|
| Deposits | 1970 | 38.2 | 30.6 | 66.1 | 63.3 | 32.9 | 57.5 | 60.2 |
| notes | 1980 | 44.2 | 36.8 | 69.5 | 65.0 | 40.4 | 68.1 | 66.9 |
| coin | 1990 | 35.6 | 28.2 | 60.5 | 55.3 | 35.6 | 41.2 | 37.4 |
| | 1998 | 24.3 | 14.7 | 49.6 | 61.4 | 27.9 | 32.4 | 29.0 |
| | 2000 | 24.3 | 14.7 | 45.2 | 59.6 | 26.9 | 27.7 | 25.4 |
| Money | 1970 | 0.5 | 1.0 | 0.0 | 0.5 | 0.4 | 0.1 | 0.0 |
| market | 1980 | 0.6 | 3.8 | 0.2 | 0.4 | 2.5 | 0.0 | 9.5 |
| inst | 1990 | 0.6 | 6.7 | 0.4 | 3.2 | 6.5 | 7.9 | 12.8 |
| | 1998 | 0.8 | 6.2 | 0.1 | 0.9 | 2.5 | 3.9 | 2.4 |
| | 2000 | 0.8 | 7.5 | 0.1 | 1.1 | 4.1 | 3.6 | 1.1 |
| Bonds | 1970 | 17.7 | 21.5 | 12.0 | 7.3 | 27.5 | 9.7 | 24.1 |
| | 1980 | 18.1 | 23.5 | 16.5 | 11.3 | 21.0 | 14.9 | 10.3 |
| | 1990 | 11.5 | 33.2 | 21.5 | 11.8 | 22.7 | 16.3 | 24.3 |
| | 1998 | 16.2 | 24.4 | 19.4 | 18.2 | 24.4 | 17.5 | 28.3 |
| | 2000 | 15.8 | 24.2 | 19.1 | 19.6 | 24.8 | 14.6 | 24.3 |
| Equity | 1970 | 39.7 | 39.9 | 12.6 | 16.3 | 29.0 | 32.6 | 13.8 |
| | 1980 | 34.1 | 30.5 | 6.3 | 14.3 | 28.1 | 16.9 | 11.5 |
| | 1990 | 47.2 | 27.3 | 9.5 | 18.2 | 28.2 | 31.7 | 23.0 |
| | 1998 | 52.9 | 50.0 | 23.4 | 11.8 | 40.4 | 41.0 | 22.8 |
| | 2000 | 53.4 | 48.5 | 27.1 | 13.1 | 39.8 | 47.8 | 30.5 |

Notes: UK, French and German portfolio shares of mutual funds in 1999/2000 fixed at nearest known level (see Table 10.1).
Data do not add to 100 owing to other assets held by institutional investors (such as loans, mutual funds and real estate) and due to lack of data on assets of Italian mutual funds.

cial liberalisation in that country. France and Italy are the outliers in 2000 with low levels of debt/GDP (below 40 per cent) while elsewhere it is 60–80 per cent, equivalent to or in excess of personal incomes. Note that since mortgages are secured by housing, this implies a link from household default probability (and potential losses by banks) to house price declines, while house price inflation may permit further borrowing, with wider macroeconomic significance.

As a variant on the tables for households, we present in Table 5.5 estimates for household sector financial asset distributions which 'see through' institutional investors and allocate their portfolios to households *pro rata*. This gives a clearer picture of households' exposure in terns of instruments.

Caution is needed in interpreting the table, since the existence of guarantees, especially for defined benefit pension funds and life insurance, means that the risk accepted by the household sector from equity may be less than these data imply. Furthermore, as shown in Table 10.5, mutual fund data are not available for certain years in Italy, France, Germany and the UK. Where this is the case, the mutual funds are assumed to be held in ultimate assets comparable to the household sector's overall portfolio.

The results are nonetheless of considerable interest. The equity and bond share is naturally much higher than direct holdings shown in Table 5.1 would suggest, and imply a much more homogeneous pattern than the standard breakdown would suggest. In 2000, bond holdings were around 25 per cent in the US, Canada and Italy, and 15 per cent elsewhere. Equity holdings are 40–50 per cent in the UK, US, Canada and France, and 30 per cent in Italy and Germany. Japan is the outlier, with equity shares of below 15 per cent, reflecting historical experience (Chapter 3). In the case of deposits, German and Japanese households have over 45 per cent, while elsewhere the share is 25 per cent except for the US (15 per cent). Overall liquidity, including money market instruments, is more closely aligned in the countries other than Germany and Japan, given large money market holdings by US households. Note that this breakdown identifies Germany and Japan quite accurately as the countries which are most bank-dominated (see Section 10.1), with France and to a lesser extent Italy intermediate or transitional.

## 5.4 FLOW DATA FOR THE HOUSEHOLD SECTOR

In terms of flow data, we can see from Table 5.6 and Figure 5.2 that total net acquisitions of financial assets for households have averaged 6–8 per cent of GDP over 1995–2000 for the G-7 except Canada (5 per cent). Considering the source of these increases, there are many similarities amongst the countries. For the UK, most accumulation has been in the form of deposits and life assurance and pensions, whilst inflows to equity and bonds has been negative for our sample period. The US has also seen inflows to deposits, mutual funds and life and pension claims but has witnessed outflows from equity. This pattern may correspond to a life-cycle process, whereby heirs of estates inheriting equity sell them to other sectors (notably institutional investors and foreigners) and instead use the proceeds to invest in deposits, long-term institutional investors and mutual funds. This is quite a long-standing process, and for the US dates back several decades. To some extent, the other countries replicate these results, with inflows

Table 5.6 *Household sector acquisition of financial assets (per cent of GDP)*

| | | UK | US | Germany | Japan | Canada | France | Italy |
|---|---|---|---|---|---|---|---|---|
| Deposits notes coin | 1995 | 4.4 | 1.5 | 1.9 | 5.7 | 2.7 | 5.2 | 1.8 |
| | 1996 | 4.2 | 1.5 | 2.8 | 5.4 | 1.7 | 2.5 | 1.8 |
| | 1997 | 4.8 | 1.7 | 1.5 | 7.2 | –0.1 | 3.5 | –3.0 |
| | 1998 | 3.8 | 2.6 | 2.4 | 5.6 | 0.8 | 2.3 | –2.7 |
| | 1999 | 3.6 | 0.7 | 0.5 | 4.2 | 2.7 | 2.2 | 0.2 |
| | 2000 | 4.0 | 3.0 | –1.5 | 1.4 | 1.5 | 0.3 | 1.4 |
| Money market inst | 1995 | 0.0 | 1.5 | –0.1 | 0.0 | 0.0 | –0.1 | 1.4 |
| | 1996 | 0.1 | 0.8 | 0.0 | 0.0 | 0.0 | 0.3 | –3.0 |
| | 1997 | 0.1 | 1.1 | 0.0 | 0.0 | 0.0 | 0.3 | –3.2 |
| | 1998 | 0.1 | 2.1 | 0.0 | 0.0 | 0.0 | 0.0 | –4.9 |
| | 1999 | 0.1 | 1.5 | 0.0 | 0.0 | 0.0 | –0.4 | –2.2 |
| | 2000 | 0.0 | 1.4 | 0.0 | 0.0 | 0.0 | 0.5 | –0.4 |
| Bonds | 1995 | 0.5 | 0.3 | 1.4 | –0.7 | 0.7 | 0.5 | 2.8 |
| | 1996 | –0.6 | 1.3 | 0.1 | –0.1 | –1.3 | –0.5 | 5.0 |
| | 1997 | –0.3 | –0.3 | 0.1 | 0.3 | 0.0 | –1.8 | 3.3 |
| | 1998 | –0.2 | –0.7 | –0.7 | –1.0 | 0.4 | –0.2 | –4.5 |
| | 1999 | –0.2 | 1.5 | 0.1 | –0.2 | 1.5 | 0.5 | –2.1 |
| | 2000 | –0.2 | –1.4 | 0.3 | –0.2 | –0.7 | –0.7 | 2.6 |
| Equity | 1995 | –1.5 | –1.2 | 0.1 | 0.3 | 2.3 | 0.8 | 0.7 |
| | 1996 | –1.7 | –2.5 | 0.5 | 0.1 | 4.9 | 1.0 | 0.1 |
| | 1997 | –0.9 | –3.5 | 0.4 | 0.2 | 7.1 | 1.1 | 0.4 |
| | 1998 | –2.9 | –2.8 | 0.4 | 0.2 | 5.3 | 0.6 | –0.1 |
| | 1999 | –3.9 | –2.8 | 0.5 | –0.2 | 2.8 | –1.2 | 2.1 |
| | 2000 | –3.7 | –4.9 | 0.7 | –0.1 | 2.9 | 0.3 | –0.9 |
| Mutual funds | 1995 | 0.2 | 0.9 | 0.6 | 1.0 | na | –2.9 | –0.6 |
| | 1996 | 0.6 | 2.5 | 0.6 | 0.0 | na | –1.2 | 3.1 |
| | 1997 | 0.6 | 3.1 | 1.1 | –0.7 | na | –1.1 | 7.6 |
| | 1998 | 1.0 | 2.8 | 1.7 | 0.3 | na | 0.3 | 15.4 |
| | 1999 | 1.1 | 1.5 | 2.3 | 0.6 | na | 1.5 | 7.6 |
| | 2000 | 0.9 | 2.3 | 3.0 | 1.4 | na | 1.4 | 1.7 |
| Life and pensions | 1995 | 4.5 | 2.8 | 2.8 | 5.1 | 3.9 | 4.8 | 2.1 |
| | 1996 | 5.7 | 2.5 | 3.0 | 3.5 | 3.7 | 5.2 | 1.7 |
| | 1997 | 4.1 | 3.1 | 3.1 | 2.7 | 3.4 | 6.1 | 2.6 |
| | 1998 | 4.4 | 2.8 | 3.1 | 2.3 | 4.0 | 4.3 | 2.5 |
| | 1999 | 5.4 | 2.5 | 3.2 | 2.4 | 2.3 | 4.9 | 3.4 |
| | 2000 | 5.9 | 2.7 | 2.9 | 2.5 | 2.0 | 5.5 | 3.4 |
| Total assets | 1995 | 8.5 | 6.8 | 7.4 | 10.2 | 7.4 | 8.0 | 9.8 |
| | 1996 | 8.4 | 7.1 | 7.7 | 8.3 | 6.1 | 7.5 | 8.5 |
| | 1997 | 8.9 | 5.6 | 6.8 | 8.1 | 3.5 | 8.3 | 7.6 |
| | 1998 | 6.6 | 7.8 | 7.4 | 6.3 | 4.2 | 7.5 | 5.7 |
| | 1999 | 6.4 | 6.2 | 7.2 | 7.0 | 3.5 | 8.5 | 9.4 |
| | 2000 | 7.5 | 4.4 | 5.7 | 3.3 | 3.0 | 7.9 | 8.1 |

Table 5.6 (*Continued*)

| | UK | US | Germany | Japan | Canada | France | Italy |
|---|---|---|---|---|---|---|---|
| **1995–2000 average** | | | | | | | |
| Deposits | 4.1 | 1.8 | 1.3 | 4.9 | 1.6 | 2.7 | 0.4 |
| MMI | 0.1 | 1.4 | 0.0 | 0.0 | 0.0 | 0.1 | −1.2 |
| Bonds | −0.2 | 0.1 | 0.2 | −0.3 | 0.1 | −0.4 | 1.2 |
| Equities | −2.4 | −3.0 | 0.5 | 0.1 | 4.2 | 0.4 | 0.4 |
| Mutual funds | 0.7 | 2.2 | 1.6 | 0.4 | 0.0 | −0.3 | 5.8 |
| Life and pensions | 5.0 | 2.7 | 3.0 | 3.1 | 3.2 | 5.1 | 2.6 |
| *Total assets* | *7.7* | *6.3* | *7.0* | *7.2* | *4.6* | *7.9* | *8.2* |

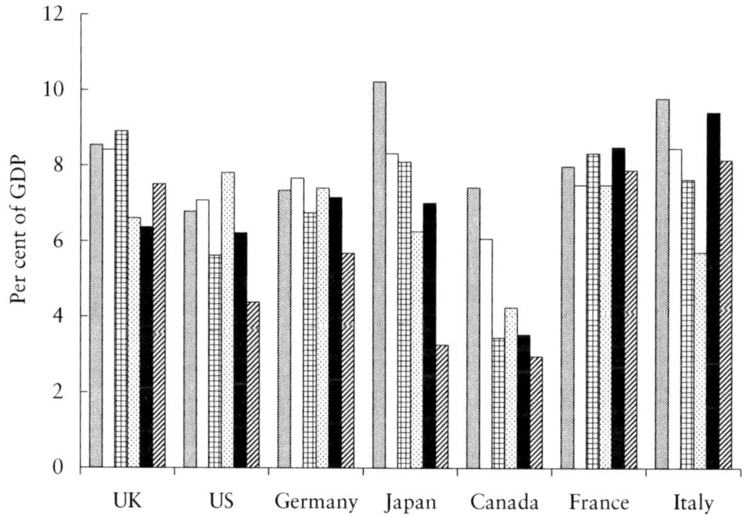


Figure 5.2 *Households' acquisition of financial assets 1995–2000*
Note: For each country each group of bars represents (from left to right) 1995, 1996, 1997, 1998, 1999, 2000.

going mainly to life and pensions, and deposits. There is little or no net inflow to equities or bonds, suggesting that, for the G-7 as a whole, recent boosts to holdings were due to price increases alone. French inflows to life and pensions, and Japanese flows to deposits, are both around 5 per cent of GDP on average.

With respect to the total level of household financial liability accumula-

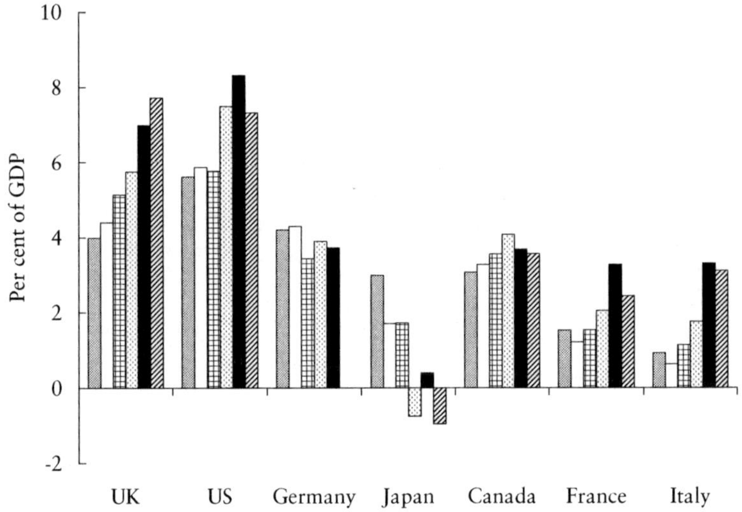


Figure 5.3 *Households' acquisition of liabilities 1995–2000*
Note: As Figure 5.2.

tion as a percentage of GDP (Table 5.7 and Figure 5.3), there are much greater differences between the countries. The UK and US have experienced much larger increases in liabilities in our sample period than the other countries, averaging 5.5–6.5 per cent of GDP, and corresponding to low or negative net financial saving (Table 3.11). As noted above, these countries have witnessed financial liberalisation and also saw buoyant housing markets and economic growth in the late 1990s. These led to a boom in borrowing, both directly for house purchase and for equity release. Rising indebtedness was offset by rising equity prices in terms of net wealth until 1998 and has continued at the time of writing to be offset by buoyant house prices. Japan is an outlier at the bottom end (0.8 per cent of GDP) and this may be due to structural balance sheet adjustment, in response to the protracted downturn in that economy.

The source of the increases in liabilities is largely through mortgage debt. Consumer credit accumulations on the other hand have made a less significant contribution. Nevertheless they have been substantial for some countries, with a sharp divide between the UK, US and Canada, where they are significant, and elsewhere where they are nugatory. Again, these are the financially liberalised and market oriented countries which stand out.

Table 5.7 *Household sector acquisition of liabilities (per cent of GDP)*

| | | UK | US | Germany | Japan | Canada | France | Italy |
|---|---|---|---|---|---|---|---|---|
| Consumer credit | 1995 | 0.9 | 1.9 | 0.2 | –0.1 | 0.8 | –0.2 | 0.0 |
| | 1996 | 1.0 | 1.7 | 0.1 | 0.1 | 0.9 | –0.1 | 0.1 |
| | 1997 | 1.2 | 1.5 | –0.2 | 0.0 | 1.0 | 0.1 | 0.1 |
| | 1998 | 1.5 | 1.2 | 0.3 | –0.2 | 1.1 | 0.0 | 0.1 |
| | 1999 | 1.5 | 1.0 | –0.1 | 0.0 | 1.1 | 0.0 | 0.2 |
| | 2000 | 2.0 | 0.8 | 0.1 | 0.1 | 1.0 | 0.3 | 0.3 |
| Housing loans | 1995 | 2.1 | 2.6 | 3.9 | 1.8 | 1.7 | 0.8 | 0.7 |
| | 1996 | 2.5 | 2.8 | 4.2 | 2.2 | 1.9 | 1.3 | 0.3 |
| | 1997 | 3.0 | 2.9 | 3.6 | 1.7 | 1.9 | 1.4 | 0.9 |
| | 1998 | 3.0 | 2.8 | 3.5 | 0.5 | 1.9 | 1.6 | 1.5 |
| | 1999 | 4.3 | 2.9 | 3.7 | 1.4 | 1.8 | 2.2 | 2.8 |
| | 2000 | 4.4 | 2.6 | 1.9 | 0.6 | 1.8 | 1.9 | 1.9 |
| Total liabilities | 1995 | 4.0 | 5.6 | 4.2 | 3.0 | 3.1 | 1.5 | 0.9 |
| | 1996 | 4.4 | 5.9 | 4.3 | 1.7 | 3.3 | 1.2 | 0.6 |
| | 1997 | 5.1 | 5.8 | 3.4 | 1.7 | 3.6 | 1.5 | 1.1 |
| | 1998 | 5.7 | 7.5 | 3.9 | –0.8 | 4.1 | 2.0 | 1.8 |
| | 1999 | 7.0 | 8.3 | 3.7 | 0.4 | 3.7 | 3.3 | 3.3 |
| | 2000 | 7.7 | 7.3 | 0.0 | –1.0 | 3.6 | 2.4 | 3.1 |
| **1995–2000 average** | | | | | | | | |
| Consumer credit | | 1.3 | 1.3 | 0.1 | 0.0 | 1.0 | 0.0 | 0.1 |
| Housing loans | | 3.2 | 2.8 | 3.5 | 1.4 | 1.8 | 1.6 | 1.4 |
| *Total liabilities* | | *5.7* | *6.7* | *3.3* | *0.8* | *3.5* | *2.0* | *1.8* |

# 6 The general government sector

## 6.1 GENERAL GOVERNMENT SECTOR – THEORETICAL AND EMPIRICAL BACKGROUND

The general government sector is distinct in many ways from the household, corporate and financial sectors. The ability to tax and the obligation to provide government goods and services are particularly important in differentiating the activity of the sector. There is little allusion to the government sector in the overall theory of financial structure and portfolio allocation as summarised in Chapter 1. Most of the extant public-finance theory concerns liabilities – there is little on assets. In the academic literature, the question of whether the overall level of government liabilities has any impact on economic activity is often discussed. This can be traced to Keynesian arguments in favour of a contra-cycle use of fiscal policy (Blanchard, 1999) which is borne out by most macro models such as the NIESR NiGEM model.

On the other hand, Barro (1974) has suggested that, under certain conditions, changes in the level of government sector liabilities are not likely to affect economic activity. These conditions include lump sum taxes which do not affect economic outcomes, free availability of credit to households and forward-looking behaviour that anticipates future taxes. This was the revival of David Ricardo's idea and is popularly known as Ricardian Equivalence. By extension the composition of debt will not affect economic activity.

The assumptions of the Ricardian Equivalence argument are not necessarily fulfilled. For example taxes are not typically lump sum, as assumed by Barro, but often distortionary. Income taxes will have economic implications and affect households' decisions between work and leisure.

Consumption taxes will affect the decision to spend or save. Fiscal changes will consequently have economic implications. Additionally, households are not always able to internalise the government's budget constraint, unlike in the Ricardian equivalence approach. This implies that households do not fully recognise that changes in debt finance costs lead to changes in future tax liabilities (or assuming finite lifetimes, agents care about the lives of future generations less than their own).

Beyond a certain point, the Ricardian effects may nevertheless become strong. Giavazzi and Pagano (1995) analyse the experience of countries such as Italy, Sweden, Ireland and Denmark that have faced fiscal crises. They suggest that private expenditure fell in periods of crisis not only due to direct effects of higher interest rates, crowding out and uncertainty generated by a fiscal crisis, but also owing to Ricardian effects, thus leading to recessionary tendencies, as well as inflation. The tightening of fiscal policy to reverse the adverse trend was in their view consequently expansionary. Other underlying factors may have been fear of inflation as it was expected that the government would seek to monetise the debt. Such fears may lead to currency crises, especially where foreign holders hold a large share of the debt.

Besides current debt, future pension liabilities may enter the perception of agents in the economy and affect their behaviour. Ricardian effects may operate in this manner also. For recent estimates of expenditures underlying such implicit debt for OECD countries see Dang *et al.* (2001).

As regards objectives in debt management, issues of risk may be important for the public sector. This can be seen as an extension of the approach of households, since they decide their optimal portfolios taking account of risk and return. Tobin (1963) is of the view that governments should ignore risk and concentrate on minimising cost and macroeconomic stability. This would suggest that sovereign governments are the least susceptible of all economic agents to default and reflects our earlier point about the unique ability of the government to tax. Nevertheless, Wheeler (1997) suggests that the government should be risk averse (following the approach of the median voter) and be concerned about the build-up of debt.

Papers discussing optimal taxation have made a contribution to the discussion about risk, and have been highly influential. This approach in the literature, dating from Lucas and Stokey (1983), suggests that the government should be risk averse (even in circumstances where the median voter is risk neutral). Consequently, the government should be prepared to accept increased debt servicing costs where tax rate fluctuations are reduced. Lucas and Stokey present a number of examples to illustrate, including the situation where the government builds up a 'war chest' up until period T when an actual war starts. Before time T the tax rate, consumption and labour income are constant, with the government accumulating bonds. It spends this accumulated wealth during the war and also additional borrowings collected in time T. These are consequently paid for by taxes after the war has ended.

Lucas and Stokey (1983) also highlight the impact of the government's portfolio on the reputation of monetary policy, in support of the attainment of low inflation or maintaining a fixed exchange rate. The case is reminiscent of the argument of Tobin (1963), in the sense that debt management should be concerned with macroeconomic stability. The objective here is to establish credibility of a particular policy (i.e. dynamic consistency). If nominal bonds with a long maturity are issued as liabilities by the government, there is a strong incentive to use unexpected inflation as a means of reducing the real value of national debt. However, Lucas and Stokey model a situation where the government can decide the maturity structure of its debt, such that there is no incentive to change policy later. Given the recent preoccupation with the reputation of monetary policy, a number of countries have separated monetary policy from fiscal policy with an independent central bank, for example the ECB, and, in the case of the UK's Debt Management Office, an operationally independent organisation in charge of organising debt holdings.

Much of the literature has tested whether changes in the structure of debt holdings have macroeconomic implications, for instance, whether debt holding has implications for the returns on assets and whether costs savings can be made. The issue here assumes a typically upward sloping yield curve, where long-term assets have higher rates of return than short-term bills due to economic uncertainty. As suggested by Campbell (1995), if the government substitutes short-term bonds for long-term bonds there may be substantial interest rate savings as the yield curve is flattened. There have been a number of studies, which consider whether debt management will have an effect on asset prices,[36] although they often do not find a substantial effect. Recent studies typically follow Frankel (1985) and adopt a portfolio balance approach. Here the concern is with whether private and public bonds are perfect substitutes and what is the covariance of changes in their value.

Where assets are not perfect substitutes, changing the number of public bonds in overall debt levels may affect asset returns. Hess (1999) finds that there is a small but significant effect from the mix of debt to yields using

36 These include Modigliani and Sutch (1967), Holland (1969), Agell and Persson (1992) and Wallace and Warner (1996).

UK data. Campbell (1999) takes a contrasting approach consistent with much of his recent work on asset pricing, but finds that Hess' results are reasonably robust.

Gale (1990) suggests that debt management neutrality is somewhat less dependent upon the assumptions of the Ricardian-equivalence model, since debt management does not affect the current mix of government revenue and expenditure.

Reinhart and Sack (2000) address the impact of the current and then-anticipated[37] decline in government liabilities due to the recent health of US government finances.[38] They use the portfolio-balance approach and find only small adjustments to the relative returns on various US financial assets. The authors found that this result would be reinforced where Agency and Corporate debt 'crowd in' to replace much of the expected decline in Treasury securities. Kashyap (1999) suggests that for the public debt structure to matter in a macroeconomic sense, we need imperfections in financial markets that violate the Modigliani-Miller theorem for banks.[39] If these are present, public debt will be preferred to private debt as a buffer stock against unexpected deposit withdrawals. In the absence of a more detailed theoretical model, much of the empirical literature in this area will be tentative.

One benefit that the government can achieve through portfolio management is the provision of specific assets to the private sector, which would not exist otherwise. Campbell and Viceira (2001) suggest that that government issue of long-term index-linked bonds would lead to substantial welfare gains for investors wishing to eliminate inflation risk (although there may be a question of risk transfers to the public sector in this case, and a commensurate increase in tax uncertainty). Gale (1990) highlights the contribution that government debt can make across generations via retirement pension income. Opportunities for a risk-free investment may increase welfare where individuals save using government bonds during their working life and consume their savings in their retirement. A risky private sector investment may not guarantee any consumption once

---

37 Since the US has now returned to deficit at the time of writing, the projections proved inaccurate.

38 No further issuance of 30 years' US Treasuries was assumed; outturns were dependent upon the extent of the downturn in 2001. See also Flemming (2000).

39 As noted in Section 4.1, the Modigliani-Miller theorem suggests that the total value of bonds and equities issued by a firm is independent of the number of bonds outstanding or their interest rate. Again the main implication of this theorem is that the nature of corporate finance is irrelevant.

workers retire, owing to credit and market risk, hence government interventions may be welfare improving. Another suggestion by Blake and Orszag (1999) is that governments should issue survivor bonds, whose return is indexed to changing longevity of cohorts of retirees. This would enable insurance companies to hedge longevity risk on annuities, see also Davis (2002b). The general objective is therefore that the government identifies areas where financial markets are missing, which can be filled with government assets and liabilities.

## 6.2 GENERAL GOVERNMENT SECTOR BALANCE SHEETS

As is the case for companies, governments need liquidity mainly for working capital, apart from any direct financial investments. Since major OECD governments are unlikely to be credit rationed, liquidity needs would be expected to be lower relative to companies.

Concerning general government financial assets, contrasts are in some ways less than for the household sector. As a percentage of total assets, there appear to be some similarities of portfolio amongst the G-7 (see Table 6.1). Notes, coins and deposits are important for government as a proportion of total assets, ranging from 8 and 11 per cent in Canada and the United States to 54 per cent in Germany, for the most recent data. As is the case for other sectors, the trend over the past 30 years has seen government demand for deposits, notes and coins decline as a proportion of assets in the US, Germany, Japan and France. This could be representative of financial innovation for the government sector, precluding the need for precautionary and transaction balances. Nevertheless, the share of liquidity has risen sharply in the UK.

Loans are important for general government in most countries and this is particularly the case for the UK, with over 50 per cent of government assets in the forms of loans. This is linked to the activism and scope of government's industrial policies. We also see high percentages of loans for the US, Canada and Italy (ranging from 25–40 per cent) but less so for France at 17 per cent and Japan at zero (public loans are held by public financial institutions included in Tables 8.1–8.4). Bond holdings are important for the US, Canada and, to a lesser extent, Japan. Government equity holdings are high for a number of countries, especially Japan and France, which have experienced substantial increases over the past 30 years and now represent over 50 per cent of total assets. This reflects finance of nationalised and part-privatised industries. Germany and Italy have also

Table 6.1 *General government sector financial assets (per cent of total)*

| | | UK | US | Germany | Japan | Canada | France | Italy |
|---|---|---|---|---|---|---|---|---|
| Deposits notes and coin | 1970 | 2.5 | 32.7 | 76.1 | 79.2 | 9.9 | 25.2 | 14.0 |
| | 1980 | 2.3 | 19.1 | 77.0 | 65.4 | 11.1 | 21.5 | 25.5 |
| | 1990 | 8.2 | 9.6 | 82.3 | 85.1 | 7.7 | 32.0 | 16.7 |
| | 1998 | 16.9 | 10.6 | 46.5 | 21.9 | 8.2 | 21.7 | 17.8 |
| | 2000 | 25.8 | 11.3 | 54.5 | 25.1 | 7.7 | 18.0 | 18.2 |
| Money Market Inst | 1970 | 1.8 | -1.0 | 1.3 | 5.2 | 0.4 | 0.0 | 0.0 |
| | 1980 | 2.1 | 3.7 | 0.0 | 5.3 | 2.4 | 0.0 | 0.5 |
| | 1990 | 0.7 | 9.8 | 0.1 | 4.1 | 9.3 | 0.0 | 0.4 |
| | 1998 | 5.3 | 18.8 | 0.0 | 4.9 | 7.0 | 1.6 | 0.4 |
| | 2000 | 6.6 | 18.3 | 0.2 | 0.7 | 8.5 | 2.2 | 0.1 |
| Loans | 1970 | 90.6 | 46.0 | 0.0 | 0.0 | 38.4 | 33.8 | 63.1 |
| | 1980 | 77.7 | 42.6 | 0.0 | 0.0 | 26.9 | 14.8 | 59.8 |
| | 1990 | 62.9 | 29.9 | 0.0 | 0.0 | 19.9 | 11.6 | 44.8 |
| | 1998 | 62.3 | 24.8 | 14.7 | 0.0 | 24.8 | 17.9 | 35.2 |
| | 2000 | 52.3 | 25.6 | 14.5 | 0.0 | 25.1 | 17.0 | 39.1 |
| Bonds | 1970 | 0.1 | 22.4 | 7.7 | 5.2 | 50.4 | 4.7 | 7.6 |
| | 1980 | 11.7 | 34.6 | 7.2 | 18.7 | 59.0 | 1.4 | 2.3 |
| | 1990 | 17.5 | 49.9 | 5.0 | 6.9 | 59.5 | 9.4 | 8.2 |
| | 1998 | 9.4 | 36.9 | 4.1 | 20.7 | 49.1 | 6.5 | 4.3 |
| | 2000 | 10.4 | 35.7 | 2.6 | 21.5 | 48.0 | 6.6 | 6.6 |
| Equity | 1970 | 5.0 | 0.0 | 14.9 | 10.4 | 0.9 | 36.3 | 15.3 |
| | 1980 | 6.2 | 0.0 | 15.8 | 10.6 | 0.6 | 61.9 | 11.9 |
| | 1990 | 10.8 | 0.4 | 10.3 | 3.9 | 3.5 | 42.5 | 29.9 |
| | 1998 | 6.0 | 7.4 | 32.0 | 50.5 | 11.0 | 48.7 | 42.3 |
| | 2000 | 4.9 | 7.4 | 24.6 | 51.3 | 10.7 | 50.9 | 34.8 |
| Mutual funds | 1970 | 0.0 | 0.0 | 0.0 | 0.0 | na | 0.0 | 0.0 |
| | 1980 | 0.0 | 0.0 | 0.0 | 0.0 | na | 0.4 | 0.0 |
| | 1990 | 0.0 | 0.4 | 2.3 | 0.0 | na | 4.5 | 0.0 |
| | 1998 | 0.0 | 1.5 | 2.6 | 2.0 | na | 3.6 | 0.0 |
| | 2000 | 0.0 | 1.7 | 3.6 | 1.4 | na | 5.3 | 1.3 |

Note: the first observation for the UK is 1975 and not 1970.

seen sizeable increases in equity holdings in the past 30 years, and the portfolio share is now 25–35 per cent. Note that this is characteristic of bank-based rather than market-oriented financial systems.

The size of government assets is generally low and does not deviate much from around a quarter of GDP (Table 6.2). The UK and US are at the low end in the mid-teens in 2000 whilst France, Italy, Japan and Canada are at the high end. Note that the book-entry 'Trust fund bureau' deposits of the

Table 6.2 *General government sector financial assets (per cent of GDP)*

| | | UK | US | Germany | Japan | Canada | France | Italy |
|---|---|---|---|---|---|---|---|---|
| Deposits notes and coin | 1970 | 0.9 | 4.2 | 17.6 | 2.1 | 3.6 | 7.3 | 4.0 |
| | 1980 | 0.6 | 3.0 | 11.8 | 3.8 | 4.5 | 6.1 | 12.3 |
| | 1990 | 1.9 | 1.9 | 12.6 | 7.9 | 3.0 | 6.0 | 3.6 |
| | 1998 | 2.5 | 1.6 | 8.5 | 5.8 | 3.0 | 5.4 | 5.1 |
| | 2000 | 4.5 | 1.7 | 10.4 | 9.2 | 2.7 | 4.9 | 4.8 |
| Money market inst | 1970 | 0.6 | –0.1 | 0.3 | 0.1 | 0.1 | 0.0 | 0.0 |
| | 1980 | 0.5 | 0.6 | 0.0 | 0.3 | 1.0 | 0.0 | 0.3 |
| | 1990 | 0.2 | 2.0 | 0.0 | 0.4 | 3.6 | 0.0 | 0.1 |
| | 1998 | 0.8 | 2.9 | 0.0 | 1.3 | 2.5 | 0.4 | 0.1 |
| | 2000 | 1.1 | 2.8 | 0.0 | 0.3 | 3.0 | 0.6 | 0.0 |
| Loans | 1970 | 32.7 | 6.0 | 0.0 | 0.0 | 14.0 | 9.8 | 18.1 |
| | 1980 | 19.0 | 6.8 | 0.0 | 0.0 | 10.9 | 4.2 | 28.9 |
| | 1990 | 14.3 | 6.0 | 0.0 | 0.0 | 7.7 | 2.2 | 9.7 |
| | 1998 | 9.1 | 3.8 | 2.7 | 0.0 | 9.0 | 4.5 | 10.1 |
| | 2000 | 9.1 | 3.9 | 2.8 | 0.0 | 8.8 | 4.6 | 10.4 |
| Bonds | 1970 | 0.0 | 2.9 | 1.8 | 0.1 | 18.4 | 1.3 | 2.2 |
| | 1980 | 2.9 | 5.5 | 1.1 | 1.1 | 24.0 | 0.4 | 1.1 |
| | 1990 | 4.0 | 10.1 | 0.8 | 0.6 | 23.1 | 1.8 | 1.8 |
| | 1998 | 1.4 | 5.7 | 0.7 | 5.5 | 17.9 | 1.6 | 1.2 |
| | 2000 | 1.8 | 5.5 | 0.5 | 7.9 | 16.8 | 1.8 | 1.8 |
| Equity | 1970 | 1.8 | 0.0 | 3.5 | 0.3 | 0.3 | 10.5 | 4.4 |
| | 1980 | 1.5 | 0.0 | 2.4 | 0.6 | 0.2 | 17.6 | 5.8 |
| | 1990 | 2.5 | 0.1 | 1.6 | 0.4 | 1.4 | 8.0 | 6.5 |
| | 1998 | 0.9 | 1.1 | 5.8 | 13.3 | 4.0 | 12.2 | 12.1 |
| | 2000 | 0.9 | 1.1 | 4.7 | 18.9 | 3.8 | 13.8 | 9.3 |
| Mutual funds | 1970 | 0.0 | 0.0 | 0.0 | 0.0 | na | 0.0 | 0.0 |
| | 1980 | 0.0 | 0.0 | 0.0 | 0.0 | na | 0.1 | 0.0 |
| | 1990 | 0.0 | 0.1 | 0.4 | 0.0 | na | 0.9 | 0.0 |
| | 1998 | 0.0 | 0.2 | 0.5 | 0.5 | na | 0.9 | 0.0 |
| | 2000 | 0.0 | 0.3 | 0.7 | 0.5 | na | 1.4 | 0.4 |
| Total assets | 1970 | 36.1 | 12.9 | 23.2 | 2.6 | 36.5 | 29.0 | 28.7 |
| | 1980 | 24.5 | 15.8 | 15.4 | 5.8 | 40.6 | 28.4 | 48.4 |
| | 1990 | 22.8 | 20.2 | 15.3 | 9.3 | 38.8 | 18.7 | 21.6 |
| | 1998 | 14.5 | 15.5 | 18.2 | 26.4 | 36.5 | 25.0 | 28.6 |
| | 2000 | 17.3 | 15.4 | 19.1 | 36.8 | 35.1 | 27.1 | 26.7 |

Note: the first observation for the UK is 1975 and not 1970.

Japanese government are omitted to ensure comparability – they are sizeable at over 50 per cent of GDP. In most countries the size of government

Table 6.3 *General government sector liabilities (per cent of total)*

| | | UK | US | Germany | Japan | Canada | France | Italy |
|---|---|---|---|---|---|---|---|---|
| Deposits notes and coin | 1970 | 20.9 | 0.0 | 0.0 | 0.0 | 1.3 | 53.8 | 22.5 |
| | 1980 | 18.4 | 0.0 | 0.0 | 0.0 | 1.8 | 34.1 | 20.0 |
| | 1990 | 18.9 | 0.0 | 0.0 | 0.0 | 1.9 | 15.5 | 10.7 |
| | 1998 | 14.9 | 0.0 | 0.0 | 0.0 | 1.6 | 7.7 | 10.5 |
| | 2000 | 16.4 | 0.0 | 0.0 | 0.0 | 1.9 | 7.0 | 11.8 |
| Money market inst | 1970 | 12.1 | na | 1.5 | 12.5 | 6.6 | 13.6 | 5.9 |
| | 1980 | 7.9 | na | 1.4 | 8.2 | 10.4 | 11.3 | 20.7 |
| | 1990 | 7.3 | na | 4.0 | 7.9 | 25.7 | 19.6 | 23.9 |
| | 1998 | 1.2 | na | 1.1 | 6.2 | 13.9 | 22.3 | 9.4 |
| | 2000 | 0.8 | na | 0.9 | 6.3 | 13.0 | 22.1 | 6.8 |
| Loans | 1970 | 34.1 | 1.4 | 82.1 | 33.9 | 6.9 | 24.2 | 42.2 |
| | 1980 | 24.2 | 0.8 | 76.8 | 30.8 | 7.7 | 30.5 | 36.9 |
| | 1990 | 27.6 | 0.3 | 50.4 | 27.1 | 4.2 | 22.3 | 15.3 |
| | 1998 | 13.3 | 0.2 | 38.6 | 23.7 | 2.8 | 18.5 | 9.3 |
| | 2000 | 16.6 | 0.2 | 36.0 | 22.6 | 3.1 | 17.4 | 9.4 |
| Bonds | 1970 | 32.9 | 98.6 | 16.4 | 53.6 | 85.2 | 8.4 | 29.4 |
| | 1980 | 49.5 | 99.2 | 21.9 | 61.0 | 80.1 | 24.2 | 22.4 |
| | 1990 | 46.2 | 99.7 | 45.6 | 65.0 | 68.3 | 42.5 | 50.1 |
| | 1998 | 70.7 | 99.8 | 60.3 | 70.1 | 81.8 | 51.5 | 70.9 |
| | 2000 | 66.2 | 99.8 | 63.1 | 71.1 | 82.0 | 53.4 | 72.0 |

Note: the first observation for the UK is 1975 and not 1970.

assets has kept pace with GDP (results for Japan may reflect accounting differences) but general government financial assets in the UK declined overall.

In terms of government liabilities, these are predominantly in bonds for all the countries studied. Unfortunately, data on maturity are not available from financial accounts, so the data do not permit comment to be made on debt management strategies. Essentially, all liabilities are bonds in the United States with 99.8 per cent in this form in 2000 (the data include Treasury Bills). All other countries have more than 50 per cent of liabilities in bonds, ranging from 53 per cent in France to 82 per cent in Canada. Money market instrument and loans are sizeable in France, Japan and Germany, while National Saving deposits are high in the UK. Nevertheless, in most countries there is a tendency for the share of bonds to increase, reflecting growth of capital markets and desire to increase maturity of liabilities. The Japanese Trust Fund Bureau holds mainly government bonds on the asset side and Postal Savings deposits on the liability side, indicating

Table 6.4 *General government sector liabilities (per cent of GDP)*

| | | UK | US | Germany | Japan | Canada | France | Italy |
|---|---|---|---|---|---|---|---|---|
| Deposits notes and coin | 1970 | 13.7 | 0.0 | 0.0 | 0.0 | 0.9 | 16.4 | 12.6 |
| | 1980 | 10.3 | 0.0 | 0.0 | 0.0 | 1.2 | 8.9 | 18.5 |
| | 1990 | 7.9 | 0.0 | 0.0 | 0.0 | 1.7 | 6.7 | 11.5 |
| | 1998 | 8.9 | 0.0 | 0.0 | 0.0 | 1.6 | 5.4 | 14.3 |
| | 2000 | 8.4 | 0.0 | 0.0 | 0.0 | 1.6 | 4.7 | 14.9 |
| Money market inst | 1970 | 8.0 | na | 0.3 | 3.2 | 4.6 | 4.2 | 3.3 |
| | 1980 | 4.5 | na | 0.4 | 7.1 | 7.3 | 3.0 | 19.0 |
| | 1990 | 3.1 | na | 1.7 | 6.7 | 23.8 | 8.5 | 25.5 |
| | 1998 | 0.7 | na | 0.7 | 6.6 | 14.2 | 15.7 | 12.8 |
| | 2000 | 0.4 | na | 0.6 | 8.1 | 11.4 | 14.6 | 8.6 |
| Loans | 1970 | 22.4 | 0.6 | 14.9 | 8.8 | 4.8 | 7.4 | 23.5 |
| | 1980 | 13.6 | 0.3 | 23.1 | 26.7 | 5.4 | 8.0 | 34.0 |
| | 1990 | 11.6 | 0.2 | 20.8 | 23.0 | 3.9 | 9.6 | 16.3 |
| | 1998 | 8.0 | 0.1 | 24.6 | 25.4 | 2.8 | 13.1 | 12.6 |
| | 2000 | 8.5 | 0.1 | 21.8 | 29.2 | 2.7 | 11.5 | 12.0 |
| Bonds | 1970 | 21.6 | 42.1 | 3.0 | 13.9 | 59.3 | 2.6 | 16.4 |
| | 1980 | 27.8 | 36.7 | 6.6 | 52.8 | 55.9 | 6.3 | 20.6 |
| | 1990 | 19.4 | 59.5 | 18.8 | 55.2 | 63.2 | 18.3 | 53.5 |
| | 1998 | 42.3 | 55.1 | 38.4 | 75.0 | 83.5 | 36.4 | 96.7 |
| | 2000 | 33.7 | 46.0 | 38.2 | 91.8 | 71.9 | 35.3 | 91.4 |
| Total liabilities | 1970 | 65.8 | 42.7 | 18.1 | 25.9 | 69.6 | 30.5 | 55.7 |
| | 1980 | 56.2 | 37.0 | 30.1 | 86.5 | 69.8 | 26.2 | 92.1 |
| | 1990 | 42.0 | 59.7 | 41.2 | 84.9 | 92.6 | 43.1 | 106.8 |
| | 1998 | 59.8 | 55.2 | 63.6 | 107.0 | 102.2 | 70.7 | 136.4 |
| | 2000 | 51.0 | 46.1 | 60.6 | 129.1 | 87.6 | 66.1 | 126.9 |
| Memo: estimated net pension liabilities 1994 | OECD estimate | −24 | −23 | −62 | −70 | −101 | −102 | −60 |
| | IMF estimate | −5 | −26 | −111 | −107 | −68 | −114 | −76 |

Note: the first observation for the UK is 1975 and not 1970.

that the consolidated public sector in that country has shorter-term liabilities than this table suggests.

The stock of liabilities relative to GDP is naturally driven by fiscal policy, although it is also affected by unanticipated inflation for long-maturity fixed rate instruments. For example, liabilities/GDP fell in the UK and US in the

1970s when inflation was rapid, despite sizeable deficits.

For the EMU countries, the early 1990s witnessed an increase in government liabilities. Total liabilities fell as a percentage of GDP in the late 1990s (Table 6.4), reflecting fiscal consolidation, although Italian debt has fallen slowly and remains above 120 per cent of GDP. There were also declines in the UK, US and Canada due to fiscal surpluses at the end of the 1990s. Owing to attempts to end its protracted slump by fiscal means, Japan broke the general trend across countries at the end of the 1990s with an increase in liabilities as a percentage of national income. This led public debt to exceed that of Italy in 2000 at 129 per cent of GDP, generating considerable concern about default risk and possible Ricardian effects, notably in the context of rapid population ageing (see Davis, 2002d). Note that since government assets and liabilities are nominal, the change in net assets is a close approximation to the fiscal flow position (Table 3.9).

Some perspective is given to the data on general government liabilities by the estimated net liabilities of public pension systems. These are the difference between the present value of contributions (with the contribution rate fixed at current levels) and the corresponding present value of benefits. Reflecting population ageing, this figure is in sizeable deficit, and shows a need for pension reform in the future, according to OECD and IMF estimates shown in Roseveare *et al.* (1996), IMF (1996) and Dang *et al.* (2001).

## 6.3 OWNERSHIP OF GOVERNMENT BONDS

The breakdown of the sectoral holdings of government bonds is shown in Table 6.5. Note that in Germany and France, data cover all bonds. The largest holder in all cases is the financial sector, within which it is life insurers and pension funds which predominate in the UK, US, Canada and France, and banks in Germany, Japan and Italy. Such assets correspond to nominal fixed liabilities. Foreign holdings are over 19 per cent except in Japan (5 per cent) – which foreigners may avoid due to perceptions of market risk, as well as owing to high demand by domestic investors. Italy stands out with 40 per cent of bonds held by investors from outside the country, a trend probably accelerated by EMU. The domestic non-financial sectors do not tend to hold large shares of government bonds, although companies in Canada hold 33 per cent of them, and households in the US, Germany and Italy hold 10–20 per cent.

Table 6.5 *Government bondholders by sector end–2000 (per cent of total)*

| | UK | US | Germany | Japan | Canada | France | Italy |
|---|---|---|---|---|---|---|---|
| Households | 7 | 14 | 14 | 5 | 6 | 5 | 18 |
| Companies | 1 | 1 | 5 | 0 | 33 | 3 | 2 |
| Public sector | 0 | 5 | 0 | 3 | 7 | 2 | 1 |
| Foreign | 20 | 19 | 27 | 5 | 19 | 21 | 40 |
| Financial | 71 | 61 | 53 | 87 | 35 | 69 | 39 |
| Banks | 3 | 15 | 37 | 40 | 9 | 33 | 18 |
| Life/pension | 62 | 16 | 4 | 23 | 18 | 36 | 8 |
| Mutual funds | 7 | 12 | 12 | 3 | 3 | 15 | 13 |
| Total | 100 | 100 | 100 | 100 | 100 | 100 | 100 |

Note: All bonds for Germany and France, 'other financial intermediaries' used for mutual funds in Germany.

# 7 The foreign sector

## 7.1 FOREIGN SECTOR – THEORETICAL AND EMPIRICAL BACKGROUND

While countries have always held external assets and liabilities vis-à-vis one another, the importance of the international balance sheet has increased due to the pace of global economic integration. Recent decades have seen rapid growth in international capital markets and, to a slightly lesser extent, in international trade. These developments reflect both regulatory and technological factors. International capital markets have grown due to removal of capital controls and substantial technological developments, for example, improved international communication systems. Similarly, international trade has grown due to negotiated removal of tariff and quota barriers as well as reduced transportation costs. (See Obstfeld, 1998, for an interesting discussion of international integration and technological development.)

Besides showing changes in net national wealth, the foreign balance sheet is useful since it gives an indication of sovereign risk exposure. For emerging market economies, there has been increasing attention paid to this source of information since the Asian crisis of 1997, leading to widespread dissemination of the IMF's set of key indicators of external vulnerability which emphasise the importance of the balance sheet. Countries with large foreign currency exposure carry substantial risks from abrupt changes in the exchange rate. Indeed, Mishkin (2001) points out that one of the main differences in financial markets between developed and emerging market economies is the large proportion of debt contracts denominated in foreign currency in the latter. For developed countries, where the chances of substantial changes in the external value of the domestic currency are in any case smaller, the balance sheet can nonetheless help to identify current account disequilibria, which could conceivably lead to more widespread confidence problems. The balance sheet is also useful to identify the impact of external shocks on particular sectors. For example, Senior and Westwood (2000) suggest that two important factors contributing to recent changes in the UK balance sheet have been the current account deficit and revaluation effects (i.e. changes in the exchange rate and in other asset prices).

As regards the composition of external assets, the benefits of international portfolio holdings have been discussed in the literature since Grubel (1968) and Levy and Sarnat (1970) and the reasons for holding foreign assets and liabilities are widely recognised. Whereas holding a diversified portfolio of assets in a domestic market can eliminate unsystematic, diversifiable risk resulting from the different performance of individual firms and industries, it cannot eliminate systematic, undiversifiable risk resulting from the performance of the economy as a whole.[40] In an efficient and integrated world capital market, systematic risk would be minimised by holding a global portfolio, wherein assets are held in proportion to their distribution by current value between the national markets. In effect, the improvement in the risk-return position from diversification more than compensates for the additional element of volatility arising from currency movements. Benefits are particularly marked for institutional investors, as discussed in Chapter 10.

Several ways may be envisaged whereby a strategy of international diversification should reduce risk (Davis and Steil, 2001). Crucially, to the extent that national trade cycles are not correlated and shocks to equity markets tend to be country-specific, the investment of part of the portfolio in other markets can reduce systematic risk for the same return.[41] In the medium term, the profit share in national economies may move differentially, which implies that international investment hedges the risk of a decline in domestic profit share and hence in equity values.[42] In the very long term, imperfect correlation of demographic shifts should offer

---

40 See Section 1.1 and Frost and Henderson (1983).

41 Consistent with this, Harvey (1991), shows that markets tend to have correlations of 0.16–0.86, with a majority in the range 0.4–0.7.

42 This will be of particular importance to defined benefit pension funds in which liabilities are tied to wages and hence rise as the profit share falls. Similarly, at an individual firm level, investment in competitors' shares hedges against a loss of profits due to partial loss of the domestic market.

protection against the effects on the domestic economy of the ageing of the population.[43]

Although the economic arguments are well-rehearsed in favour of it, there does appear to be 'aberrant' behaviour displayed by the more developed countries, inconsistent with the benefits of international portfolio diversification. Most important is the home-bias puzzle whereby domestic residents hold a disproportionate amount of their wealth in domestic assets. This low level of international diversification is considered in French and Poterba (1991). These authors find that US investors hold 94 per cent of their equity wealth in domestic assets. The figure is even higher for Japan and only slightly lower for the United Kingdom; these two countries have 98 per cent and 82 per cent respectively of equity wealth in domestic securities. Tesar and Werner (1995) find similar results with more recent data, although smaller countries often display more evidence of integration.[44]

Lewis (1995) considers the evidence as to whether the home bias of large industrial countries can be considered optimal in some sense. She uses a partial equilibrium Capital Asset Pricing Model (CAPM) and finds that the optimal holding of domestic US assets is less than 50 per cent. Flavin and Wickens (2000) implement an approach taking account of time-varying risk for the UK and find that the optimal holding is 57 per cent. These figures, far above actual levels, highlight the low level of actual international diversification of wealth holding.

Some of the disparity here may be explained by the location of multinational firms. Domestic firms will often have foreign operations and hence a foreign income stream which reduces the need for portfolio investment in foreign assets. NIESR (1997) shows that marked foreign

---

43 Erb *et al.* (1997) show how asset returns vary systematically with a country's demographic characteristics, with an older population being more risk averse and demanding a higher premium on equity investment.

44 Additionally, integration has increased rapidly in the 1990s with both assets and liabilities increasing for a number of the G-7 countries (US, UK, France and Italy). Assets have doubled in Germany and liabilities have doubled in Canada. This may have led to decreases in the home-bias problem reported by French and Poterba, using 1989 data, and Tesar and Werner (1995), examining data from 1990. Senior and Westwood (2000) report that just under 70 per cent of domestic equity was held by overseas investors in 1999 in the UK (their definitions differ from Table 4.7). The authors report figures for the United States consistent with French and Poterba, suggesting integration has not reduced home bias in that country.

exposure may arise from such international activities of domestic companies, and hence home bias may be exaggerated at an aggregate level. In the UK and Germany, for example, around 25 per cent of firms' activities is conducted abroad. Mitra-Stiff (1995) and Obstfeld (1998) review why foreign direct investment is substantial and increasing in this context. In their recent study of the UK balance sheet, Senior and Westwood (2000) draw attention to the role of international mergers and acquisitions as contributing to the growth of FDI at the end of the 1990s.

For countries, the benefits of international openness and investment also include the ability to tap into growth in other countries, allowing nations' risks to be pooled and access foreign borrowing in times of recession, or as an investment for long-term development. Foreign assets offer the opportunity for exchange rate risk to be hedged (although this is reduced in a European context with the introduction of the euro). An alternative benefit, from a general welfare perspective, is the discipline that international portfolios impose on policymakers. The assumption here is that profligate monetary or fiscal policy would precipitate capital flight, with foreigners and residents selling domestic assets. Governments under such circumstance have a disincentive from pursuing overly expansionary macroeconomic policy.

There may also be disadvantages to openness. These include exposure to rapid reversals in international capital flows, which can provoke macroeconomic disruption. Such behaviour may originate both in international banks and institutional investors. On potentially disruptive effects of banking flows via the international interbank market, with particular reference to Asia, see Bernard and Bisignano (2000). Concerning institutional investors (Davis and Steil, 2001), there is an important asymmetry between the location and size of institutional investors – very large in cash terms and mainly in OECD countries – and the emerging markets and their relatively small size. In the context of the cyclical nature of investment in emerging markets, a marginal portfolio adjustment in the context of global investment by institutions can thus be a first-order event for the emerging market.

Recent research has focused on whether and how portfolio flows disrupt capital markets. Froot *et al.* (1999) found that flows into and out of countries are highly correlated across international investors and seem to occur in response to global trends such as inflation and exchange rate expectations rather than changes in local conditions in the country concerned. Also, although investors' withdrawal did not strongly correlate with falls in prices (i.e., it was not direct pullouts that caused price collapses), a marked deceleration in inflows did tend to depress prices, consistent with the idea that they are often marked up in the expectation that recent trends in inflows will continue. The results are not entirely conclusive in suggesting that foreign institutions destabilise emerging markets but offer strong circumstantial evidence. Underlying such patterns may be the tendency for institutional investors to treat emerging markets as a separate asset class (Buckberg, 1996). Institutional investors or their portfolio managers who are uninformed[45] about individual countries, or who do not seek to differentiate, may allocate funds evenly across emerging markets to ensure diversification. Inflows thus tend to lead to increases in stock prices across all emerging markets, regardless of the variation in underlying structural and macroeconomic performance.

Judgements on emerging market investments are often undertaken in a manner that is both correlated across markets and also on the basis of historical evidence of correlations and returns, without reference to the effects of recent inflows on such patterns. As inflows themselves lead to price rises, the process may become self-generating, destabilising the market. The corollary is that, when there is a crisis in one emerging market, such as Mexico in 1994, a reassessment occurs, and the allocation across the asset class as a whole is reduced. Given the size of institutional investors relative to the emerging markets, this generates volatility across the sector as a whole. Such behaviour is contrary to the efficient markets hypothesis, with allocation not following the fundamentals of an individual asset but rather investor sentiment about the class of assets as a whole, whose fundamentals may be unrelated. Indeed, such behaviour is likely to drive prices away from fundamentals in many markets.

## 7.2 FOREIGN SECTOR BALANCE SHEETS

Looking at foreign sector financial assets for our sample of seven OECD countries (Table 7.1), the majority are placed in deposits, equity, bonds and, to a lesser extent, loans. The theory outlined above has little to say about portfolio composition by instrument, on which we now comment. Patterns will partly reflect the locus of international intermediation – banking or

45 The use of managers with general expertise in emerging markets rather than specialists in individual countries is reportedly partly driven by the difficulty of comparing the performance of such narrowly defined specialists. In contrast, general or balanced expertise in emerging markets may be readily compared. But the latter may generate herd behaviour, as managers seek not to diverge from mainstream asset allocation for fear of performing below the median.

Table 7.1 *Foreign sector financial assets (per cent of total)*

| | | UK | US | Germany | Japan | Canada | France | Italy |
|---|---|---|---|---|---|---|---|---|
| Deposits | 1970 | 68.1 | 29.8 | 47.8 | na | 24.1 | 41.6 | 0.2 |
| | 1980 | 76.8 | 12.5 | 60.4 | na | 34.9 | 62.7 | 0.9 |
| | 1990 | 57.1 | 11.2 | 47.8 | na | 20.6 | 45.8 | 29.8 |
| | 1998 | 45.3 | 9.4 | 36.5 | 6.9 | 13.7 | 28.8 | 18.8 |
| | 2000 | 39.8 | 7.8 | 34.8 | 3.9 | 13.0 | 24.7 | 18.5 |
| Money market inst | 1970 | 6.8 | 4.3 | 3.3 | na | 2.4 | 0.1 | 0.0 |
| | 1980 | 0.5 | 3.1 | 1.0 | na | 3.3 | 0.0 | 0.0 |
| | 1990 | 7.9 | 1.6 | 0.1 | na | 7.7 | 4.5 | 1.9 |
| | 1998 | 3.1 | 3.6 | 1.4 | 0.5 | 6.8 | 6.3 | 5.3 |
| | 2000 | 4.2 | 3.0 | 2.5 | 1.2 | 4.7 | 7.5 | 5.5 |
| Loans | 1970 | 18.4 | 0.3 | 0.0 | na | 7.3 | 3.1 | 68.4 |
| | 1980 | 3.7 | 1.0 | 0.0 | na | 8.2 | 5.8 | 82.6 |
| | 1990 | 13.7 | 9.2 | 0.0 | na | 11.8 | 6.6 | 43.2 |
| | 1998 | 17.9 | 2.7 | 9.2 | 52.8 | 7.5 | 6.2 | 16.5 |
| | 2000 | 19.0 | 1.7 | 13.7 | 41.6 | 8.2 | 6.4 | 16.3 |
| Bonds | 1970 | 4.1 | 25.3 | 6.6 | na | 44.4 | 9.4 | 0.5 |
| | 1980 | 4.1 | 38.6 | 9.0 | na | 41.6 | 6.4 | 0.9 |
| | 1990 | 6.2 | 37.8 | 25.8 | na | 53.2 | 13.7 | 12.0 |
| | 1998 | 9.1 | 43.8 | 32.9 | 20.3 | 61.7 | 13.3 | 38.6 |
| | 2000 | 7.7 | 40.6 | 27.3 | 16.7 | 59.8 | 11.1 | 39.8 |
| Equity | 1970 | 2.5 | 27.0 | 40.8 | na | 21.9 | 45.8 | 31.0 |
| | 1980 | 2.0 | 16.7 | 23.8 | na | 12.0 | 25.1 | 15.6 |
| | 1990 | 15.0 | 13.1 | 18.2 | na | 6.6 | 29.3 | 13.1 |
| | 1998 | 24.6 | 22.6 | 19.3 | 19.6 | 10.4 | 44.7 | 20.3 |
| | 2000 | 29.3 | 25.4 | 19.8 | 36.5 | 14.3 | 49.6 | 19.5 |
| Mutual funds | 1970 | 0.0 | 0.0 | 0.0 | na | na | 0.0 | 0.0 |
| | 1980 | 0.0 | 0.0 | 0.0 | na | na | 0.0 | 0.0 |
| | 1990 | 0.1 | 0.0 | 1.0 | na | na | 0.1 | 0.0 |
| | 1998 | 0.1 | 0.0 | 0.2 | 0.0 | na | 0.7 | 0.5 |
| | 2000 | 0.1 | 0.0 | 0.8 | 0.0 | na | 0.7 | 0.4 |
| FDI | 1970 | na | 13.2 | na | na | na | na | na |
| | 1980 | na | 28.1 | na | na | na | na | na |
| | 1990 | na | 27.1 | na | na | na | na | na |
| | 1998 | na | 17.8 | na | na | na | na | na |
| | 2000 | na | 21.4 | na | na | na | na | na |
| Central Bank reserves | 1970 | na | na | 1.4 | na | na | na | na |
| | 1980 | 12.9 | na | 5.8 | na | na | na | na |
| | 1990 | na | na | 7.1 | na | na | na | na |
| | 1998 | na | na | 0.5 | na | na | na | na |
| | 2000 | na | na | 1.2 | na | na | na | na |

Note: the first observation for the UK is 1975 and not 1970.

Table 7.2 *Foreign sector financial assets (per cent of GDP)*

| | | UK | US | Germany | Japan | Canada | France | Italy |
|---|---|---|---|---|---|---|---|---|
| Deposits | 1970 | 58.4 | 2.8 | 5.4 | na | 7.0 | 7.2 | 0.0 |
| | 1980 | 68.2 | 1.9 | 10.2 | na | 14.9 | 21.9 | 0.2 |
| | 1990 | 96.8 | 3.6 | 14.4 | na | 10.6 | 33.0 | 10.9 |
| | 1998 | 122.2 | 5.5 | 34.7 | 2.8 | 9.8 | 32.7 | 14.8 |
| | 2000 | 135.8 | 5.2 | 45.4 | 1.6 | 7.8 | 40.9 | 18.0 |
| Money Market Inst | 1970 | 5.8 | 0.4 | 0.4 | na | 0.7 | 0.0 | 0.0 |
| | 1980 | 0.5 | 0.5 | 0.2 | na | 1.4 | 0.0 | 0.0 |
| | 1990 | 13.3 | 0.5 | 0.0 | na | 3.9 | 3.2 | 0.7 |
| | 1998 | 8.4 | 2.1 | 1.3 | 0.2 | 4.9 | 7.1 | 4.2 |
| | 2000 | 14.2 | 2.0 | 3.2 | 0.5 | 2.8 | 12.5 | 5.4 |
| Loans | 1970 | 15.8 | 0.0 | 0.0 | na | 2.1 | 0.5 | 13.7 |
| | 1980 | 3.3 | 0.2 | 0.0 | na | 3.5 | 2.0 | 17.3 |
| | 1990 | 23.3 | 2.9 | 0.0 | na | 6.0 | 4.8 | 15.8 |
| | 1998 | 48.3 | 1.6 | 8.8 | 21.2 | 5.4 | 7.0 | 12.9 |
| | 2000 | 64.8 | 1.2 | 17.9 | 16.7 | 4.9 | 10.6 | 15.9 |
| Bonds | 1970 | 3.5 | 2.4 | 0.7 | na | 13.0 | 1.6 | 0.1 |
| | 1980 | 3.6 | 5.9 | 1.5 | na | 17.8 | 2.2 | 0.2 |
| | 1990 | 10.5 | 12.1 | 7.8 | na | 27.3 | 9.9 | 4.4 |
| | 1998 | 24.5 | 25.4 | 31.2 | 8.1 | 44.2 | 15.1 | 30.3 |
| | 2000 | 26.1 | 27.0 | 35.7 | 6.7 | 35.8 | 18.4 | 38.8 |
| Equity | 1970 | 2.1 | 2.6 | 4.6 | na | 6.4 | 7.9 | 6.2 |
| | 1980 | 1.7 | 2.6 | 4.0 | na | 5.1 | 8.8 | 3.3 |
| | 1990 | 25.4 | 4.2 | 5.5 | na | 3.4 | 21.2 | 4.8 |
| | 1998 | 66.4 | 13.1 | 18.3 | 7.9 | 7.4 | 50.8 | 15.9 |
| | 2000 | 99.8 | 16.9 | 25.8 | 14.6 | 8.6 | 82.0 | 19.0 |
| Mutual Funds | 1970 | 0.0 | 0.0 | 0.0 | na | na | 0.0 | 0.0 |
| | 1980 | 0.0 | 0.0 | 0.0 | na | na | 0.0 | 0.0 |
| | 1990 | 0.1 | 0.0 | 0.3 | na | na | 0.1 | 0.0 |
| | 1998 | 0.2 | 0.0 | 0.2 | 0.0 | na | 0.8 | 0.4 |
| | 2000 | 0.2 | 0.0 | 1.0 | 0.0 | na | 1.1 | 0.4 |
| FDI | 1970 | na | 1.3 | na | na | na | na | na |
| | 1980 | na | 4.3 | na | na | na | na | na |
| | 1990 | na | 8.6 | na | na | na | na | na |
| | 1998 | na | 10.3 | na | na | na | na | na |
| | 2000 | na | 14.3 | na | na | na | na | na |
| Central Bank reserves | 1970 | na | na | 0.2 | na | na | na | na |
| | 1980 | 11.5 | na | 1.0 | na | na | na | na |
| | 1990 | na | na | 2.1 | na | na | na | na |
| | 1998 | na | na | 0.5 | na | na | na | na |
| | 2000 | na | na | 1.6 | na | na | na | na |

Table 7.2 (*Continued*)

| | | UK | US | Germany | Japan | Canada | France | Italy |
|---|---|---|---|---|---|---|---|---|
| Total assets | 1970 | 85.6 | 9.5 | 11.2 | na | 29.2 | 17.4 | 20.0 |
| | 1980 | 88.9 | 15.3 | 16.9 | na | 42.8 | 35.0 | 20.9 |
| | 1990 | 169.4 | 31.9 | 30.1 | na | 51.2 | 72.2 | 36.7 |
| | 1998 | 269.9 | 58.0 | 95.0 | 40.1 | 71.7 | 113.5 | 78.5 |
| | 2000 | 341.0 | 66.5 | 130.7 | 40.0 | 59.9 | 165.5 | 97.4 |

Note: the first observation for UK is 1975 and not 1970.

institutional investors – but also the activities of multinational enterprises (MNEs).

Deposit holdings are sizeable as a proportion of foreigners' claims on the UK (40 per cent) and Germany (35 per cent). France and Italy also have an important role for deposits with 25 per cent and 19 per cent respectively. For Continental European countries, this reflects the bank-based nature of the financial system, while for the UK it is more a reflection of London as an international financial centre. For the US and Canada, securities predominate. Equity is also important for foreign investors in France, Japan and the UK, and bonds in Germany and Italy. FDI is shown to be high for the US, but the data are not available from national balance sheets elsewhere. (An alternative presentation of the international investment position is given in Section 7.3, which comments on balance-of-payments portfolio data. There we see that the US indeed has the largest FDI, but stocks for other countries are not negligible.)

From Table 7.2 and Figure 1.4 it can be seen that foreign sector assets are considerable in the UK, at more than three times GDP, and this may reflect the City of London's role in the British economy. They are also considerable for France and Germany, albeit far below the UK. Foreign deposits alone represent 135 per cent of UK GDP. The upward trend in foreign assets in the UK, and to a lesser extent elsewhere, is also noteworthy, reflecting international financial integration. The value of foreign equity holdings relative to GDP is also notable in France and the UK, where foreigners hold domestic shares equivalent to 80 per cent and 100 per cent of GDP, respectively. Elsewhere the estimate is 25 per cent of GDP or less. The bond figures are much more comparable, ranging from around 35 per cent in Germany, Canada and Italy to 25 per cent in the UK and US and 18 per cent in France. Only Japan is an outlier, with high domestic demand, low yields and market risk leading to foreign holdings of only 7 per cent of GDP.

Table 7.3 *Foreign sector liabilities (per cent of total)*

| | | UK | US | Germany | Japan | Canada | France | Italy |
|---|---|---|---|---|---|---|---|---|
| Deposits | 1970 | 0.0 | 0.5 | 0.0 | na | 35.7 | 7.8 | 17.3 |
| | 1980 | 0.0 | 4.7 | 0.0 | na | 38.6 | 45.0 | 13.3 |
| | 1990 | 47.7 | 20.2 | 0.0 | na | 20.2 | 46.3 | 33.1 |
| | 1998 | 40.5 | 15.8 | 26.2 | 3.2 | 15.5 | 24.9 | 11.7 |
| | 2000 | 37.0 | 17.1 | 20.4 | 4.8 | 11.0 | 19.2 | 6.3 |
| Money market inst | 1970 | 0.8 | 0.0 | 0.1 | na | 0.0 | 0.0 | 3.2 |
| | 1980 | 0.4 | 1.0 | 0.1 | na | 0.0 | 0.0 | 4.9 |
| | 1990 | 0.9 | 5.1 | 0.2 | na | 0.0 | 0.0 | 5.4 |
| | 1998 | 1.3 | 1.8 | 0.6 | 0.0 | 0.0 | 7.7 | 1.8 |
| | 2000 | 1.4 | 2.5 | 0.4 | 0.0 | 0.0 | 10.0 | 1.1 |
| Loans | 1970 | 87.8 | 25.3 | 37.4 | na | 12.2 | 35.9 | 50.5 |
| | 1980 | 69.9 | 21.2 | 50.6 | na | 26.8 | 9.5 | 41.5 |
| | 1990 | 16.3 | 6.7 | 53.1 | na | 13.8 | 13.5 | 20.7 |
| | 1998 | 14.1 | 2.9 | 17.8 | 40.2 | 14.2 | 10.1 | 18.1 |
| | 2000 | 14.3 | 2.5 | 18.7 | 28.7 | 12.6 | 9.7 | 17.3 |
| Bonds | 1970 | 0.8 | 9.3 | 10.5 | na | na | 1.3 | 6.1 |
| | 1980 | 8.2 | 7.4 | 9.4 | na | na | 2.0 | 2.2 |
| | 1990 | 11.4 | 7.8 | 19.2 | na | na | 5.3 | 11.3 |
| | 1998 | 17.1 | 11.5 | 20.8 | 24.8 | na | 12.6 | 25.2 |
| | 2000 | 14.7 | 10.2 | 19.6 | 30.0 | na | 10.9 | 25.6 |
| Equity | 1970 | 6.8 | 4.3 | 12.4 | na | na | 40.2 | 12.7 |
| | 1980 | 0.0 | 2.8 | 14.3 | na | na | 13.0 | 7.3 |
| | 1990 | 23.6 | 13.4 | 15.7 | na | na | 25.7 | 22.3 |
| | 1998 | 27.0 | 36.6 | 29.7 | 14.9 | na | 42.1 | 35.6 |
| | 2000 | 32.6 | 36.4 | 35.8 | 27.5 | na | 48.5 | 41.2 |
| Mutual funds | 1970 | 0.0 | 0.0 | 0.0 | na | na | 0.0 | 0.0 |
| | 1980 | 0.0 | 0.0 | 0.0 | na | na | 0.0 | 0.0 |
| | 1990 | 0.1 | 0.0 | 1.8 | na | na | 0.6 | 0.0 |
| | 1998 | 0.0 | 0.0 | 5.0 | 0.0 | na | 1.0 | 4.8 |
| | 2000 | 0.1 | 0.0 | 5.1 | 0.0 | na | 0.5 | 6.5 |
| FDI | 1970 | 0.7 | 58.9 | na | na | 12.4 | na | na |
| | 1980 | 15.5 | 60.8 | na | na | 17.9 | na | na |
| | 1990 | na | 42.6 | na | na | 35.9 | na | na |
| | 1998 | na | 29.9 | na | 8.8 | 49.3 | na | na |
| | 2000 | na | 30.4 | na | 9.0 | 53.6 | na | na |
| Central Bank reserves | 1970 | 3.0 | 1.7 | 39.6 | na | 39.7 | 14.8 | 10.1 |
| | 1980 | 6.0 | 2.0 | 25.6 | na | 16.6 | 30.5 | 30.8 |
| | 1990 | na | 4.2 | 9.9 | na | 30.1 | 8.6 | 7.3 |
| | 1998 | na | 1.5 | na | 8.1 | 21.0 | 1.7 | 2.8 |
| | 2000 | na | 0.9 | na | na | 22.8 | 1.2 | 2.0 |

Note: the first observation for the UK is 1975 and not 1970.

Table 7.4 *Foreign sector liabilities (per cent of GDP)*

| | | UK | US | Germany | Japan | Canada | France | Italy |
|---|---|---|---|---|---|---|---|---|
| Deposits | 1970 | 0.0 | 0.1 | 0.0 | na | 9.6 | 1.3 | 4.6 |
| | 1980 | 0.0 | 1.1 | 0.0 | na | 7.2 | 18.7 | 3.8 |
| | 1990 | 78.9 | 5.1 | 0.0 | na | 4.3 | 28.5 | 10.5 |
| | 1998 | 103.3 | 7.1 | 23.9 | 2.0 | 5.9 | 30.6 | 8.3 |
| | 2000 | 121.1 | 8.3 | 26.0 | 3.0 | 4.4 | 32.7 | 6.5 |
| Money market inst | 1970 | 0.7 | 0.0 | 0.0 | na | na | 0.0 | 0.9 |
| | 1980 | 0.4 | 0.2 | 0.0 | na | na | 0.0 | 1.4 |
| | 1990 | 1.5 | 1.3 | 0.1 | na | na | 0.0 | 1.7 |
| | 1998 | 3.2 | 0.8 | 0.6 | 0.0 | na | 9.4 | 1.3 |
| | 2000 | 4.5 | 1.2 | 0.5 | 0.0 | na | 17.0 | 1.2 |
| Loans | 1970 | 72.8 | 3.6 | 7.3 | na | 3.3 | 6.1 | 13.4 |
| | 1980 | 66.9 | 4.8 | 11.0 | na | 5.0 | 4.0 | 11.9 |
| | 1990 | 27.0 | 1.7 | 23.5 | na | 3.0 | 8.3 | 6.6 |
| | 1998 | 35.9 | 1.3 | 16.3 | 24.8 | 5.4 | 12.4 | 12.8 |
| | 2000 | 46.9 | 1.2 | 23.9 | 17.6 | 5.1 | 16.4 | 17.7 |
| Bonds | 1970 | 0.7 | 1.3 | 2.0 | na | na | 0.2 | 1.6 |
| | 1980 | 7.9 | 1.7 | 2.1 | na | na | 0.8 | 0.6 |
| | 1990 | 18.8 | 2.0 | 8.5 | na | na | 3.3 | 3.6 |
| | 1998 | 43.8 | 5.2 | 19.0 | 15.3 | na | 15.5 | 17.8 |
| | 2000 | 48.0 | 5.0 | 25.0 | 18.4 | na | 18.5 | 26.3 |
| Equity | 1970 | 5.6 | 0.6 | 2.4 | na | na | 6.8 | 3.4 |
| | 1980 | 0.0 | 0.6 | 3.1 | na | na | 5.4 | 2.1 |
| | 1990 | 39.0 | 3.4 | 7.0 | na | na | 15.8 | 7.1 |
| | 1998 | 69.1 | 16.4 | 27.2 | 9.2 | na | 51.7 | 25.1 |
| | 2000 | 106.7 | 17.7 | 45.7 | 16.8 | na | 82.3 | 42.3 |
| Mutual funds | 1970 | 0.0 | 0.0 | 0.0 | na | na | 0.0 | 0.0 |
| | 1980 | 0.0 | 0.0 | 0.0 | na | na | 0.0 | 0.0 |
| | 1990 | 0.2 | 0.0 | 0.8 | na | na | 0.4 | 0.0 |
| | 1998 | 0.1 | 0.0 | 4.5 | 0.0 | na | 1.2 | 3.4 |
| | 2000 | 0.2 | 0.0 | 6.5 | 0.0 | na | 0.9 | 6.7 |
| FDI | 1970 | 0.6 | 8.5 | na | na | 3.3 | na | na |
| | 1980 | 14.8 | 13.8 | na | na | 3.3 | na | na |
| | 1990 | na | 10.8 | na | na | 7.7 | na | na |
| | 1998 | na | 13.4 | na | 5.5 | 18.7 | na | na |
| | 2000 | na | 14.8 | na | 5.5 | 21.6 | na | na |
| Central Bank reserves | 1970 | 2.5 | 0.2 | 7.7 | na | 10.6 | 2.5 | 2.7 |
| | 1980 | 5.8 | 0.4 | 5.6 | na | 3.1 | 12.7 | 8.8 |
| | 1990 | na | 1.0 | 4.4 | na | 6.4 | 5.3 | 2.3 |
| | 1998 | na | 0.7 | na | 5.0 | 8.0 | 2.0 | 2.0 |
| | 2000 | na | 0.4 | na | 0.0 | 9.2 | 2.0 | 2.0 |

Table 7.4 (*Continued*)

| | | UK | US | Germany | Japan | Canada | France | Italy |
|---|---|---|---|---|---|---|---|---|
| Total | 1970 | 82.9 | 14.4 | 19.4 | na | 26.7 | 16.9 | 26.5 |
| | 1980 | 95.8 | 22.8 | 21.8 | na | 18.6 | 41.6 | 28.6 |
| | 1990 | 165.3 | 25.2 | 44.2 | na | 21.4 | 61.5 | 31.7 |
| | 1998 | 255.5 | 44.9 | 91.5 | 61.7 | 38.0 | 122.9 | 70.7 |
| | 2000 | 327.5 | 48.5 | 127.6 | 61.4 | 40.3 | 169.8 | 102.6 |

Note: the first observation for the UK is 1975 and not 1970.

The pattern of foreign liabilities differs somewhat from that of assets, although this partly reflects omissions, such as for foreign securities held by Canadians. In Table 7.4, foreign sector liabilities are again sizeable for the UK. The other European countries also have substantial foreign liabilities. These characteristics contrast with the experience on the other side of the Atlantic – and in Japan where lower foreign assets may reflect less open economies in a financial sense. In terms of instruments, UK and French investors match their foreign counterparts in holding 110 per cent and 80 per cent equivalents of their own GDP in foreign equities. This puts into perspective any view that these countries are dominated by foreign investors, as might have been drawn from Table 4.7. German and Italian investors hold the equivalent of 45 per cent each. US and Japanese holdings are much smaller relative to GDP, although in absolute terms they are sizeable.

Net positions in foreign assets are much smaller than gross ones. According to the data, Germany, Japan and Italy had net positive positions, which is particularly large in the case of Japan. The UK, US and Canada had net foreign liabilities of 15–30 per cent of GDP. Whereas these levels are sustainable for such OECD countries, in a way that might not be the case for emerging market economies, they do indicate a potential vulnerability, at least of the exchange rate, to an adverse macroeconomic situation (e.g. twin deficits in the balance of payments and the public sector).

## 7.3 INTERNATIONAL INVESTMENT POSITIONS DERIVED FROM THE BALANCE OF PAYMENTS DATA

Stepping outside the flow of funds balance sheets framework, Tables 7.5–7.9 show the data from the IMF for capital account international investor positions. These are harmonised by IMF statisticians and stated in US dollars. We focus mainly on data for end-2000.

Table 7.5 *International investment position end-2000 (US$ billion)*

| | UK | US | Germany | Japan | Canada | France | Italy |
|---|---|---|---|---|---|---|---|
| *Financial account total assets* | 4402 | 7190 | 2530 | 3012 | 519 | 2407 | 1114 |
| Direct investment abroad | 911 | 2468 | 425 | 278 | 201 | 1006 | 180 |
| Portfolio investment assets of which: | 1299 | 2407 | 1009 | 1245 | 141 | 614 | 581 |
| – equity securities assets | 610 | 1828 | 577 | 262 | 118 | 197 | 260 |
| – debt securities assets | 690 | 578 | 432 | 983 | 23 | 417 | 321 |
| Financial derivatives: assets | | | | 4 | | 120 | 4 |
| Other investment assets of which: | 2148 | 2187 | 1009 | 1124 | 145 | 603 | 302 |
| – monetary authority | | | 6 | | | 17 | –7 |
| – general govt | 15 | 85 | 61 | 210 | 22 | 27 | 23 |
| – banks | 1572 | 1277 | 679 | 566 | 65 | 427 | 140 |
| – other sectors | 562 | 825 | 262 | 349 | 58 | 53 | 146 |
| Reserve assets | 43 | 128 | 87 | 361 | 31 | 64 | 47 |
| *Financial account total liabilities* | 4515 | 9377 | 2461 | 1854 | 681 | 2347 | 1071 |
| Direct investment in domestic economy | 457 | 2737 | 422 | 50 | 194 | 703 | 113 |
| Portfolio investment liabilities of which: | 1500 | 4368 | 1035 | 872 | 331 | 869 | 570 |
| – equity securities liabilities | 914 | 1665 | 299 | 559 | 57 | 461 | 53 |
| – debt securities liabilities | 587 | 2702 | 737 | 313 | 274 | 408 | 517 |

Table 7.5 (*Continued*)

| | UK | US | Germany | Japan | Canada | France | Italy |
|---|---|---|---|---|---|---|---|
| Financial derivatives: liabilities | | | | 3 | | 119 | 3 |
| Other investment liabilities of which: | 2558 | 2272 | 1004 | 929 | 157 | 655 | 384 |
| – monetary authority | | 252 | 14 | | | 2 | 1 |
| – general govt | 6 | 14 | 18 | 10 | 2 | 16 | 7 |
| – banks | 1885 | 1284 | 845 | 607 | 103 | 528 | 265 |
| – other sectors | 664 | 723 | 127 | 313 | 52 | 43 | 112 |

Table 7.5 shows that the US has the largest absolute international position, and also the largest imbalance, with assets of $7.2 trillion and liabilities of $9.4 trillion. The UK also has large claims on both sides of the balance sheet, around $4.5 trillion, accounted for to a considerable extent by the international banking sector (monetary assets are counted in 'other investment assets'). According to these figures, the UK and Canada also have a small negative net position, while Japan has a marked surplus, and the others are in rough balance. Direct investment patterns are dominated by the US, which has the largest direct investment abroad, as well as foreign investment in the US. The very large foreign portfolio investment in the US is another key feature of the table, amounting to almost $4.5 trillion.

Table 7.6 shows the shares of assets and liabilities within their respective totals. On the asset side, for the UK and Germany other investments (largely monetary claims) on foreigners have the largest share, while in the US, France and Canada it is FDI, and portfolio claims in Japan and Italy. The high share of FDI in Canada as well as the US is noteworthy, showing a high level of cross-border activity by domestic corporations. As regards composition of portfolio investment, investors from the US, Germany and Canada hold mainly foreign equities, while elsewhere most foreign portfolio investment is in debt securities. Of course, other (monetary) investment is short-term debt, while FDI is typically a form of equity claim.

On the liability side (i.e. foreigners' holdings of domestic assets), other (monetary) investment dominates in the UK and Japan, while elsewhere most foreign claims are accounted for by portfolio investment. Foreign investment in equity has a higher share than debt in the UK, Japan and France, while elsewhere, it is largely debt that foreigners hold.

Table 7.6 *International investment position end-2000 (per cent of total)*

| | UK | US | Germany | Japan | Canada | France | Italy |
|---|---|---|---|---|---|---|---|
| *Financial account total assets* | | | | | | | |
| Direct investment abroad | 21 | 34 | 17 | 9 | 39 | 42 | 16 |
| Portfolio investment assets of which: | 30 | 33 | 40 | 41 | 27 | 26 | 52 |
| – equity securities assets | 14 | 25 | 23 | 9 | 23 | 8 | 23 |
| – debt securities assets | 16 | 8 | 17 | 33 | 4 | 17 | 29 |
| Financial derivatives: assets | 0 | 0 | 0 | 0 | 0 | 5 | 0 |
| Other investment assets of which: | 49 | 30 | 40 | 37 | 28 | 25 | 27 |
| – monetary authority | 0 | 0 | 0 | 0 | 0 | 1 | –1 |
| – general govt | 0 | 1 | 2 | 7 | 4 | 1 | 2 |
| – banks | 36 | 18 | 27 | 19 | 13 | 18 | 13 |
| – other sectors | 13 | 11 | 10 | 12 | 11 | 2 | 13 |
| Reserve assets | 1 | 2 | 3 | 12 | 6 | 3 | 4 |
| *Financial account total liabilities* | | | | | | | |
| Direct investment in domestic economy | 10 | 29 | 17 | 3 | 28 | 30 | 11 |
| Portfolio investment liabilities of which: | 33 | 47 | 42 | 47 | 49 | 37 | 53 |
| – equity securities liabilities | 20 | 18 | 12 | 30 | 8 | 20 | 5 |
| – debt securities liabilities | 13 | 29 | 30 | 17 | 40 | 17 | 48 |
| Financial derivatives: liabilities | 0 | 0 | 0 | 0 | 0 | 5 | 0 |
| Other investment liabilities of which: | 57 | 24 | 41 | 50 | 23 | 28 | 36 |
| – monetary authority | 0 | 3 | 1 | 0 | 0 | 0 | 0 |
| – general govt | 0 | 0 | 1 | 1 | 0 | 1 | 1 |
| – banks | 42 | 14 | 34 | 33 | 15 | 22 | 25 |
| – other sectors | 15 | 8 | 5 | 17 | 8 | 2 | 10 |

Table 7.7 *International investment position end-2000 (per cent of GDP)*

| | UK | US | Germany | Japan | Canada | France | Italy |
|---|---|---|---|---|---|---|---|
| *Financial account total assets* | 312 | 73 | 134 | 68 | 74 | 184 | 103 |
| Direct investment abroad | 65 | 25 | 23 | 6 | 29 | 77 | 17 |
| Portfolio investment assets of which: | 92 | 24 | 54 | 28 | 20 | 47 | 54 |
| – equity securities assets | 43 | 19 | 31 | 6 | 17 | 15 | 24 |
| – debt securities assets | 49 | 6 | 23 | 22 | 3 | 32 | 30 |
| Financial derivatives: assets | 0 | 0 | 0 | 0 | 0 | 9 | 0 |
| Other investment assets of which: | 152 | 22 | 54 | 25 | 21 | 46 | 28 |
| – monetary authority | 0 | 0 | 0 | 0 | 0 | 1 | –1 |
| – general govt | 1 | 1 | 3 | 5 | 3 | 2 | 2 |
| – banks | 112 | 13 | 36 | 13 | 9 | 33 | 13 |
| – other sectors | 40 | 8 | 14 | 8 | 8 | 4 | 13 |
| Reserve assets | 3 | 1 | 5 | 8 | 4 | 5 | 4 |
| *Financial account total liabilities* | 320 | 95 | 131 | 42 | 97 | 179 | 99 |
| Direct investment in domestic economy | 32 | 28 | 22 | 1 | 28 | 54 | 10 |
| Portfolio investment liabilities of which: | 106 | 44 | 55 | 20 | 47 | 66 | 53 |
| – equity securities liabilities | 65 | 17 | 16 | 13 | 8 | 35 | 5 |
| – debt securities liabilities | 42 | 27 | 39 | 7 | 39 | 31 | 48 |
| Financial derivatives: liabilities | 0 | 0 | 0 | 0 | 0 | 9 | 0 |
| Other investment liabilities of which: | 181 | 23 | 53 | 21 | 22 | 50 | 35 |
| – monetary authority | 0 | 3 | 1 | 0 | 0 | 0 | 0 |
| – general govt | 0 | 0 | 1 | 0 | 0 | 1 | 1 |
| – banks | 134 | 13 | 45 | 14 | 15 | 40 | 24 |
| – other sectors | 47 | 7 | 7 | 7 | 7 | 3 | 10 |
| Net foreign assets | –8 | –22 | 4 | 26 | –23 | 5 | 4 |

Table 7.8 *International investment position (per cent of total)*

| | | UK | US | Germany | Japan | Canada | France | Italy |
|---|---|---|---|---|---|---|---|---|
| Assets | | | | | | | | |
| FDI | 1980 | 14 | 28 | 12 | 13 | 26 | na | 5 |
| | 1990 | 13 | 32 | 11 | 11 | 37 | 15 | 15 |
| | 1998 | 14 | 36 | 18 | 9 | 37 | 18 | 16 |
| | 2000 | 21 | 34 | 17 | 9 | 39 | 42 | 16 |
| Portfolio investment | 1980 | 8 | 8 | 8 | 13 | 9 | na | 4 |
| | 1990 | 22 | 15 | 17 | 32 | 15 | 11 | 17 |
| | 1998 | 32 | 33 | 32 | 35 | 22 | 31 | 39 |
| | 2000 | 30 | 33 | 40 | 41 | 27 | 26 | 52 |
| Other assets | 1980 | 72 | 41 | 64 | 58 | 62 | na | 46 |
| | 1990 | 62 | 46 | 65 | 53 | 39 | 52 | 44 |
| | 1998 | 52 | 28 | 46 | 48 | 35 | 43 | 39 |
| | 2000 | 49 | 30 | 40 | 37 | 28 | 25 | 27 |
| Liabilities | | | | | | | | |
| FDI | 1980 | 12 | 17 | 11 | 2 | 29 | na | 10 |
| | 1990 | 13 | 22 | 10 | 1 | 25 | 11 | 13 |
| | 1998 | 9 | 29 | 10 | 1 | 22 | 15 | 10 |
| | 2000 | 10 | 29 | 17 | 3 | 28 | 30 | 11 |
| Portfolio investment | 1980 | 6 | 35 | 17 | 29 | 34 | na | 5 |
| | 1990 | 21 | 38 | 28 | 26 | 45 | 28 | 11 |
| | 1998 | 31 | 46 | 47 | 45 | 52 | 41 | 53 |
| | 2000 | 33 | 47 | 42 | 47 | 49 | 37 | 53 |
| Other liabilities | 1980 | 82 | 48 | 72 | 69 | 37 | na | 85 |
| | 1990 | 67 | 40 | 62 | 73 | 29 | 60 | 76 |
| | 1998 | 60 | 25 | 43 | 64 | 25 | 40 | 36 |
| | 2000 | 57 | 24 | 41 | 50 | 23 | 28 | 36 |

Looking at ratios to GDP in Table 7.7, the UK stands out with assets and liabilities both accounting for over three times GDP. Note that, given the harmonised data, we consider that these data offer a more precise comparison than the data in Tables 7.2 and 7.4. Although the nominal size of US claims is large, it is put in perspective by the size of the US economy, with assets being 73 per cent and liabilities 95 per cent of GDP. Canadian, Italian, German and French claims are larger relative to GDP on both sides of the balance sheet than in the US. Interestingly, Japan has the lowest holdings relative to GDP for both assets and liabilities, despite the publicity given to Japanese investors' international activities. Net foreign assets are shown to be sizeable in absolute terms in the US, Canada and Japan, with

Table 7.9 *International investment position (per cent of GDP)*

| | | UK | US | Germany | Japan | Canada | France | Italy |
|---|---|---|---|---|---|---|---|---|
| Assets | 1980 | 100 | 26 | 34 | 16 | 35 | na | 33 |
| | 1990 | 161 | 39 | 67 | 66 | 39 | 58 | 33 |
| | 1998 | 248 | 66 | 99 | 69 | 73 | 103 | 80 |
| | 2000 | 312 | 73 | 134 | 68 | 74 | 184 | 103 |
| of which: | | | | | | | | |
| FDI | 1980 | 14 | 7 | 4 | 2 | 9 | na | 2 |
| | 1990 | 22 | 13 | 8 | 7 | 15 | 9 | 5 |
| | 1998 | 35 | 24 | 17 | 6 | 27 | 18 | 13 |
| | 2000 | 65 | 25 | 23 | 6 | 29 | 77 | 17 |
| Portfolio | 1980 | 8 | 2 | 3 | 2 | 3 | na | 1 |
| investment | 1990 | 35 | 6 | 11 | 21 | 6 | 6 | 5 |
| | 1998 | 80 | 22 | 32 | 24 | 16 | 32 | 32 |
| | 2000 | 92 | 24 | 54 | 28 | 20 | 47 | 54 |
| Other assets | 1980 | 72 | 10 | 22 | 10 | 22 | na | 15 |
| | 1990 | 100 | 18 | 43 | 35 | 15 | 30 | 14 |
| | 1998 | 129 | 19 | 46 | 33 | 26 | 44 | 31 |
| | 2000 | 152 | 22 | 54 | 25 | 21 | 46 | 28 |
| Liabilities | 1980 | 92 | 17 | 30 | 15 | 71 | na | 24 |
| | 1990 | 163 | 42 | 46 | 54 | 77 | 60 | 40 |
| | 1998 | 262 | 83 | 97 | 43 | 109 | 101 | 82 |
| | 2000 | 320 | 95 | 131 | 42 | 97 | 179 | 99 |
| of which: | | | | | | | | |
| FDI | 1980 | 11 | 3 | 3 | 0 | 21 | na | 2 |
| | 1990 | 20 | 9 | 5 | 0 | 20 | 7 | 5 |
| | 1998 | 23 | 24 | 10 | 1 | 24 | 15 | 8 |
| | 2000 | 32 | 28 | 22 | 1 | 28 | 54 | 10 |
| Portfolio | 1980 | 5 | 6 | 5 | 4 | 24 | na | 1 |
| investment | 1990 | 34 | 16 | 13 | 14 | 35 | 17 | 5 |
| | 1998 | 81 | 38 | 45 | 19 | 57 | 42 | 44 |
| | 2000 | 106 | 44 | 55 | 20 | 47 | 66 | 53 |
| Other | 1980 | 76 | 8 | 21 | 10 | 26 | na | 20 |
| liabilities | 1990 | 108 | 17 | 29 | 40 | 23 | 36 | 30 |
| | 1998 | 158 | 21 | 42 | 27 | 28 | 40 | 30 |
| | 2000 | 181 | 23 | 53 | 21 | 22 | 50 | 35 |
| Net foreign | 1980 | 8 | 9 | 4 | 1 | −36 | na | 9 |
| assets | 1990 | −1 | −3 | 21 | 12 | −38 | −2 | −7 |
| | 1998 | −14 | −17 | 1 | 27 | −36 | 2 | −2 |
| | 2000 | −8 | −22 | 4 | 26 | −23 | 5 | 4 |

net assets of 26 per cent of GDP in Japan and net liabilities of 22–23 per cent in the US and Canada. Elsewhere the discrepancy is below 10 per cent of GDP, with a deficit in the UK and a surplus in the Continental European countries.

Whereas the IMF data are too detailed to give a full time-series representation, it is useful to show trends in shares and in ratios to GDP of the major subcomponents. Accordingly, Table 7.8 shows the shares of total assets and liabilities of FDI, portfolio and other (monetary) assets and liabilities since 1980. On the asset side the share of FDI and portfolio investment has tended to rise and monetary claims to fall, consistent with the growing securitisation of international financial markets as well as the growth of multinational enterprises. There are broadly similar patterns on the liabilities side.

As regards ratios to GDP (Table 7.9), a growing volume of foreign assets relative to GDP is apparent, as in Table 7.2, which is apparent in all the subcomponents. The shift from net foreign assets to liabilities in the US, and the growth of net foreign assets in Japan, are noteworthy features.

# 8 The financial sector

## 8.1 THE FINANCIAL SECTOR – THEORETICAL AND EMPIRICAL BACKGROUND

The economics of financial institutions has already been largely covered in Chapter 1. There we showed that financial institutions can be understood as developing in response to problems of transactions costs, asymmetric information and incomplete contracts. Meanwhile, financial systems tend to be categorised between those where banks are the main financiers of the corporate sector via loans, and those where households and institutional investors play a major role via securities.

In this context, the determination of the portfolio distribution of the financial sector is largely a matter of its institutional composition. The main components of the financial sector are, respectively, depository institutions and institutional investors. As detailed in Chapters 9 and 10, their asset portfolios differ largely as a consequence of the nature of their liabilities, with banks meeting short-term liquidity needs on the part of their investors, while institutional investors are rather focused on long-term saving and insurance needs. Banks accordingly tend to hold a more sizeable proportion of liquid assets than institutions. But, in addition, banks tend to hold significant proportions of non-traded loans in their investment portfolios, while the investments of institutional investors tend to be dominated by securities. Banks have a duration mismatch which is absent for institutional investors. As discussed below, this links to the comparative advantage of banks in resolving asymmetric information problems.

It remains useful to provide here some general theoretical points relating to the determination of financial sector portfolios, prior to the discussion of banks and institutional investors in Chapters 9 and 10. Even more than for the non-financial sectors, the most basic aim of financial institutions on both the asset and liability sides is to achieve an optimal trade-off of risk and return by allocation of the portfolio to appropriately diversified combinations of assets (and in some cases liabilities, i.e. leveraging the portfolio by borrowing). The precondition for such an optimal trade-off is the ability to attain the frontier of efficient portfolios, where there is no possibility of increasing return without increasing risk, or of reducing risk without reducing return (Section 1.1). Any portfolio where it is possible to increase return without raising risk is inefficient and is dominated by a portfolio with more return for the same risk. The exact trade-off chosen will depend on objectives, preferences and constraints on investors. Financial institutions differ from most other sectors in having quite precise liabilities, which enable them to focus largely on investment *per se*. Moreover, compared with non-financial sectors, institutional investors, and to a lesser extent banks, have lower relative needs for transactions and precautionary balances.

There are common features of all types of investment by financial institutions (see Trzcinka, 1997, 1998; Bodie *et al.*, 1999) which form a further useful introduction to an assessment of portfolios. First, there is identification of the investors' objectives/preferences and constraints.

In terms of objectives, there is a need to assess where on the above-mentioned optimal risk-return trade-off the institution wishes to be, in other words its risk tolerance in pursuit of return.

As regards constraints, extending the framework set out in Section 1.1, these may include liquidity, investment horizon, inflation sensitivity, regulations, tax and accounting considerations and unique needs. All of these may link to the nature of the liabilities, for example:

- liquidity-based constraints link to the right for investors to withdraw funds as a lump sum (as for banks or life insurers), or the current needs for regular disbursement (for pension funds);
- the investment horizon relates to the planned liquidation date of the investment (e.g. maturity of a bank deposit, retirement for pensions or maturity of a life contract), and is often measured by the concept of effective maturity or duration;[46]
- inflation sensitivity relates to the need to hold assets as inflation hedges, such as index-linked bonds (or in their absence, equities or real estate) – these are typically more important for institutional investors than for banks;
- tax considerations may change the nature of the trade-off;

46 Duration is the average time to an asset's discounted cash flows.

- accounting rules can generate different 'optimal' portfolios, although market value accounting is needed to produce an appropriate portfolio in an economic sense. Finding a market value may itself be problematic for illiquid assets such as loans, art works and even real estate. Usually, bank portfolios are measured at book value and institutional investors' at market value;
- finally there is the influence of regulations *per se*. Besides those linking to asset allocation, there are sometimes liability restrictions, which may affect desired asset allocations. The best known types of regulation for banks are capital adequacy regulations and reserve–asset ratios (Greenbaum and Thakor, 1995; Freixas and Rochet, 1999) while for institutional investors there are typically regulations on portfolio composition and on minimum funding levels (Davis 2001a, 2002c).

## 8.2 FINANCIAL INSTITUTIONS SECTOR BALANCE SHEETS

Assets for the G-7 financial sectors, aggregating all financial institutions including the central bank, are generally concentrated in loans and securities (see Table 8.1). Loans account for 56 per cent of assets in bank-dominated Japan and 45 per cent in Germany, while in the UK and France they are below 30 per cent. Bonds plus equities are over 50 per cent in the US, and over 40 per cent in Canada and Italy. Deposits (including interbank deposits and those by other financial institutions) are over 20 per cent in the UK and France, reflecting structural aspects of banking, notably the importance of the interbank market, although note also that interbank loans and deposits are netted out in Germany and the US, hence understating the importance of deposits in those countries (Bank of Japan 2000). (As noted, we have sought to correct for this in the US.) Across a number of countries, we have seen a move towards more holding of bonds and equity and a move away from loans, although loans were still the largest single category in 2000, except in France and the UK where deposits predominate.

Total assets of the financial sector as a percentage of GDP are a good reflection of the size of each country's financial sector and the corresponding scope of financial intermediation (Table 8.2 and Figure 1.5). The United Kingdom has the largest; financial assets are six times as large as domestic output. Even if the estimated size[47] of the international banking sector is

47 The foreign currency assets and liabilities of UK monetary financial institutions at end-2000 were each around £1500 billion, i.e. around 150 per cent of GDP.

Table 8.1 *Financial sector financial assets (per cent of total)*

| | | UK | US | Germany | Japan | Canada | France | Italy |
|---|---|---|---|---|---|---|---|---|
| Deposits | 1970 | 17.2 | 3.9 | 3.2 | 0.3 | 10.4 | 22.0 | 15.2 |
| | 1980 | 17.9 | 3.7 | 4.0 | 0.5 | 9.1 | 30.4 | 20.9 |
| | 1990 | 30.1 | 3.0 | 6.2 | 0.4 | 4.5 | 28.1 | 19.4 |
| | 1998 | 27.3 | 2.0 | 12.7 | 7.2 | 4.3 | 26.0 | 12.3 |
| | 2000 | 27.6 | 1.9 | 12.6 | 7.6 | 3.7 | 25.1 | 12.6 |
| Money market inst | 1970 | 5.4 | 1.1 | 1.2 | 6.1 | 4.7 | 3.3 | 3.0 |
| | 1980 | 2.4 | 3.3 | 0.4 | 5.2 | 5.8 | 1.8 | 7.4 |
| | 1990 | 4.6 | 6.6 | 0.4 | 5.6 | 10.3 | 7.3 | 3.4 |
| | 1998 | 3.6 | 6.1 | 0.3 | 6.1 | 9.9 | 8.7 | 2.4 |
| | 2000 | 3.3 | 7.2 | 0.6 | 4.0 | 9.9 | 8.7 | 0.9 |
| Loans | 1970 | 57.1 | 48.0 | 72.7 | 74.4 | 46.9 | 65.5 | 60.9 |
| | 1980 | 56.1 | 52.6 | 78.4 | 64.3 | 59.1 | 53.0 | 43.2 |
| | 1990 | 36.3 | 45.0 | 69.3 | 64.5 | 54.2 | 43.0 | 50.2 |
| | 1998 | 26.5 | 33.7 | 49.0 | 56.9 | 41.1 | 26.5 | 40.2 |
| | 2000 | 27.2 | 34.7 | 44.9 | 55.8 | 40.8 | 23.7 | 41.3 |
| Bonds | 1970 | 7.9 | 30.1 | 12.2 | 13.0 | 23.9 | 3.4 | 17.2 |
| | 1980 | 12.1 | 27.4 | 11.3 | 19.2 | 17.5 | 4.9 | 20.9 |
| | 1990 | 9.3 | 31.9 | 15.8 | 20.0 | 18.5 | 12.0 | 19.5 |
| | 1998 | 16.0 | 28.6 | 22.4 | 22.6 | 23.9 | 16.5 | 28.7 |
| | 2000 | 7.0 | 27.2 | 20.0 | 25.2 | 23.7 | 14.6 | 24.4 |
| Equity | 1970 | 12.0 | 15.4 | 3.3 | 6.2 | 10.2 | 3.3 | 1.8 |
| | 1980 | 10.0 | 11.9 | 2.4 | 10.7 | 7.4 | 3.7 | 1.7 |
| | 1990 | 18.1 | 11.8 | 4.7 | 8.9 | 10.7 | 5.5 | 5.9 |
| | 1998 | 24.2 | 25.4 | 12.2 | 5.8 | 19.0 | 15.5 | 14.8 |
| | 2000 | 24.1 | 25.0 | 15.6 | 7.0 | 19.9 | 20.8 | 18.5 |
| Mutual funds | 1970 | 0.4 | 0.4 | 0.0 | 0.1 | na | 0.0 | 0.0 |
| | 1980 | 1.4 | 0.3 | 0.0 | 0.1 | na | 0.0 | 0.0 |
| | 1990 | 1.7 | 1.1 | 1.6 | 0.6 | na | 2.1 | 0.0 |
| | 1998 | 2.4 | 4.0 | 3.3 | 0.3 | na | 4.7 | 0.6 |
| | 2000 | 2.3 | 3.8 | 5.9 | 0.4 | na | 6.6 | 1.5 |
| Central Bank reserves | 1970 | 0.0 | 1.2 | 7.4 | 0.0 | 4.1 | 2.6 | 2.0 |
| | 1980 | 0.0 | 0.7 | 3.4 | 0.0 | 1.0 | 6.3 | 5.8 |
| | 1990 | 0.0 | 0.6 | 2.0 | 0.0 | 1.9 | 2.0 | 1.6 |
| | 1998 | 0.0 | 0.2 | 0.1 | 1.0 | 1.7 | 0.6 | 0.9 |
| | 2000 | 0.0 | 0.2 | 0.5 | 0.0 | 2.0 | 0.5 | 0.8 |

Note: the first observation for the UK is 1975 and not 1970.

Table 8.2 *Financial sector financial assets (per cent of GDP)*

| | | UK | US | Germany | Japan | Canada | France | Italy |
|---|---|---|---|---|---|---|---|---|
| Deposits | 1970 | 35.1 | 5.8 | 3.3 | 0.4 | 13.5 | 29.5 | 20.8 |
| | 1980 | 38.3 | 5.8 | 6.5 | 1.3 | 13.9 | 61.7 | 31.9 |
| | 1990 | 119.1 | 6.6 | 13.8 | 1.3 | 7.5 | 75.3 | 28.6 |
| | 1998 | 155.8 | 6.0 | 38.8 | 36.5 | 10.2 | 91.4 | 27.0 |
| | 2000 | 172.8 | 6.3 | 43.8 | 38.1 | 8.6 | 102.7 | 30.2 |
| Money market inst | 1970 | 11.1 | 1.7 | 1.2 | 9.3 | 6.1 | 4.4 | 4.1 |
| | 1980 | 5.1 | 5.2 | 0.6 | 14.0 | 8.7 | 3.7 | 11.3 |
| | 1990 | 18.3 | 14.5 | 1.0 | 19.5 | 17.4 | 19.5 | 5.0 |
| | 1998 | 20.3 | 18.9 | 0.9 | 31.1 | 23.7 | 30.6 | 5.3 |
| | 2000 | 20.4 | 23.3 | 1.9 | 20.2 | 22.8 | 35.5 | 2.2 |
| Loans | 1970 | 116.4 | 71.3 | 75.1 | 113.5 | 61.1 | 88.0 | 83.4 |
| | 1980 | 119.6 | 82.4 | 127.1 | 174.3 | 89.6 | 107.3 | 65.8 |
| | 1990 | 143.4 | 98.3 | 153.4 | 222.9 | 91.6 | 115.4 | 73.8 |
| | 1998 | 151.2 | 104.1 | 149.2 | 288.0 | 98.3 | 93.1 | 88.4 |
| | 2000 | 170.3 | 112.7 | 156.2 | 280.7 | 94.3 | 97.1 | 99.0 |
| Bonds | 1970 | 16.0 | 44.7 | 12.6 | 19.9 | 31.1 | 4.5 | 23.5 |
| | 1980 | 25.9 | 43.0 | 18.4 | 52.1 | 26.5 | 9.9 | 31.9 |
| | 1990 | 36.6 | 69.8 | 35.0 | 69.1 | 31.3 | 32.0 | 28.7 |
| | 1998 | 91.0 | 88.2 | 68.2 | 114.6 | 57.2 | 57.9 | 63.1 |
| | 2000 | 97.1 | 88.3 | 69.5 | 126.7 | 54.9 | 60.0 | 58.5 |
| Equity | 1970 | 24.4 | 22.9 | 3.5 | 9.4 | 13.3 | 4.4 | 2.4 |
| | 1980 | 21.4 | 18.7 | 3.9 | 29.1 | 11.2 | 7.5 | 2.6 |
| | 1990 | 71.5 | 25.9 | 10.3 | 30.7 | 18.1 | 14.9 | 8.7 |
| | 1998 | 138.0 | 78.4 | 37.0 | 29.2 | 45.5 | 54.6 | 32.6 |
| | 2000 | 150.7 | 81.0 | 54.1 | 35.4 | 45.9 | 85.2 | 44.5 |
| Mutual funds | 1970 | 0.9 | 0.5 | 0.0 | 0.1 | na | 0.0 | 0.0 |
| | 1980 | 3.0 | 0.5 | 0.0 | 0.3 | na | 0.0 | 0.0 |
| | 1990 | 6.6 | 2.3 | 3.5 | 2.2 | na | 5.7 | 0.0 |
| | 1998 | 13.6 | 12.4 | 10.1 | 1.7 | na | 16.6 | 1.4 |
| | 2000 | 14.4 | 12.5 | 20.6 | 1.9 | na | 27.1 | 3.5 |
| Central Bank reserves | 1970 | 0.0 | 1.8 | 7.7 | 0.0 | 5.3 | 3.5 | 2.7 |
| | 1980 | 0.0 | 1.1 | 5.6 | 0.0 | 1.6 | 12.7 | 8.8 |
| | 1990 | 0.0 | 1.3 | 4.4 | 0.0 | 3.2 | 5.3 | 2.3 |
| | 1998 | 0.0 | 0.7 | 0.5 | 5.0 | 4.0 | 2.0 | 2.0 |
| | 2000 | 0.0 | 0.6 | 1.6 | 0.0 | 4.6 | 2.1 | 2.0 |
| Total assets | 1970 | 203.8 | 148.7 | 103.4 | 152.6 | 130.4 | 134.4 | 137.0 |
| | 1980 | 213.2 | 156.7 | 162.0 | 271.2 | 151.5 | 202.7 | 152.3 |
| | 1990 | 395.5 | 218.6 | 221.4 | 345.7 | 169.2 | 268.1 | 147.1 |
| | 1998 | 569.9 | 308.8 | 304.7 | 506.1 | 238.9 | 350.9 | 219.9 |
| | 2000 | 625.6 | 324.6 | 347.7 | 503.1 | 231.2 | 409.7 | 239.9 |

Note: the first observation for the UK is 1975 and not 1970.

Table 8.3 *Financial sector liabilities (per cent of total)*

| | | UK | US | Germany | Japan | Canada | France | Italy |
|---|---|---|---|---|---|---|---|---|
| Deposits | 1970 | 70.2 | 53.4 | 73.5 | 71.2 | 52.8 | 63.9 | 67.2 |
| | 1980 | 70.9 | 49.6 | 69.5 | 70.8 | 61.0 | 67.0 | 72.0 |
| | 1990 | 53.1 | 34.0 | 59.6 | 58.4 | 49.0 | 50.5 | 63.1 |
| | 1998 | 41.9 | 18.0 | 46.1 | 50.3 | 35.7 | 50.0 | 41.0 |
| | 2000 | 42.2 | 16.8 | 43.7 | 51.9 | 33.1 | 47.6 | 38.3 |
| Money market inst | 1970 | 4.5 | 2.4 | 0.9 | 4.6 | 0.0 | 0.3 | 0.0 |
| | 1980 | 0.4 | 5.9 | 0.2 | 3.3 | 0.0 | 0.3 | 0.0 |
| | 1990 | 6.9 | 6.5 | 0.1 | 5.1 | 0.0 | 5.5 | 0.0 |
| | 1998 | 4.1 | 6.3 | 0.5 | 5.3 | 0.0 | 5.0 | 0.0 |
| | 2000 | 4.7 | 7.0 | 1.3 | 2.5 | 0.0 | 5.5 | 0.0 |
| Loans | 1970 | 2.1 | 3.2 | 0.3 | 0.0 | 3.8 | 16.9 | 13.3 |
| | 1980 | 2.2 | 3.0 | 0.4 | 0.0 | 6.0 | 14.0 | 10.5 |
| | 1990 | 6.5 | 2.7 | 0.5 | 0.0 | 4.0 | 5.8 | 9.6 |
| | 1998 | 9.4 | 3.2 | 0.3 | 18.5 | 5.4 | 2.2 | 9.2 |
| | 2000 | 10.3 | 3.5 | 0.3 | 18.5 | 5.9 | 2.2 | 9.3 |
| Bonds | 1970 | 0.5 | 4.7 | 12.4 | 6.9 | 1.9 | 5.2 | 13.6 |
| | 1980 | 0.5 | 8.8 | 15.9 | 6.9 | 3.1 | 5.4 | 11.4 |
| | 1990 | 2.1 | 16.5 | 16.4 | 7.1 | 4.2 | 9.1 | 7.3 |
| | 1998 | 3.8 | 17.9 | 20.6 | 4.7 | 6.0 | 7.0 | 11.0 |
| | 2000 | 4.4 | 19.1 | 19.3 | 4.1 | 6.4 | 5.3 | 10.1 |
| Equity | 1970 | 5.9 | 8.6 | 2.0 | 1.8 | 14.5 | 8.1 | 3.2 |
| | 1980 | 5.3 | 3.1 | 1.9 | 2.1 | 8.5 | 8.1 | 4.2 |
| | 1990 | 5.5 | 3.1 | 4.2 | 1.3 | 12.6 | 11.6 | 12.1 |
| | 1998 | 8.6 | 8.7 | 9.0 | 3.2 | 11.4 | 8.3 | 15.9 |
| | 2000 | 9.2 | 8.8 | 10.6 | 3.7 | 12.8 | 9.3 | 18.2 |
| Mutual funds | 1970 | 1.3 | 3.3 | 0.0 | 1.3 | 2.5 | 0.0 | 0.0 |
| | 1980 | 1.2 | 3.3 | 0.0 | 1.3 | 1.0 | 1.3 | 0.0 |
| | 1990 | 1.9 | 9.1 | 4.6 | 4.2 | 3.0 | 10.9 | 2.5 |
| | 1998 | 4.1 | 17.2 | 10.0 | 1.9 | 13.5 | 13.3 | 15.7 |
| | 2000 | 4.9 | 18.2 | 11.8 | 2.3 | 14.5 | 15.4 | 15.2 |
| Life and pension claims | 1970 | 15.5 | 24.5 | 10.7 | 14.3 | 24.4 | 5.5 | 2.6 |
| | 1980 | 19.7 | 26.3 | 11.3 | 15.6 | 20.5 | 3.9 | 1.9 |
| | 1990 | 24.1 | 28.1 | 13.6 | 23.9 | 27.2 | 6.5 | 5.5 |
| | 1998 | 28.1 | 28.7 | 13.4 | 16.1 | 27.9 | 14.1 | 7.2 |
| | 2000 | 24.2 | 26.5 | 13.1 | 17.0 | 27.3 | 14.7 | 8.9 |

Note: the first observation for the UK is 1975 and not 1970.

deducted, assets would still be 4.5 times GDP. Japan and France also have substantial financial sectors, while the smallest sectors are in Canada and Italy. Additionally, financial assets of the financial sector are increasing rapidly for all the G-7 countries as a percentage of GDP. As noted in Davis and Steil (2001) it is an interesting counterpart to the growth of securities markets that total financial intermediation – including institutional investors – is tending to rise.

In Table 8.3, the most important category of liabilities is typically deposits, which as a percentage of total liabilities is 40–50 per cent in Japan, France, Germany, the UK and Italy. Whereas these countries are for the most part bank-dominated, so a large share of deposits is unsurprising, the UK joins as a consequence of the scope of international banking activity in that country. In the US, deposits are only 17 per cent of financial sector liabilities, showing the low relative importance of depository financial institutions.

Also important are the liabilities of life insurance and pensions (see also Figure 1.7). The point has been made earlier that these are particularly important for the US, the UK and Canada, which have larger private pension schemes. They are smaller in Italy, France, Japan and Germany (where pension provision is more on the basis of pay-as-you-go social security) but has been increasing as a percentage of total liabilities and as a percentage of GDP over the past 30 years (see Table 8.4). Mutual funds have also grown, and are particularly important in the US and France. There is a contrast with the size of households' assets in mutual funds (Table 5.2) because here we include the gross assets of mutual funds, some of which are held by sectors other than households. Note finally from Table 8.4 that the liabilities of the financial system are virtually identical to the assets. This is to be expected, as financial institutions have few fixed assets.

Table 8.4 *Financial sector liabilities (per cent of GDP)*

| | | UK | US | Germany | Japan | Canada | France | Italy |
|---|---|---|---|---|---|---|---|---|
| Deposits | 1970 | 143.9 | 72.2 | 88.6 | 97.4 | 63.4 | 86.7 | 89.4 |
| | 1980 | 155.4 | 71.1 | 107.6 | 162.2 | 91.3 | 134.3 | 99.7 |
| | 1990 | 216.9 | 70.5 | 126.1 | 191.9 | 86.8 | 143.5 | 91.1 |
| | 1998 | 258.4 | 57.6 | 138.7 | 229.7 | 88.6 | 169.1 | 91.1 |
| | 2000 | 279.3 | 57.1 | 148.9 | 239.7 | 82.2 | 181.9 | 96.9 |
| Money market inst | 1970 | 9.3 | 3.2 | 1.1 | 6.2 | 0.0 | 0.4 | 0.0 |
| | 1980 | 0.8 | 8.4 | 0.3 | 7.6 | 0.0 | 0.7 | 0.0 |
| | 1990 | 28.0 | 13.5 | 0.2 | 16.7 | 0.0 | 15.5 | 0.0 |
| | 1998 | 25.4 | 20.3 | 1.6 | 24.2 | 0.0 | 17.0 | 0.0 |
| | 2000 | 31.3 | 23.8 | 4.4 | 11.7 | 0.0 | 20.9 | 0.0 |
| Loans | 1970 | 4.2 | 4.3 | 0.4 | 0.0 | 4.6 | 23.0 | 17.7 |
| | 1980 | 4.7 | 4.2 | 0.7 | 0.0 | 9.0 | 28.0 | 14.5 |
| | 1990 | 26.7 | 5.6 | 1.0 | 0.0 | 7.2 | 16.5 | 13.8 |
| | 1998 | 58.1 | 10.1 | 0.8 | 84.2 | 13.4 | 7.5 | 20.3 |
| | 2000 | 68.3 | 12.0 | 0.9 | 85.7 | 14.7 | 8.4 | 23.6 |
| Bonds | 1970 | 1.1 | 6.4 | 14.9 | 9.5 | 2.3 | 7.1 | 18.1 |
| | 1980 | 1.0 | 12.6 | 24.7 | 15.8 | 4.6 | 10.7 | 15.8 |
| | 1990 | 8.6 | 34.1 | 34.6 | 23.4 | 7.4 | 25.8 | 10.5 |
| | 1998 | 23.2 | 57.3 | 62.1 | 21.5 | 14.9 | 23.7 | 24.3 |
| | 2000 | 29.4 | 65.1 | 65.7 | 18.9 | 16.0 | 20.2 | 25.7 |
| Equity | 1970 | 12.2 | 11.6 | 2.4 | 2.4 | 17.4 | 11.0 | 4.3 |
| | 1980 | 11.6 | 4.4 | 3.0 | 4.7 | 12.7 | 16.3 | 5.8 |
| | 1990 | 22.3 | 6.5 | 8.9 | 4.3 | 22.4 | 33.0 | 17.5 |
| | 1998 | 52.8 | 27.8 | 27.2 | 14.7 | 28.3 | 28.1 | 35.3 |
| | 2000 | 61.0 | 30.0 | 36.2 | 17.1 | 31.7 | 35.5 | 46.0 |
| Mutual funds | 1970 | 2.6 | 4.4 | 0.0 | 1.8 | 3.0 | 0.0 | 0.0 |
| | 1980 | 2.6 | 4.7 | 0.0 | 3.0 | 1.5 | 2.6 | 0.0 |
| | 1990 | 7.9 | 18.8 | 9.8 | 13.8 | 5.3 | 31.1 | 3.6 |
| | 1998 | 25.6 | 55.0 | 30.2 | 8.6 | 33.4 | 44.8 | 34.9 |
| | 2000 | 32.6 | 62.0 | 40.4 | 10.7 | 36.1 | 58.9 | 38.6 |
| Life and pension claims | 1970 | 31.7 | 33.2 | 12.9 | 19.5 | 29.3 | 7.5 | 3.5 |
| | 1980 | 43.2 | 37.7 | 17.5 | 35.7 | 30.7 | 7.8 | 2.6 |
| | 1990 | 98.3 | 58.3 | 28.9 | 78.5 | 48.2 | 18.6 | 7.9 |
| | 1998 | 173.5 | 91.8 | 40.3 | 73.4 | 69.2 | 47.7 | 16.1 |
| | 2000 | 160.3 | 90.3 | 44.6 | 78.4 | 67.8 | 56.1 | 22.4 |
| Total | 1970 | 205.1 | 135.3 | 120.5 | 136.9 | 119.9 | 135.7 | 133.0 |
| | 1980 | 219.3 | 143.2 | 154.7 | 229.1 | 149.8 | 200.4 | 138.4 |
| | 1990 | 408.7 | 207.3 | 211.7 | 328.6 | 177.2 | 284.1 | 144.4 |
| | 1998 | 617.0 | 319.9 | 300.9 | 456.3 | 247.9 | 338.0 | 222.0 |
| | 2000 | 662.2 | 340.3 | 341.1 | 462.2 | 248.6 | 381.9 | 253.2 |

Note: the first observation for the UK is 1975 and not 1970

# 9 The banking sector

## 9.1 THE BANKING SECTOR – THEORETICAL AND EMPIRICAL BACKGROUND

We noted in Section 1.2 that the economic theory of banking suggests that banks specialise in holding liquid liabilities and illiquid assets, with the consequent risk of runs when depositors lose confidence, unless the lender of last resort intervenes. Since, in the G-7 countries, there is such a safety net, banks need prudential supervision such as capital adequacy regulations to prevent them having an incentive to take risk at the expense of the taxpayer.

The portfolio decision of the banking sector has a number of aspects (Greenbaum and Thakor, 1995; Tobin and Golub, 1998). On the asset side the aim is traditionally seen as influenced by, on the one hand, desire for sufficient liquidity to ensure that demand for funds by depositors can be met without recourse to borrowing from the authorities' discount window, and on the other by desire to maximise risk-adjusted return in a standard portfolio manner.

Liquidity could be provided either by balances with central banks, money market securities such as Treasury bills, short-term government bonds or by interbank deposits. In many countries, it is set at a level enforced by reserve requirements, although these have tended to decline as an instrument of prudential policy, with their main function nowadays being related to the role of reserve requirements as a monetary policy instrument. One may add that the function of interbank deposits is traditionally seen as partly linked to banking structure, and thus varies across countries in line with bank structure. For example, depositors may prefer to hold funds with larger rather than smaller banks, and the latter borrow on the interbank market to finance lending, or it can be a means of geographical diversification for banks in local markets.

Meanwhile, banks' comparative advantage in overcoming problems of information asymmetry has traditionally led them to focus on non-traded loans made to borrowers about whom they had private information, although there would generally also be some securities held, offering a second line of liquidity at a higher return. Desire for diversification and focus on fee income has led to a growth of securitisation of loans, notably in North America, leading banks to reduce their loan allocation and either shrink the portfolio or hold resulting securities instead. Banks may also hold equity as an asset, either as a direct investment or more commonly in bank-dominated countries as a consequence of past rescues of companies.

On the liability side, banks' traditional liabilities have been retail sight deposits, but banks are increasingly diversifying their liability portfolios across a range of instruments to protect against the risk of liquidity crises (so-called liability management). Other short-term liabilities include time deposits, interbank deposits and certificates of deposit. As an alternative to deposits, there may be fixed-rate long-term bonds as a liability, which may offer superior duration matching for loans compared with classical deposits. Subordinated debt may also underpin bank regulation by allowing forms of market discipline on banks to operate (Evanoff and Wall, 2002).

Liabilities also include capital *per se*. In this context, a further factor influencing banks' portfolios is capital requirements, which impose a certain level of equity on banks' liabilities side. As noted by Bernanke and Lown (1991), shocks to bank capital, either due to losses or tightening of regulation, may contribute to financing constraints on the non-financial sectors independently of the balance sheets of the latter, especially for borrowers confined to banks in the credit channel (see Section 4.2).

In some countries, regulation also implies a separation of commercial from investment banking that affects banks' portfolios. For example, universal banks are more likely to hold equity stakes, although Japanese commercial bank equity stakes show that the orientation of the financial system is the key determinant. Meanwhile, off-balance-sheet activity has burgeoned in all OECD countries, but especially in the US.

One of the factors underlying changes in bank portfolios, as noted by Davis and Tuori (2001), is technology. The above mentioned development of loan trading and packaging has enabled banks to refocus their activities on fee earning activity – under the influence of capital requirements that the authorities impose on banks' liabilities. To some extent, banks have been able to specialise in information production and monitoring of credit exposures as agents rather than principals (e.g. in the context of loan securitisation). On the other hand, banks' profits have come under pressure in some areas, such as lending to large firms, because, owing to technical progress, these areas are also open to competition from inside the domestic banking sector, cross-border and from other financial institutions willing to hold bonds issued by such firms. Note that the development of institutional investors has been facilitated by technological changes reducing the cost of collecting saving, gathering and disseminating public information and assessing risk.[48]

Competition linked to innovation is not confined to the assets side of banks' balance sheets. Technological innovations also impact on the cost of funds by facilitating economy in liquid balances and competition in provision of liquidity. For wholesale, corporate deposits the main threat is directly from markets (such as repos and commercial paper for companies) and for households it is non-banks (such as money market funds), which has even led to part of banks' traditional function, the provision of liquidity, being increasingly undertaken by other institutions or markets. While there will be ongoing demand for nominal value in certain saving instruments (deposits), the amount is declining. Meanwhile, innovations in financial products have facilitated a reshaping of the balance sheets and income structures of banks considerably. The related possibility of separating risks from capital has led to a massive increase in off-balance sheet activities (Metais, 1997), which has also changed the income structure.

The effect on banks of the growth of securities markets can be larger than the share of external financing from the market would suggest. The existence of market financing could have affected terms and conditions of bank lending, in the sense that banks are more clearly only one possible supplier of external funding for all but the smallest firms. In other words, the market for external financing has become contestable, with potential competition from market financing limiting the scope for banks to profit from lending relationships. One may add that banks have been encouraged to take part in the process of securitisation by undertaking investment banking activities such as underwriting, which employs their capacities of information gathering as well as private information based on existing credit relations.

Liberalisation of banks' activities has until recently gone further in the EU than in the US or Japan. In the EU, liberalisation gained momentum

48 While we have noted that institutional investors have started to compete with traditional banking in respect of both assets and liabilities, in the G-7 these institutional investors are often part of banking groups, or banks own the asset management firms which undertake portfolio management for institutions.

with the Single Market programme. The single most influential act has been the Second Banking Co-ordination Directive, providing a passport for banks to offer services across the Union on the basis of home country authorisation. Banks – and their competitors – were also able to take advantage in the area of investment banking of the Investment Services Directive, which granted the cross-border passport to securities firms, portfolio managers and investment advisors. At present, liberalisation and deregulation in the EU financial services sector is very extensive[49] and, rather than anticipating new acts of liberalisation, ongoing incremental adjustment of the regulatory environment implemented in the 1980s and early 1990s seems more likely. The US is catching up, with the abolition of restrictions on interstate banking and the barriers between commercial and investment banking both taking place in the 1990s.

The impact of deregulation and liberalisation on banking may go much further because of the way they *facilitate* change. In effect, the process allows other driving forces to 'leverage' and have a more profound effect on the financial system. One of the factors which is facilitated by liberalisation is globalisation, which is occurring in most private sectors of the economy. As companies and individuals requiring financial services are becoming more globally oriented, they demand appropriate financial services. Globalisation is seen to increase competition in most areas of financial services, but also it could increase economies of scale and scope. Many markets which have previously been segmented, be it on or off balance sheet, face more competition and reduced margins. At the same time, globalisation has opened up new markets for banks particularly in trading, asset management and investment banking activities. Therefore we might expect banks to get more trading and investment banking income, possibly to reduce on balance sheet lending, and to face some further reduction of interest margins. Furthermore, globalisation may be expected to make portfolios and financial markets more similar, since international banks compete in the same markets to some extent.

The regulatory environment has also affected the banking system directly, not merely by inducing competition. The clearest example is the effect from capital requirements, and different risk weights therein. Since capital requirements are imposed by international agreement, they are another

49 One may add that deregulation and liberalisation have a global perspective, which is linked to the increased scope of world trade in goods and services and liberalisation in that area in general. Rather than always leading this process, the financial services industry has in some ways been forced to adjust to the development in other sectors of the economy.

force for convergence. It has been argued that the huge increase in off-balance sheet items largely results from lower capital requirements attached to off balance sheet items than for activities conducted on balance sheet. One consequence has been the increase in securitisation in terms of packaging of loans and their resale in the form of bonds. In the income structure this is reflected in the increase in the relative share of non-interest income. Similarly, lower risk weights attached to interbank loans have most likely increased their share in balance sheets and, as they have lower margins than loans to non-financial clients, have reduced overall interest income relative to assets (albeit in this case with no major implications for overall profitability).

## 9.2 BANKING SECTOR BALANCE SHEETS

We sought to construct an equivalent to 'monetary financial institutions' in the banking tables, including the central bank (although, in all of the G-7, the central bank is much smaller than commercial banks). On the asset side (Table 9.1), loans are the main asset, accounting for over 50 per cent except in the UK and France, and putting into perspective the move to securitisation. A key difference between countries is the scope of interbank activity. It can be seen that the UK, Italy and France have sizeable shares of deposits among bank assets, amounting to over 30 per cent in the UK and France and almost 20 per cent for Italy. For France in particular, loans are a correspondingly lower proportion of assets than elsewhere. US banks' estimated interbank assets are only 2 per cent of gross assets. This pattern does not correspond to traditional views of the bank-dominated versus market-oriented split.

France and Japan also have a high proportion of money market instruments as a bank asset – around 10 per cent, corresponding to high liquidity, while in the UK and Canada it is around 5 per cent and it is negligible in the US, Germany and Italy. Bonds are a marked feature of US banks' assets, amounting to almost 30 per cent (including holdings of securitised assets). Germany and Japan also have sizeable bond portfolios (around 20 per cent), while elsewhere the shares are quite small.

As regards banks' equity holdings, Germany and Japan do not stand out in the way that might be expected, in line with the paradigm's suggestion that sizeable holdings are maintained in order to cement corporate governance (Section 1.5). Holdings of French and Italian banks exceed them in terms of portfolio share for most years. US banks, meanwhile, are shown to hold considerable amounts of mutual funds, unlike other countries (it

Table 9.1 *Banking sector financial assets (per cent of total)*

| | | UK | US | Germany | Japan | Canada | France | Italy |
|---|---|---|---|---|---|---|---|---|
| Deposits | 1970 | 23.1 | 4.7 | 1.3 | 1.6 | 14.1 | 22.0 | 16.6 |
| | 1980 | 25.0 | 3.3 | 0.5 | 2.0 | 10.1 | 31.2 | 23.0 |
| | 1990 | 38.0 | 3.1 | 0.3 | 1.5 | 4.2 | 35.1 | 27.0 |
| | 1998 | 36.5 | 2.3 | 8.4 | 10.9 | 3.8 | 36.7 | 16.0 |
| | 2000 | 34.9 | 2.3 | 9.0 | 11.1 | 2.6 | 35.0 | 16.2 |
| Money market inst | 1970 | 6.6 | 1.0 | 1.1 | 7.0 | 5.5 | 3.4 | 3.8 |
| | 1980 | 2.5 | 1.9 | 0.4 | 9.5 | 4.9 | 1.9 | 8.4 |
| | 1990 | 5.8 | 1.9 | 0.5 | 9.3 | 9.7 | 3.5 | 4.3 |
| | 1998 | 4.8 | 0.9 | 0.4 | 7.5 | 7.1 | 10.5 | 2.2 |
| | 2000 | 4.2 | 1.0 | 0.8 | 8.1 | 5.7 | 9.3 | 0.7 |
| Loans | 1970 | 66.9 | 55.1 | 79.7 | 72.3 | 55.3 | 68.6 | 54.7 |
| | 1980 | 69.1 | 64.1 | 83.4 | 61.1 | 72.0 | 55.9 | 36.3 |
| | 1990 | 49.9 | 62.3 | 80.7 | 70.7 | 77.1 | 54.1 | 46.5 |
| | 1998 | 44.6 | 58.7 | 61.7 | 59.8 | 72.2 | 33.8 | 57.2 |
| | 2000 | 45.8 | 60.6 | 59.5 | 50.0 | 72.5 | 32.3 | 58.9 |
| Bonds | 1970 | 2.5 | 27.6 | 9.1 | 14.0 | 18.5 | 1.2 | 20.8 |
| | 1980 | 2.0 | 24.0 | 10.1 | 16.1 | 8.5 | 2.5 | 24.0 |
| | 1990 | 4.8 | 26.3 | 13.3 | 12.3 | 3.9 | 5.1 | 18.3 |
| | 1998 | 11.7 | 27.5 | 20.7 | 17.2 | 10.1 | 7.7 | 17.6 |
| | 2000 | 7.0 | 27.1 | 19.5 | 19.0 | 10.4 | 7.6 | 14.6 |
| Equity | 1970 | 1.0 | 9.4 | 1.9 | 5.1 | 0.5 | 2.0 | 1.6 |
| | 1980 | 0.0 | 5.3 | 1.6 | 11.1 | 3.2 | 1.9 | 1.5 |
| | 1990 | 1.4 | 3.8 | 2.4 | 5.6 | 2.5 | 1.6 | 1.6 |
| | 1998 | 2.3 | 4.7 | 6.4 | 4.3 | 3.5 | 9.2 | 5.4 |
| | 2000 | 2.9 | 4.0 | 7.9 | 11.3 | 4.4 | 13.3 | 7.9 |
| Mutual funds | 1970 | 0.0 | 0.4 | 0.0 | 0.1 | na | 0.0 | 0.0 |
| | 1980 | 1.3 | 0.2 | 0.0 | 0.1 | na | 0.0 | 0.0 |
| | 1990 | 0.0 | 1.2 | 0.3 | 0.6 | na | 0.6 | 0.0 |
| | 1998 | 0.0 | 5.0 | 2.2 | 0.4 | na | 1.3 | 0.1 |
| | 2000 | 0.1 | 4.3 | 2.7 | 0.5 | na | 1.9 | 0.3 |
| Central Bank reserves | 1970 | na | 1.9 | 6.8 | na | 6.1 | 2.8 | 2.5 |
| | 1980 | na | 1.2 | 3.9 | na | 1.3 | 6.6 | 6.9 |
| | 1990 | na | 1.4 | 2.5 | na | 2.6 | 0.0 | 2.3 |
| | 1998 | na | 0.9 | 0.2 | na | 3.3 | 0.8 | 1.4 |
| | 2000 | na | 0.7 | 0.6 | na | 4.3 | 0.7 | 1.3 |

Note: the first observation for the UK is 1975 and not 1970.

Table 9.2 *Banking sector financial assets (per cent of GDP)*

| | | UK | US | Germany | Japan | Canada | France | Italy |
|---|---|---|---|---|---|---|---|---|
| Deposits | 1970 | 65.3 | 4.3 | 1.5 | 1.2 | 12.3 | 28.1 | 17.6 |
| | 1980 | 33.7 | 3.0 | 0.7 | 2.3 | 12.3 | 60.2 | 29.5 |
| | 1990 | 99.9 | 2.8 | 0.5 | 2.4 | 5.2 | 73.5 | 26.7 |
| | 1998 | 115.1 | 2.0 | 19.5 | 27.5 | 4.6 | 91.4 | 22.4 |
| | 2000 | 120.8 | 2.0 | 22.6 | 30.5 | 2.7 | 96.6 | 24.6 |
| Money market inst | 1970 | 18.6 | 0.9 | 1.2 | 5.2 | 4.8 | 4.4 | 4.0 |
| | 1980 | 3.4 | 1.7 | 0.6 | 10.6 | 6.0 | 3.6 | 10.7 |
| | 1990 | 15.3 | 1.7 | 0.9 | 15.0 | 12.1 | 7.4 | 4.2 |
| | 1998 | 15.3 | 0.8 | 0.9 | 18.9 | 8.4 | 26.3 | 3.1 |
| | 2000 | 14.6 | 0.8 | 1.9 | 22.2 | 6.0 | 25.6 | 1.1 |
| Loans | 1970 | 189.3 | 50.6 | 89.6 | 54.0 | 47.9 | 88.0 | 58.1 |
| | 1980 | 93.0 | 58.2 | 118.9 | 68.0 | 88.0 | 108.0 | 46.6 |
| | 1990 | 131.4 | 56.7 | 143.8 | 113.4 | 96.2 | 113.2 | 46.0 |
| | 1998 | 140.5 | 50.1 | 143.2 | 151.5 | 86.5 | 84.2 | 80.1 |
| | 2000 | 158.5 | 52.1 | 149.9 | 137.8 | 76.7 | 89.2 | 89.1 |
| Bonds | 1970 | 7.0 | 25.3 | 10.2 | 10.4 | 16.0 | 1.5 | 22.1 |
| | 1980 | 2.7 | 21.8 | 14.3 | 17.9 | 10.4 | 4.9 | 30.8 |
| | 1990 | 12.7 | 23.9 | 23.7 | 19.7 | 4.9 | 10.6 | 18.1 |
| | 1998 | 36.9 | 23.5 | 48.0 | 43.6 | 12.0 | 19.2 | 24.7 |
| | 2000 | 42.0 | 23.3 | 49.0 | 52.3 | 11.0 | 20.9 | 22.1 |
| Equity | 1970 | 2.9 | 8.6 | 2.2 | 3.8 | 0.4 | 2.6 | 1.7 |
| | 1980 | 0.0 | 4.8 | 2.3 | 12.4 | 3.9 | 3.7 | 1.9 |
| | 1990 | 3.7 | 3.4 | 4.3 | 9.0 | 3.1 | 3.3 | 1.6 |
| | 1998 | 7.3 | 4.0 | 14.9 | 10.8 | 4.2 | 23.1 | 7.6 |
| | 2000 | 9.9 | 3.5 | 20.0 | 31.1 | 4.7 | 36.7 | 12.0 |
| Mutual funds | 1970 | 0.0 | 0.4 | 0.0 | 0.0 | na | 0.0 | 0.0 |
| | 1980 | 1.7 | 0.2 | 0.0 | 0.1 | na | 0.0 | 0.0 |
| | 1990 | 0.1 | 1.1 | 0.5 | 0.9 | na | 1.3 | 0.0 |
| | 1998 | 0.2 | 4.3 | 5.1 | 1.1 | na | 3.3 | 0.2 |
| | 2000 | 0.2 | 3.7 | 6.8 | 1.5 | na | 5.4 | 0.4 |
| Central Bank reserves | 1970 | na | 1.8 | 7.7 | na | 5.3 | 3.5 | 2.7 |
| | 1980 | na | 1.1 | 5.6 | na | 1.6 | 12.7 | 8.8 |
| | 1990 | na | 1.3 | 4.4 | na | 3.2 | 0.0 | 2.3 |
| | 1998 | na | 0.7 | 0.5 | na | 4.0 | 2.0 | 2.0 |
| | 2000 | na | 0.6 | 1.6 | na | 4.6 | 2.0 | 2.0 |
| Total assets | 1970 | 283.1 | 91.9 | 112.4 | 74.7 | 86.6 | 128.1 | 106.1 |
| | 1980 | 134.6 | 90.7 | 142.5 | 111.2 | 122.2 | 193.0 | 128.3 |
| | 1990 | 263.2 | 90.9 | 178.2 | 160.4 | 124.8 | 209.4 | 98.9 |
| | 1998 | 315.2 | 85.3 | 232.0 | 253.4 | 119.8 | 249.3 | 140.2 |
| | 2000 | 346.0 | 85.9 | 251.8 | 275.4 | 105.8 | 276.3 | 151.4 |

Note: the first observation for the UK is 1975 and not 1970.

should be borne in mind that US banks have trust departments which hold securities on behalf of clients).

The above comments are focused on ongoing structural differences between balance sheets. It may be added that in Germany, Japan, the UK and France there is a marked downward trend in the share of loans, the classic bank asset, with an offsetting rise in deposits, money market instruments (for France), bonds and shares. Elsewhere the banking sector portfolio is remarkably stable, despite the scope of financial change, including liberalisation, structural change and instability, over the 30-year period covered (Berger and Udell, 1995). This is particularly noteworthy for the US, where small shifts into mutual funds seem to be the main changes observable.

Looking at the data relative to GDP, a striking feature is the size of bank assets in the UK, amounting to over 3.5 times GDP and reflecting the scope of international banking activity in London. (As noted above, purely domestic-currency banking assets are around twice GDP.) Bank assets are also sizeable in bank-dominated Germany, Japan and France, at over 2.5 times GDP. If international business were to be excluded, the size of the UK sector would be below that of Germany, Japan and France. Note that for most countries, the size of banking sectors is much more comparable than the financial sectors commented on above. This reflects the more diverse range of financial activities in countries such as the UK, where capital markets and institutional investors are much larger than elsewhere.

The US and Canadian banking sectors stand out, in contrast, as extremely small relative to the size of the economy, reflecting the relatively minor role of banks in corporate financing compared with other countries, and securitisation of many household mortgages (despite inclusion of savings institutions and monetary authorities in the data). Italy is in an intermediate position. In most countries, the banking sector has grown over time relative to GDP, the exceptions being the US and Canada where the ratio to GDP has declined. This underlines the very different patterns in those countries, which should not perhaps be taken as typical of the evolution of financial sectors generally.

Banks in Japan hold bonds equivalent to 50 per cent of GDP, while their equity holdings, unrealised gains in which count as capital, have been extremely volatile. This underlines the current exposure of Japanese banks to rises in bond yields from their exceptionally low levels. German and UK banks also have bond holdings of around half of GDP, while the largest equity holder relative to GDP is the French banking sector (37 per cent of GDP).

Turning to the portfolio share of bank liabilities, it can be seen that the

Table 9.3 *Banking sector liabilities (per cent of total)*

| | | UK | US | Germany | Japan | Canada | France | Italy |
|---|---|---|---|---|---|---|---|---|
| Deposits | 1970 | 89.4 | 96.4 | 82.8 | 79.6 | 56.6 | 67.6 | 86.1 |
| | 1980 | 95.9 | 85.0 | 79.2 | 79.8 | 53.7 | 70.7 | 86.2 |
| | 1990 | 83.8 | 83.0 | 75.2 | 78.7 | 52.7 | 65.0 | 91.2 |
| | 1998 | 82.9 | 75.2 | 65.3 | 77.6 | 51.2 | 75.9 | 61.3 |
| | 2000 | 83.7 | 73.3 | 62.1 | 79.8 | 51.1 | 74.6 | 59.7 |
| Money market inst | 1970 | 6.8 | 1.8 | 1.0 | 8.0 | 0.0 | 0.3 | 0.0 |
| | 1980 | 0.1 | 7.9 | 0.2 | 7.2 | 0.3 | 0.4 | 0.0 |
| | 1990 | 10.6 | 7.5 | 0.1 | 9.3 | 0.0 | 7.0 | 0.0 |
| | 1998 | 7.7 | 10.9 | 0.7 | 5.5 | 0.0 | 7.2 | 0.0 |
| | 2000 | 8.5 | 12.0 | 1.8 | 4.3 | 0.0 | 7.3 | 0.0 |
| Loans | 1970 | 0.3 | 1.4 | 0.3 | 1.1 | 34.5 | 18.2 | 12.1 |
| | 1980 | 0.0 | 2.1 | 0.1 | 0.2 | 40.9 | 15.0 | 11.1 |
| | 1990 | 0.4 | 2.7 | 0.5 | 0.6 | 44.2 | 7.5 | 2.1 |
| | 1998 | 0.3 | 4.6 | 0.0 | 10.3 | 41.8 | 0.9 | 6.1 |
| | 2000 | 0.2 | 5.8 | 0.0 | 9.3 | 41.6 | 1.2 | 6.2 |
| Bonds | 1970 | 0.3 | 0.4 | 13.9 | 8.8 | 8.6 | 5.5 | 0.0 |
| | 1980 | 0.4 | 1.1 | 18.2 | 9.5 | 3.3 | 5.7 | 0.0 |
| | 1990 | 2.2 | 2.5 | 20.6 | 9.2 | 1.6 | 11.7 | 0.0 |
| | 1998 | 4.2 | 3.2 | 29.2 | 4.0 | 4.9 | 9.0 | 16.4 |
| | 2000 | 4.6 | 3.5 | 27.4 | 3.8 | 4.8 | 8.5 | 14.4 |
| Equity | 1970 | 3.2 | 0.0 | 1.8 | 2.5 | 0.3 | 7.9 | 1.8 |
| | 1980 | 3.7 | 3.9 | 1.7 | 3.3 | 1.8 | 8.3 | 2.7 |
| | 1990 | 3.0 | 4.3 | 2.3 | 2.2 | 1.4 | 8.8 | 6.7 |
| | 1998 | 4.9 | 6.1 | 4.8 | 2.6 | 2.1 | 7.0 | 16.1 |
| | 2000 | 2.9 | 5.4 | 8.7 | 2.9 | 2.6 | 8.4 | 19.8 |

Note: the first observation for the UK is 1975 and not 1970.

traditional liability, deposits, remains dominant, accounting for 70–80 per cent in most countries. As noted, these include interbank as well as non-bank deposits. An exception is Canada, where loans as a liability count for over 40 per cent of liabilities, and Germany, where issuance of bank bonds has been an important source of bank financing (over 25 per cent of liabilities). German banks effectively intermediate by this means between final borrowers and investors, providing maturity matching between assets and liabilities. Italian banks also rely on bond financing to a considerable extent; this form of bond-based intermediation has received little attention in the literature. As regards equity, the data suggest that for most countries, shares account for less than 10 per cent of liabilities. The data for liabilities

Table 9.4 *Banking sector liabilities (per cent of GDP)*

| | | UK | US | Germany | Japan | Canada | France | Italy |
|---|---|---|---|---|---|---|---|---|
| Deposits | 1970 | 119.1 | 72.2 | 88.5 | 58.8 | 78.5 | 86.8 | 87.0 |
| | 1980 | 129.8 | 71.1 | 107.6 | 82.1 | 115.4 | 133.8 | 96.8 |
| | 1990 | 216.9 | 70.5 | 126.1 | 121.3 | 114.6 | 143.3 | 85.6 |
| | 1998 | 258.4 | 57.6 | 138.7 | 229.7 | 105.8 | 166.9 | 91.1 |
| | 2000 | 279.3 | 57.1 | 148.9 | 239.7 | 94.0 | 178.7 | 96.9 |
| Money market inst | 1970 | 9.1 | 1.3 | 1.1 | 5.9 | 0.0 | 0.4 | 0.0 |
| | 1980 | 0.1 | 6.6 | 0.3 | 7.4 | 0.6 | 0.7 | 0.0 |
| | 1990 | 27.5 | 6.4 | 0.2 | 14.3 | 0.0 | 15.5 | 0.0 |
| | 1998 | 24.0 | 8.3 | 1.6 | 16.4 | 0.0 | 15.7 | 0.0 |
| | 2000 | 28.4 | 9.3 | 4.4 | 12.8 | 0.0 | 17.4 | 0.0 |
| Loans | 1970 | 0.4 | 1.0 | 0.3 | 0.8 | 47.9 | 23.4 | 12.2 |
| | 1980 | 0.0 | 1.8 | 0.1 | 0.2 | 87.9 | 28.3 | 12.4 |
| | 1990 | 0.9 | 2.3 | 0.8 | 1.0 | 96.2 | 16.5 | 1.9 |
| | 1998 | 0.9 | 3.5 | 0.0 | 30.6 | 86.4 | 2.0 | 9.1 |
| | 2000 | 0.8 | 4.5 | 0.0 | 27.9 | 76.5 | 2.9 | 10.1 |
| Bonds | 1970 | 0.4 | 0.3 | 14.9 | 6.5 | 12.0 | 7.1 | 0.0 |
| | 1980 | 0.5 | 0.9 | 24.7 | 9.8 | 7.0 | 10.7 | 0.0 |
| | 1990 | 5.7 | 2.1 | 34.6 | 14.1 | 3.4 | 25.8 | 0.0 |
| | 1998 | 13.1 | 2.5 | 62.1 | 11.7 | 10.1 | 19.9 | 24.3 |
| | 2000 | 15.4 | 2.8 | 65.7 | 11.4 | 8.8 | 20.3 | 23.3 |
| Equity | 1970 | 4.2 | 0.0 | 1.9 | 1.8 | 0.4 | 10.2 | 1.9 |
| | 1980 | 4.9 | 3.3 | 2.3 | 3.4 | 3.9 | 15.7 | 3.0 |
| | 1990 | 7.7 | 3.7 | 3.9 | 3.4 | 3.1 | 19.5 | 6.3 |
| | 1998 | 15.3 | 4.7 | 10.2 | 7.7 | 4.2 | 15.4 | 23.9 |
| | 2000 | 9.7 | 4.2 | 20.9 | 8.6 | 4.7 | 20.2 | 32.1 |
| Total | 1970 | 133.2 | 74.9 | 106.9 | 73.8 | 138.8 | 128.4 | 101.0 |
| | 1980 | 135.3 | 83.6 | 135.9 | 102.9 | 214.8 | 189.4 | 112.2 |
| | 1990 | 258.7 | 84.9 | 167.8 | 154.1 | 217.4 | 220.6 | 93.8 |
| | 1998 | 311.7 | 76.6 | 212.6 | 296.1 | 206.6 | 220.0 | 148.4 |
| | 2000 | 333.5 | 77.9 | 239.9 | 300.4 | 184.0 | 239.5 | 162.4 |

Note: the first observation for the UK is 1975 and not 1970.

are of course not risk-weighted, so a low equity share is still consistent with a Basel ratio of over 8 per cent, especially with high shares of OECD interbank and government bonds. Italian banks stand out as having exceptionally high equity–asset ratios, of around 20 per cent.

The overall ratio of liabilities to GDP is naturally comparable to the assets – the difference largely reflects the unclassified assets and liabilities shown in Tables 2.3 and 2.4 as well as fixed assets.

# 10 Insurance companies, pension funds and mutual funds

## 10.1 PORTFOLIO BEHAVIOUR OF INSTITUTIONAL INVESTORS

Institutional investors may be defined as specialised financial institutions that manage savings collectively on behalf of small investors towards a specific objective in terms of acceptable risk, return maximisation, and maturity of claims (Davis and Steil, 2001). Asset management defines the process whereby assets collected by institutional investors are actually invested in the capital markets. Whereas conceptually these aspects are often bundled together, in fact the asset manager may or may not be a part of the institutional investor in a legal sense. In effect, asset management may be either internal or external to the institution itself.

Given the twin separations between beneficiary and institutional investor and between institutional investor and asset manager, important principal-agent issues may arise. Self-interested behaviour of agents (such as asset managers) may not always be fully in line with the interests of those bearing the risks (such as retail investors in mutual funds, or the corporate sponsors of defined benefit pension funds). These agency problems give rise in turn to some of the distinctive effects of institutional investors on capital markets.

A key point to make regarding institutional investors is that their asset choices need not reflect the mean-variance model, which assumes that the investor chooses an asset allocation based solely on average return and its volatility (Section 1.1). Certain considerations in respect of liabilities give rise to alternative paradigms of institutional asset allocation, which may imply a very different approach to investment (Borio *et al.*, 1997):

(1) Immunisation is a special case of the mean-variance approach which implies that the investor tries to stabilise the value of the investment at the end of the holding period, i.e. to hold an entirely riskless position; this is done typically in respect of interest rate risk by appropriately adjusting the duration of the assets held to that of the liabilities. It necessitates a constant rebalancing of the portfolio – as well as the existence of assets which have a similar duration to liabilities.
(2) Matching is a particular case of immunisation where the assets precisely replicate the cash flows of the liabilities, including any related option characteristics.
(3) Shortfall risk[50] and portfolio insurance approaches put a particular stress on avoiding downward moves, e.g. in the context of minimum solvency levels for pension funds or insurance companies. Hence, unlike mean-variance and immunisation they are not symmetric in respect to the weight put on upward and downward asset price moves.
(4) A further issue is whether the benchmark for investment is seen in nominal terms, as implicitly assumed above, or real terms. The benchmark may also be defined relative to the liabilities of the institution such as defined benefit pension or insurance claims. Asset management techniques which take into account the nature of liabilities are known as asset-liability management techniques (ALM) (see also Blake, 1999), of which immunisation is a special case.

Following the analysis of Section 8.1, there are a variety of constraints which apply to life insurers or pension funds, all of which may have a marked effect on optimal portfolios, even abstracting from regulation. Notably, the nature of the liabilities is the key to understanding how institutional investors differ in their operations. Such liabilities differ in certainty and timing, from known outlay and timing (bank deposit) through known outlay but uncertain timing (traditional life insurance), uncertain outlay and known timing (floating rate debt) and uncertain outlay and uncertain timing (pension funds, endowment/unit linked life insurance, property and casualty insurance). Certainty needs will vary within groups, e.g. a pension fund may require lesser certainty than a life insurer in nominal terms.

After these considerations are taken into account, investment strategies are developed and implemented. A primary decision is to choose the asset categories to be included in the portfolio – usually money market instruments, shares, bonds, real estate, loans and foreign assets. Market conditions are monitored, using historic data on macroeconomic and

---

50 See Leibowitz and Kogelman (1991).

financial variables as well as economic forecasts, to determine expectations of rates of return over the holding period. The efficient frontier can be derived between risk and return, depending on the probability distribution of holding period returns. Below the frontier the asset allocation is inefficient in the sense that risk can be reduced or return increased with no change to the other variable. An optimal asset mix may then be derived, selecting the portfolio that is efficient, which meets the required trade-off of risk and return and satisfies the constraints. Portfolio adjustments are made as appropriate when relevant variables change (such as market conditions, relative asset values and forecasts thereof, and the evolving nature of investor circumstances).

The investment process is often divided into several components, with asset allocation (or strategic asset allocation)[51] referring to the long-term decision on the disposition of the overall portfolio, while tactical asset allocation relates to short-term adjustments to this basic choice between asset categories in the light of short-term profit opportunities, so-called 'market timing'. Meanwhile security selection relates to the choice of individual assets to be held within each asset class, which may be both strategic and tactical. Regulatory investment restrictions (Davis, 2002c) typically apply most strongly to asset allocation between instruments but may also affect security selection (e.g. if there is a limit on exposures as a proportion of the institution's balance sheet, or as a proportion of the equity of the firm invested in).

## 10.2 INVESTMENT CONSIDERATIONS FOR THE DIFFERING TYPES OF INSTITUTIONAL INVESTOR

Both the risk tolerance and the return requirement of mutual funds are predefined for each fund and can vary sharply between funds. Hence investment objectives for mutual funds are straightforward in that they design investment strategies to allow their shareholders control over overall allocations by instrument or asset class. They are more specialised than pension funds or insurance companies. They have to maintain their declared profile of investments, designing the portfolio process directly for the asset class. Changes in the composition of the mutual fund sectors' assets will then reflect changes in the portfolio preferences of the household sector,

51 Note that strategic choices include not only the disposition of the portfolio but also the choice of active versus passive management and domestic versus international.

which the household sector chooses in light of the remaining assets and liabilities, see Chapter 5. There are major differences between mutual funds in their portfolio strategies. A key distinction is between actively managed and passive or index funds. Within actively managed funds, there are a large number of subcategories dividing strategies, notably value versus growth strategies. And there are, of course, subdivisions with respect to the type of assets funds may invest in – and the strictness with which such subdivisions are to be maintained.

For life insurance (Dickinson, 1998), it is fundamentally a matter of actuarial calculation (notably using mortality tables as well as assumptions on asset returns) to assess and project how much a policyholder may be paid in the case of a claim. Life insurance company traditional liabilities, such as term policies and annuities, tend to be defined in nominal terms, and hence could be matched or immunised, usually by using long-term bonds. However, life companies are increasingly also offering variable policies such as variable-life policies, variable annuities, endowment, and unit (mutual fund) linked policies. These typically combine a term policy with a saving element aimed at capital appreciation, where for the latter there is no explicit guarantee as to the size of the bonus to be disbursed. Such policies may offer higher returns – and also risks – to policyholders, while posing less shortfall risk to the surplus of the life insurer (see below). In many countries, including the United States, there is a deferred-taxation benefit to such investment. Besides the popularity of variable policies, another factor increasing equity investment is that insurance companies are heavily involved in investing pension monies. This may occur directly on a defined contribution basis or externally as asset managers invest in so-called 'segregated accounts' on behalf of defined contribution or defined benefit funds. An additional feature affecting life companies' portfolios is that they need some short-term liquidity to cover early surrender of policies and policy loans.

Asset allocation considerations, linked notably to the bond/equity choice, arise strongly for pension funds.[52] The crucial point is that for pension funds, the portfolio distribution and the corresponding return and risk on the assets held, in relation to the growth of average labour earnings, determine the replacement ratio (pension as a proportion of final earnings) obtainable by purchase of an annuity at retirement financed via an occupational or personal defined contribution fund[53] as well as the cost to a company of

52 For an extensive set of readings on the topic of pension finance see Bodie and Davis (2000).

53 The growth of receipts under funding with defined contributions depends on the

providing a pension in a defined benefit plan.[54] This link of liabilities to labour earnings points to a crucial difference with insurance companies as well as households, in that pension funds face the risk of increasing nominal liabilities (for example, due to wage increases), as well as the risk of holding assets, and hence need to trade volatility with return. In effect, their liabilities are typically denominated in real terms and are not fixed in nominal terms. Hence, they must also focus on real assets that offer some form of inflation protection. This implies a particular focus on equities and property. An additional factor that will influence the portfolio distributions of an individual pension fund is maturity – the ratio of active to retired members. The duration of liabilities (that is, the average time to discounted pension payment requirements) is much longer for an immature fund having few pensions in payment than for a mature fund for which sizeable repayments are required. A fund that is closing down (or winding up) will have even shorter-duration liabilities. Further key distinctions arise in the investment approach of defined contribution and defined benefit funds:

In a defined contribution pension fund, the sponsors are responsible only for making contributions to the plan. There is no guarantee regarding assets at retirement, which depend on growth in the assets of the plan. In some cases, the portfolio distribution is chosen solely by the sponsor and the investment managers it employs. But increasingly (e.g., 401(k) plans in the United States), employees are left also to decide the asset allocation. As regards portfolio objectives, a defined contribution pension plan should in principle seek to maximise return for a given risk, so as to attain as high as possible a replacement ratio at retirement. This implies following closely the standard mean-variance portfolio optimisation schema. Until the approach of retirement necessitates a shift to bonds, the superior returns on equity will likely ensure that a significant share of the portfolio is accounted for by equities, depending on the degree of risk aversion.

Defined benefit fund liabilities are, owing to the sponsor's guarantee, basically a form of corporate debt (Bodie, 1990). Appropriate investment strategies will depend on the nature of the obligation incurred. If the sponsor seeks to fund the accumulated benefit obligation and the obligation is purely

---

rate of return on the assets accumulated during the working life. The actual pension received per annum varies with the number of years of retirement relative to working age (the passivity ratio).

54 Under full funding, the contribution rate to obtain a given defined benefit replacement rate depends on the difference between the growth rate of wages (which determines the pension needed for a given replacement rate) and the return on assets, as well as the passivity ratio (the proportion of life spent after retirement).

nominal, with a minimum-funding requirement in place, it will be appropriate, as for life insurers, to immunise the liabilities with bonds of the same duration to hedge the interest rate risk of these liabilities. With a projected benefit obligation target, an investment policy based on diversification may be most appropriate, in the belief that risk reduction depends on a maximum diversification of the pension fund relative to the firm's operating investments (Ambachtsheer, 1988). Moreover, it is normal for defined benefit schemes that offer a certain link to salary at retirement for the liability to include an element of indexation. Then fund managers and actuaries typically assume that it may be appropriate to include a significant proportion of real assets such as equities and property in the portfolio as well as bonds. There are also tax considerations, arising from the exemption of contributions and asset returns from tax. For example, as Black (1980) showed, for both defined benefit and defined contribution funds, there is a fiscal incentive to maximise the tax advantage of pension funds by investing in assets with the highest possible spread between pre-tax and post-tax returns. In many countries, this tax effect gives an incentive to hold bonds.

## 10.3 EMPIRICAL WORK ON AGGREGATE INSTITUTIONAL PORTFOLIOS

The choice in regulating institutional investor portfolios is between quantitative portfolio restrictions, which limit holdings of assets with high volatility, and prudent person rules, which enjoin diversification and defensible investment procedures.[55] Davis (2002c) set out to consider how long-term institutional portfolios differ, depending on whether there are quantitative restrictions, as well as seeing whether the restrictions actually bind. He also noted some other key influences on portfolios. Portfolios with prudent person rules have fewer bonds, more equities and foreign assets than those with quantitative restrictions. The differences for domestic assets are slightly greater for pension funds than for life insurance, and markedly so for foreign assets. Such a contrast would be much greater if the countries which have recently switched to a prudent person approach for pension funds (such as Japan) were excluded, as they are slowly adjusting to the new regime.

55 The managers have to be able to defend the strategy in court against any accusation that it is inconsistent with the investment behaviour of a prudent person undertaking investment on his or her own behalf.

Also of interest are the econometric results of Davis (1988) concerning the scope of tactical asset allocation for life insurers and pension funds in the US, UK, Germany, Japan and Canada. These estimates showed that changing portfolios are strongly influenced by relative asset returns (implying tactical asset allocation) where there are few regulations governing portfolio distributions and low transactions costs, as in the US and UK. Adjustment to a change in such returns in these countries is generally rapid. Assuming adequate information and appropriate incentives to fund managers, this should imply an efficient allocation of funds and correct valuation of securities. In Davis' research, these results did not all hold where transactions costs were high and portfolio regulations were strict – e.g., in Germany, Japan and Canada. In these countries, adjustment to a change in returns was somewhat slower, implying that portfolios were relatively invariant to changes in asset market conditions. These estimates illustrate a certain inflexibility of portfolios to market conditions when portfolio restrictions apply. These could apply either directly, owing to the limits themselves, or indirectly if portfolio regulations promote a cautious and uncompetitive asset management sector.

Davis (1995a, 2001a) also highlighted a number of other influences on institutional investors' portfolios:

- solvency and minimum funding rules and their interaction with associated accounting arrangements may play a crucial role in influencing portfolios, and may account for the non-binding nature of the portfolio restrictions themselves. This is because they determine the size and volatility of the surplus, as well as defining the rules for dealing with a corresponding deficit. They thus influence the likelihood and cost of any deficiency, and hence the importance for life insurers and pension funds of maintaining a stable valuation of assets relative to liabilities, independent of portfolio limits;
- minimum rates of return set annually by regulation can constrain diversification even when quantitative limits are not stringent (OECD 2000). This is because they limit holdings of volatile assets which could reduce returns below the limit in one year, even if they offer a high mean return;
- as regards accounting standards, application of accounting principles, which insist on positive net worth of the fund at all times, carry equities on the balance sheet at the lower of book value and market value and calculate returns net of unrealised capital gains (as in Germany and Switzerland) and restrain equity holdings by life insurers and pension funds independently of the portfolio regulations (see Hepp, 1992);

- liabilities have a major influence, for example on the share of bonds, in that:
  (a) inflation sensitivity of liabilities will determine the demand for assets acting as inflation hedges such as index linked bonds, as well as assets whose return is unaffected by inflation such as real estate and equities; nominal liabilities require only money fixed assets;
  (b) the need for cash flow will play an important role by determining the need for liquidity to meet (known or uncertain) cash flows, for example in the context of growing maturity of pension funds, and policy loans/early surrender for life insurers;
  (c) duration of liabilities in combination with the strictness of minimum funding and solvency rules will set a benchmark for the duration of assets – or if they are not matched, to the scope of interest rate risk;
  Note that besides differing between countries, these factors will differ strongly between individual life companies and pension funds.
- as noted, higher taxation on bonds than equities makes the former an attractive investment to tax-exempt investors such as pension funds;
- ownership and control of pension funds may influence portfolios, via the degree of risk aversion of those controlling the fund and the degree to which those holding residual risks (i.e. benefiting from a surplus or funding a deficit) can control asset distributions. Similar differences may exist between mutual and listed insurance companies, where the latter may be more aggressive in risk-taking;
- concerning international diversification, in small countries, the assets of institutional investors often in practice exceed the entire domestic equity market, and hence simple liquidity considerations necessitate international investment, abstracting from risk/return considerations, if regulations permit;
- the structure of insurance and asset management markets and related levels of competition is likely to impact on the efficiency of investment. In particular, protection of fund managers from external competition may lead to a sub-optimal investment strategy from the point of view of beneficiaries, with low yielding assets held as well as high commissions charged;
- whereas in principle capital market activity should ensure that asset returns are equalised across countries, owing to international investment restrictions, exchange controls etc. this has not always been the case in the past, resulting in markedly different real returns on assets. In this context, inter-country differences in strategic bond holding may also relate to asset returns;
- financial structure more generally may have an important role to play.

In traditionally bank-dominated economies, where capital markets play a subordinate role, it may be loans that dominate the portfolios of long-term institutional investors.

## 10.4 LIFE INSURANCE AND PENSION FUND BALANCE SHEETS

Turning to the balance sheet data for the combined insurance and pension fund sectors, aggregated data for portfolio shares are shown in Table 10.1. The most sizeable difference is in the share of equities as opposed to that of bonds. In the UK, the combined sector holds 60 per cent of assets in equity, and in the US 45 per cent. Elsewhere, the share of equity is much lower, 30–35 per cent in Canada and Italy and below 25 per cent in Germany, Japan and France. In most countries, the offset is a larger share of bonds, with over 45 per cent of the portfolio being held in bonds in Japan, France, Canada, and Italy. In Germany, long-term institutional investors hold a relatively small proportion of bonds also, and hold a considerable proportion of deposits, mutual funds, and (until recently) loans. These patterns reflect the main financing instruments in the currency. Mutual fund holdings are also sizeable in France, and are growing in the US, UK and Italy.

In general, these patterns reflect two factors. First, there is the relative size of life insurance companies compared with pension funds. In the US, UK and Canada, the pension fund sector is large, whereas elsewhere the life insurance sector predominates. Pension funds tend to hold more aggressive portfolios than life insurers, because their liabilities are defined in terms of average earnings (real liabilities), and hence they need to obtain a return in excess of average earnings growth. The second factor is the portfolio regulations that apply to the sectors as noted above. In the US and UK, these are based on 'prudent person' rules, which require diversification but do not insist on maxima for any given instrument (Davis, 2001a). Elsewhere, portfolio regulations, which usually limit holdings of equity, tend to apply to both life insurers and pension funds.

Table 10.2 shows the size of long-term institutional investors relative to GDP. The UK stands out with assets equivalent to 170 per cent of GDP, followed by the US with 100 per cent of GDP (note that the total institutional sector in the US is comparable to the UK, since, as shown below, mutual funds in the US are extremely large). In other countries, long-term institutions account for 50–80 per cent of GDP, and in Italy only 20 per cent. These in turn reflect the scope of social security pensions.

Table 10.1 *Insurance and pension assets (per cent of total)*

| | | UK | US | Germany | Japan | Canada | France | Italy |
|---|---|---|---|---|---|---|---|---|
| Deposits | 1970 | 3.1 | 2.7 | 14.5 | 3.6 | 2.1 | 22.3 | 15.5 |
| | 1980 | 3.7 | 3.8 | 29.3 | 3.2 | 3.6 | 16.4 | 16.5 |
| | 1990 | 7.5 | 3.7 | 36.1 | 4.9 | 1.3 | 2.5 | 3.8 |
| | 1998 | 4.4 | 1.7 | 35.5 | 5.8 | 1.1 | 2.0 | 2.2 |
| | 2000 | 3.9 | 1.5 | 33.6 | 4.7 | 1.3 | 2.0 | 3.5 |
| Money market inst | 1970 | 0.7 | 0.8 | 0.0 | 1.1 | 1.3 | 1.1 | 0.0 |
| | 1980 | 1.2 | 3.5 | 0.0 | 1.0 | 4.1 | 0.3 | 0.0 |
| | 1990 | 1.0 | 5.0 | 0.0 | 7.3 | 8.4 | 6.2 | 0.7 |
| | 1998 | 1.2 | 4.7 | 0.0 | 1.5 | 5.4 | 3.9 | 1.3 |
| | 2000 | 1.2 | 5.0 | 0.0 | 1.9 | 7.1 | 2.9 | 0.5 |
| Loans | 1970 | 14.6 | 24.5 | 57.1 | 69.5 | 36.5 | 0.9 | 21.3 |
| | 1980 | 4.4 | 15.3 | 41.7 | 46.5 | 29.4 | 0.6 | 30.5 |
| | 1990 | 3.5 | 10.2 | 28.2 | 40.5 | 20.6 | 0.2 | 3.5 |
| | 1998 | 2.3 | 3.9 | 12.0 | 25.9 | 11.8 | 6.3 | 0.8 |
| | 2000 | 2.5 | 3.8 | 10.6 | 22.4 | 10.7 | 4.3 | 0.4 |
| Bonds | 1970 | 40.0 | 46.0 | 18.5 | 5.0 | 46.2 | 47.5 | 39.0 |
| | 1980 | 34.4 | 47.9 | 20.8 | 16.9 | 47.7 | 47.3 | 34.2 |
| | 1990 | 21.1 | 50.9 | 14.8 | 20.3 | 48.1 | 54.9 | 63.9 |
| | 1998 | 25.9 | 36.5 | 12.7 | 48.5 | 50.0 | 51.6 | 64.5 |
| | 2000 | 26.9 | 35.7 | 8.4 | 52.2 | 51.2 | 45.1 | 50.3 |
| Equity | 1970 | 41.0 | 25.6 | 9.9 | 20.6 | 14.0 | 28.3 | 24.2 |
| | 1980 | 52.5 | 28.9 | 8.2 | 32.0 | 15.3 | 35.3 | 18.9 |
| | 1990 | 59.9 | 28.3 | 12.2 | 26.4 | 21.5 | 20.9 | 28.0 |
| | 1998 | 58.2 | 45.1 | 18.7 | 17.5 | 31.6 | 20.2 | 28.6 |
| | 2000 | 57.3 | 45.1 | 23.1 | 18.3 | 29.7 | 23.6 | 35.9 |
| Mutual funds | 1970 | 0.6 | 0.4 | 0.0 | 0.1 | na | 0.0 | 0.0 |
| | 1980 | 3.7 | 0.7 | 0.0 | 0.4 | na | 0.0 | 0.0 |
| | 1990 | 7.1 | 1.9 | 8.6 | 0.6 | na | 15.2 | 0.0 |
| | 1998 | 7.9 | 8.1 | 21.0 | 0.7 | na | 16.1 | 2.6 |
| | 2000 | 8.3 | 8.9 | 24.3 | 0.5 | na | 22.2 | 9.5 |

Nevertheless, a feature of all countries is growth of institutions, owing to growing wealth and population ageing as well as pension reform. Comparing Table 10.2 and Table 9.2, it is apparent that growth has been more rapid than for banks. In the US, life companies and pension funds alone are larger than banks in terms of assets. The size of the sectors carries across to the subcomponents, where UK institutions hold equities equivalent to 100 per cent of GDP. Bond holdings of sectors such as the UK, US, Japan

Table 10.2 *Insurance and pension assets (per cent of GDP)*

| | | UK | US | Germany | Japan | Canada | France | Italy |
|---|---|---|---|---|---|---|---|---|
| Deposits | 1970 | 1.2 | 1.1 | 1.8 | 0.7 | 0.6 | 1.4 | 0.3 |
| | 1980 | 1.4 | 1.6 | 5.7 | 1.2 | 1.0 | 1.3 | 0.4 |
| | 1990 | 6.7 | 2.4 | 12.3 | 2.8 | 0.6 | 0.5 | 0.3 |
| | 1998 | 7.4 | 1.7 | 17.1 | 4.3 | 0.7 | 1.2 | 0.4 |
| | 2000 | 6.6 | 1.4 | 18.8 | 3.8 | 0.7 | 1.4 | 0.8 |
| Money market inst | 1970 | 0.3 | 0.3 | 0.0 | 0.2 | 0.4 | 0.1 | 0.0 |
| | 1980 | 0.4 | 1.5 | 0.0 | 0.4 | 1.2 | 0.0 | 0.0 |
| | 1990 | 0.9 | 3.2 | 0.0 | 4.1 | 3.6 | 1.1 | 0.1 |
| | 1998 | 2.0 | 4.8 | 0.0 | 1.1 | 3.1 | 2.3 | 0.2 |
| | 2000 | 2.0 | 4.9 | 0.0 | 1.5 | 3.9 | 2.0 | 0.1 |
| Loans | 1970 | 5.7 | 9.6 | 7.3 | 13.3 | 10.1 | 0.1 | 0.4 |
| | 1980 | 1.6 | 6.4 | 8.1 | 17.9 | 8.4 | 0.0 | 0.7 |
| | 1990 | 3.1 | 6.5 | 9.6 | 22.9 | 8.9 | 0.0 | 0.2 |
| | 1998 | 3.9 | 4.0 | 5.8 | 19.3 | 6.8 | 3.7 | 0.1 |
| | 2000 | 4.2 | 3.7 | 5.9 | 17.9 | 5.9 | 3.0 | 0.1 |
| Bonds | 1970 | 15.6 | 17.9 | 2.4 | 1.0 | 12.8 | 3.0 | 0.8 |
| | 1980 | 12.6 | 20.2 | 4.1 | 6.5 | 13.6 | 3.6 | 0.8 |
| | 1990 | 18.9 | 32.3 | 5.0 | 11.5 | 20.7 | 10.1 | 4.4 |
| | 1998 | 43.1 | 36.8 | 6.1 | 36.1 | 28.5 | 30.3 | 11.3 |
| | 2000 | 45.3 | 35.1 | 4.7 | 41.8 | 28.4 | 31.3 | 11.4 |
| Equity | 1970 | 16.0 | 10.0 | 1.3 | 3.9 | 3.9 | 1.8 | 0.5 |
| | 1980 | 19.3 | 12.2 | 1.6 | 12.3 | 4.4 | 2.7 | 0.5 |
| | 1990 | 53.7 | 18.0 | 4.2 | 14.9 | 9.2 | 3.9 | 1.9 |
| | 1998 | 96.7 | 45.4 | 9.0 | 13.1 | 18.1 | 11.9 | 5.0 |
| | 2000 | 96.3 | 44.3 | 12.9 | 14.7 | 16.5 | 16.3 | 8.1 |
| Mutual funds | 1970 | 0.2 | 0.2 | 0.0 | 0.0 | na | 0.0 | 0.0 |
| | 1980 | 1.4 | 0.3 | 0.0 | 0.2 | na | 0.0 | 0.0 |
| | 1990 | 6.3 | 1.2 | 2.9 | 0.4 | na | 2.8 | 0.0 |
| | 1998 | 13.1 | 8.2 | 10.1 | 0.5 | na | 9.4 | 0.5 |
| | 2000 | 13.9 | 8.8 | 13.6 | 0.4 | na | 15.4 | 2.1 |
| Total assets | 1970 | 39.1 | 39.0 | 12.7 | 19.1 | 27.8 | 6.3 | 2.1 |
| | 1980 | 36.7 | 42.1 | 19.5 | 38.5 | 28.6 | 7.6 | 2.5 |
| | 1990 | 89.6 | 63.6 | 33.9 | 56.5 | 43.0 | 18.4 | 6.9 |
| | 1998 | 166.2 | 100.7 | 48.1 | 74.4 | 57.1 | 58.7 | 17.5 |
| | 2000 | 168.2 | 98.3 | 55.9 | 80.1 | 55.5 | 69.3 | 22.6 |

Note: UK data for 1970 include general insurance.

Table 10.3 *Insurance and pension liabilities (per cent of total)*

| | | UK | US | Germany | Japan | Canada | France | Italy |
|---|---|---|---|---|---|---|---|---|
| Loans | 1970 | 0.0 | 0.0 | 0.2 | 0.0 | 0.0 | 0.2 | 1.8 |
| | 1980 | 0.0 | 0.0 | 0.4 | 0.0 | 0.4 | 0.1 | 1.7 |
| | 1990 | 1.0 | 0.0 | 0.2 | 0.0 | 0.6 | 0.0 | 1.9 |
| | 1998 | 0.9 | 0.0 | 0.6 | 0.0 | 0.6 | 5.2 | 2.1 |
| | 2000 | 1.2 | 0.0 | 0.6 | 0.0 | 0.3 | 4.6 | 1.2 |
| Bonds | 1970 | 0.0 | 0.0 | 0.0 | 0.0 | 0.0 | 0.0 | 0.0 |
| | 1980 | 0.0 | 0.0 | 0.0 | 0.0 | 0.0 | 0.0 | 0.0 |
| | 1990 | 0.0 | 0.0 | 0.0 | 0.2 | 0.0 | 0.0 | 0.0 |
| | 1998 | 0.0 | 0.0 | 0.0 | 0.1 | 0.0 | 0.1 | 0.0 |
| | 2000 | 0.0 | 0.0 | 0.0 | 0.1 | 0.0 | 0.3 | 0.9 |
| Equity | 1970 | 0.0 | 0.0 | 4.0 | 0.9 | 0.2 | 9.5 | 9.6 |
| | 1980 | 0.0 | 0.0 | 1.4 | 1.4 | 0.2 | 6.3 | 19.1 |
| | 1990 | 4.5 | 0.0 | 14.6 | 0.4 | 0.5 | 42.1 | 52.2 |
| | 1998 | 5.0 | 0.0 | 19.9 | 1.9 | 0.7 | 11.5 | 37.1 |
| | 2000 | 5.0 | 0.0 | 24.1 | 2.1 | 1.3 | 11.6 | 33.9 |
| Life and pension claims | 1970 | 100.0 | 100.0 | 95.8 | 99.1 | 99.8 | 90.3 | 88.6 |
| | 1980 | 100.0 | 100.0 | 98.2 | 98.6 | 99.4 | 93.6 | 79.2 |
| | 1990 | 94.6 | 100.0 | 84.0 | 99.4 | 98.9 | 57.8 | 45.9 |
| | 1998 | 94.2 | 100.0 | 73.5 | 98.0 | 98.7 | 83.2 | 60.8 |
| | 2000 | 93.8 | 100.0 | 69.9 | 97.8 | 98.4 | 83.5 | 64.0 |

and France are over 30 per cent of GDP, equivalent to a sizeable proportion of government debt (although bear in mind that bonds held are also private and foreign).

Liabilities of long-term institutions (Table 10.3) are mainly in the form of life and pension claims *per se*. On the other hand, reflecting the role of life insurance companies, equity accounts for over 10 per cent of liabilities in France, and over 20 per cent in Germany and Italy. A solvency margin between assets and liabilities is thus maintained. Debt financing of institutional investors is not, however, common. Liabilities relative to GDP are virtually identical to assets (Table 10.4).

## 10.5 MUTUAL FUND BALANCE SHEETS

Turning to mutual funds (Table 10.5), asset-distribution data for Italy are not available from the flow of funds balance sheets and some years are missing for the UK, Germany and France. The portfolio choice of mutual

Table 10.4 *Insurance and pension liabilities (per cent of GDP)*

| | | UK | US | Germany | Japan | Canada | France | Italy |
|---|---|---|---|---|---|---|---|---|
| Loans | 1970 | 0.0 | 0.0 | 0.0 | 0.0 | 0.0 | 0.0 | 0.1 |
| | 1980 | 0.0 | 0.0 | 0.1 | 0.0 | 0.1 | 0.0 | 0.1 |
| | 1990 | 1.0 | 0.0 | 0.1 | 0.0 | 0.3 | 0.0 | 0.2 |
| | 1998 | 1.6 | 0.0 | 0.3 | 0.0 | 0.4 | 3.0 | 0.5 |
| | 2000 | 2.1 | 0.0 | 0.0 | 0.0 | 0.2 | 3.1 | 0.4 |
| Bonds | 1970 | 0.0 | 0.0 | 0.0 | 0.0 | 0.0 | 0.0 | 0.0 |
| | 1980 | 0.0 | 0.0 | 0.0 | 0.0 | 0.0 | 0.0 | 0.0 |
| | 1990 | 1.0 | 0.0 | 0.0 | 0.1 | 0.0 | 0.0 | 0.0 |
| | 1998 | 1.6 | 0.0 | 0.0 | 0.1 | 0.0 | 0.0 | 0.0 |
| | 2000 | 2.1 | 0.0 | 0.0 | 0.1 | 0.0 | 0.2 | 0.3 |
| Equity | 1970 | 0.0 | 0.0 | 0.5 | 0.2 | 0.1 | 0.8 | 0.4 |
| | 1980 | 0.0 | 0.0 | 0.3 | 0.4 | 0.1 | 0.5 | 0.6 |
| | 1990 | 0.0 | 0.0 | 5.0 | 0.3 | 0.2 | 13.6 | 6.4 |
| | 1998 | 0.0 | 0.0 | 10.9 | 1.4 | 0.5 | 6.6 | 8.7 |
| | 2000 | 0.0 | 0.0 | 15.3 | 1.6 | 0.9 | 7.8 | 11.0 |
| Life and pension claims | 1970 | 47.0 | 33.2 | 0.5 | 16.5 | 29.3 | 7.5 | 3.5 |
| | 1980 | 43.2 | 37.7 | 0.3 | 29.3 | 30.7 | 7.8 | 2.6 |
| | 1990 | 98.3 | 58.3 | 5.0 | 71.7 | 48.2 | 18.6 | 5.6 |
| | 1998 | 173.5 | 91.8 | 10.9 | 73.4 | 69.2 | 47.7 | 14.3 |
| | 2000 | 160.3 | 90.3 | 44.6 | 78.4 | 67.8 | 56.1 | 20.7 |
| Total | 1970 | 47.0 | 33.2 | 12.9 | 16.6 | 29.3 | 8.3 | 3.9 |
| | 1980 | 43.2 | 37.7 | 18.7 | 29.7 | 30.9 | 8.4 | 3.2 |
| | 1990 | 103.9 | 58.3 | 28.9 | 72.1 | 48.7 | 32.2 | 12.2 |
| | 1998 | 184.2 | 91.8 | 40.3 | 74.9 | 70.1 | 57.4 | 23.4 |
| | 2000 | 170.9 | 90.3 | 63.8 | 80.2 | 68.9 | 67.2 | 32.4 |

funds is of course largely driven by the preferences of the household sector, who choose to buy money market, bond or equity funds according to their risk and liquidity preferences (Davis and Steil, 2001). There are also balanced funds which hold at their discretion a variety of financial assets.

The data suggest that mutual fund holders in the UK and US have the strongest risk preference, with over 50 per cent in equities, although the figure has also been rising elsewhere (except in Japan, perhaps reflecting poor performance of shares in the 1990s). Rising equity shares possibly reflect a decline in risk aversion or merely a belief that equities will continue to do as well as they did in the 1990s. An interesting feature is that, in the US and Canada, equity holdings were even higher in 1970, before the bear market of the mid-1970s led to increased risk aversion. This was also,

Table 10.5 *Mutual fund assets (per cent of total)*

| | | UK | US | Germany | Japan | Canada | France | Italy |
|---|---|---|---|---|---|---|---|---|
| Deposits | 1970 | 2.1 | 0.0 | na | 0.0 | 15.0 | 10.5 | na |
| | 1980 | 2.4 | 19.3 | na | 0.0 | 6.7 | 7.5 | na |
| | 1990 | 5.0 | 5.2 | 11.6 | 0.0 | 2.5 | 4.1 | na |
| | 1998 | 4.0 | 3.1 | 7.3 | 19.1 | 3.8 | 10.0 | na |
| | 2000 | na | 3.6 | na | 5.0 | 3.9 | na | na |
| Money market inst | 1970 | 3.0 | 5.3 | na | 14.2 | 2.4 | 0.6 | na |
| | 1980 | 1.0 | 28.7 | na | 14.5 | 6.9 | 0.8 | na |
| | 1990 | 1.9 | 26.0 | 0.5 | 27.3 | 22.6 | 36.1 | na |
| | 1998 | 1.3 | 13.8 | 0.5 | 19.5 | 24.7 | 26.8 | na |
| | 2000 | na | 15.9 | na | 21.9 | 24.9 | na | na |
| Loans | 1970 | 0.0 | 0.0 | na | 0.0 | 0.5 | 1.6 | na |
| | 1980 | 0.0 | 0.0 | na | 0.0 | 38.9 | 0.6 | na |
| | 1990 | 0.0 | 0.0 | 0.0 | 0.0 | 10.3 | 7.2 | na |
| | 1998 | 0.0 | 0.0 | 0.0 | 0.0 | 3.4 | 0.0 | na |
| | 2000 | na | 0.0 | na | 0.0 | 2.1 | na | na |
| Bonds | 1970 | 6.1 | 11.7 | na | 39.5 | 6.5 | 42.3 | na |
| | 1980 | 5.1 | 19.4 | na | 32.9 | 14.6 | 50.3 | na |
| | 1990 | 5.5 | 46.9 | 68.1 | 28.8 | 21.7 | 37.3 | na |
| | 1998 | 8.4 | 32.2 | 51.8 | 41.1 | 25.2 | 28.8 | na |
| | 2000 | na | 28.3 | na | 45.5 | 22.5 | na | na |
| Equity | 1970 | 88.7 | 83.1 | na | 46.3 | 75.6 | 45.0 | na |
| | 1980 | 91.6 | 32.5 | na | 52.6 | 33.0 | 40.8 | na |
| | 1990 | 87.6 | 21.8 | 19.8 | 44.0 | 42.8 | 15.3 | na |
| | 1998 | 86.3 | 51.0 | 40.4 | 20.3 | 42.9 | 34.3 | na |
| | 2000 | na | 52.1 | na | 27.5 | 46.7 | na | na |

however, before the advent of money market mutual funds. Of the other assets, money market instruments are indeed sizeable in Japan, Canada, France and to a lesser extent the US. High shares of deposits and money market instruments are a notable feature of Japanese mutual funds, which parallels the asset price turbulence of the 1990s and accompanying shifts by households themselves to deposits (Table 5.1).

The relative size of the mutual fund sectors is apparent from Table 10.6, which compares assets to GDP. It can be seen that those in the US and France are far larger than those elsewhere, although rapid growth is also apparent in Germany and Italy. French and US mutual funds are over 50 per cent of GDP, while in Italy, Germany and Canada they are around 35–45 per cent. Table 10.7 shows that mutual funds tend not to leverage

Table 10.6 *Mutual fund assets (per cent of GDP)*

| | | UK | US | Germany | Japan | Canada | France | Italy |
|---|---|---|---|---|---|---|---|---|
| Deposits | 1970 | 0.1 | 0.0 | na | 0.0 | 0.3 | 0.2 | na |
| | 1980 | 0.1 | 1.0 | na | 0.0 | 0.1 | 0.2 | na |
| | 1990 | 0.6 | 1.0 | 1.1 | 0.0 | 0.1 | 1.2 | na |
| | 1998 | 1.0 | 1.7 | 2.0 | 1.6 | 0.9 | 4.5 | na |
| | 2000 | na | 2.3 | na | 0.5 | 0.9 | na | na |
| Money market inst | 1970 | 0.2 | 0.3 | na | 0.3 | 0.0 | 0.0 | na |
| | 1980 | 0.1 | 1.4 | na | 0.7 | 0.1 | 0.0 | na |
| | 1990 | 0.2 | 5.1 | 0.0 | 3.1 | 1.0 | 11.0 | na |
| | 1998 | 0.3 | 7.7 | 0.1 | 1.6 | 6.0 | 12.1 | na |
| | 2000 | na | 9.9 | na | 2.3 | 6.0 | na | na |
| Loans | 1970 | 0.0 | 0.0 | na | 0.0 | 0.0 | 0.0 | na |
| | 1980 | 0.0 | 0.0 | na | 0.0 | 0.4 | 0.0 | na |
| | 1990 | 0.0 | 0.0 | 0.0 | 0.0 | 0.4 | 2.2 | na |
| | 1998 | 0.0 | 0.0 | 0.0 | 0.0 | 0.8 | 0.0 | na |
| | 2000 | na | 0.0 | na | 0.0 | 0.5 | na | na |
| Bonds | 1970 | 0.3 | 0.6 | na | 0.9 | 0.1 | 0.8 | na |
| | 1980 | 0.3 | 1.0 | na | 1.6 | 0.2 | 1.4 | na |
| | 1990 | 0.6 | 9.2 | 6.3 | 3.3 | 0.9 | 11.3 | na |
| | 1998 | 2.1 | 18.0 | 14.6 | 3.3 | 6.1 | 13.0 | na |
| | 2000 | na | 17.6 | na | 4.8 | 5.4 | na | na |
| Equity | 1970 | 4.7 | 4.2 | na | 1.0 | 1.4 | 0.9 | na |
| | 1980 | 5.2 | 1.6 | na | 2.5 | 0.4 | 1.1 | na |
| | 1990 | 10.2 | 4.3 | 1.8 | 5.0 | 1.8 | 4.6 | na |
| | 1998 | 22.0 | 28.5 | 11.3 | 1.7 | 10.5 | 15.4 | na |
| | 2000 | na | 32.5 | na | 2.9 | 11.2 | na | na |
| Total assets | 1970 | 5.3 | 5.0 | na | 2.2 | 1.9 | 1.9 | na |
| | 1980 | 5.7 | 5.0 | na | 4.8 | 1.1 | 2.7 | na |
| | 1990 | 11.6 | 19.5 | 9.2 | 11.5 | 4.2 | 30.4 | 3.6 |
| | 1998 | 25.5 | 55.9 | 28.1 | 8.1 | 24.4 | 45.0 | 34.9 |
| | 2000 | 32.4 | 62.3 | 40.4 | 10.6 | 24.1 | 60.6 | 41.4 |

themselves in any of the countries shown (by taking on loans), while Table 10.8 largely repeats the information in Table 10.6.

Table 10.7 *Mutual fund liabilities (per cent of total)*

| | | UK | US | Germany | Japan | Canada | France | Italy |
|---|---|---|---|---|---|---|---|---|
| Loans | 1970 | 0.7 | 0.0 | na | 0.0 | 0.0 | 1.3 | na |
| | 1980 | 7.1 | 0.0 | na | 0.0 | 0.2 | 0.0 | na |
| | 1990 | 6.2 | 0.0 | 0.7 | 0.0 | 0.1 | 0.0 | na |
| | 1998 | 4.0 | 0.0 | 1.4 | 0.0 | 0.1 | 0.4 | na |
| | 2000 | na | 0.0 | na | 0.0 | 0.2 | 0.0 | na |
| Mutual | 1970 | 99.3 | 100.0 | na | 100.0 | 100.0 | 98.7 | na |
| Fund | 1980 | 92.9 | 100.0 | na | 100.0 | 99.8 | 100.0 | na |
| claims | 1990 | 93.8 | 100.0 | 100.0 | 100.0 | 99.9 | 100.0 | na |
| | 1998 | 96.0 | 100.0 | 100.0 | 100.0 | 99.9 | 99.6 | na |
| | 2000 | na | 100.0 | na | 100.0 | 99.8 | 0.0 | na |

Table 10.8 *Mutual fund liabilities (per cent of GDP)*

| | | UK | US | Germany | Japan | Canada | France | Italy |
|---|---|---|---|---|---|---|---|---|
| Loans | 1970 | 0.0 | 0.0 | 0.0 | 0.0 | 0.0 | 0.0 | na |
| | 1980 | 0.4 | 0.0 | 0.0 | 0.0 | 0.0 | 0.0 | na |
| | 1990 | 0.6 | 0.0 | 0.1 | 0.0 | 0.0 | 0.0 | na |
| | 1998 | 0.9 | 0.0 | 0.4 | 0.0 | 0.0 | 0.2 | na |
| | 2000 | na | 0.0 | 0.0 | 0.0 | 0.1 | na | na |
| Mutual | 1970 | 5.4 | 4.4 | 0.0 | 1.8 | 3.0 | 1.6 | na |
| Fund | 1980 | 5.8 | 4.7 | 0.0 | 3.0 | 1.5 | 2.6 | na |
| claims | 1990 | 8.5 | 18.8 | 9.8 | 13.8 | 5.3 | 31.1 | na |
| | 1998 | 20.7 | 55.0 | 30.2 | 8.6 | 33.4 | 44.8 | na |
| | 2000 | na | 62.0 | 47.0 | 10.7 | 36.1 | na | na |
| Total | 1970 | 5.4 | 4.4 | 0.0 | 1.8 | 3.0 | 1.6 | na |
| | 1980 | 6.2 | 4.7 | 0.0 | 3.0 | 1.5 | 2.6 | na |
| | 1990 | 9.1 | 18.8 | 9.8 | 13.8 | 5.3 | 31.1 | 3.6 |
| | 1998 | 21.6 | 55.0 | 30.2 | 8.6 | 33.4 | 45.0 | 34.9 |
| | 2000 | 32.6 | 62.0 | 40.4 | 10.7 | 36.2 | 60.6 | 41.4 |

# 11 Confronting theoretical paradigms with the data

In this chapter we seek to bring together some overarching issues, drawing both on the theory and the pattern of sectoral balance sheets. We assess whether structural differences are in line with the theoretical division of bank- and market-based financial systems, whether any convergence in financial structure is detectable, whether there are exceptional features in France making it a hybrid system, and the evidence for differing behaviour or performance across economies depending on financial structure.

## 11.1 ARE STRUCTURAL DIFFERENCES IN LINE WITH THE STYLISED MODELS?

On the first issue, we drew up Table 11.1, which seeks to confront some of the expectations one can derive from the literature on financial structure with the balance sheet data. Such an assessment must inevitably be rather summary and broad brush, not least given that the paradigms themselves are often lacking in clarity and precision. We have selected France, Italy, Germany and Japan as the bank-dominated countries and the UK, US and Canada as the market-based ones.

For the household sector, the theory expects the bank-dominated countries to have assets based on banks and/or money-fixed bonds, little consumer credit and relatively low asset and liability/GDP ratios. The asset pattern reflects the lack of funded pensions, the liability pattern the priority of banks given to lending to industry. In contrast, the Anglo-Saxon households are expected to have a focus on equity, life and pension funds and mutual funds, consumer credit as well as mortgages and generally large ratios to GDP on both sides of the balance sheet. Most of these predictions

Table 11.1 *An assessment of balance sheets in the light of theory – non-financial sectors*

| Sector | Expectation from theory – bank based | Expectation from theory – market based | Positive deviation | Negative deviation |
|---|---|---|---|---|
| Household assets | High bonds and deposits, low assets/GDP (unfunded pensions) | High equities, life/pensions, mutual funds, high assets/GDP | Italy, Germany high mutual funds; France high equity holdings, Japan assets/GDP high | UK low direct equity holdings, France low direct bond holdings, Canada assets/GDP low |
| Household liabilities | Low debt, mainly mortgages | High debt, with high consumer credit | Germany and Japan debt/GDP comparable to market based. Italy high share of consumer credit | |
| Corporate assets | No strong predictions, possibly focus on bank deposits (compensating balances) and equity (crossholdings) | No strong predictions, possibly focus on MMIs, bonds for liquidity. Higher liquidity due to lack of relationship banks | UK high equity holdings; Canada and US high deposit share, Germany high bonds, Japan high liquidity/GDP | UK low MMIs and bonds, US low liquidity/GDP |

Table 11.1 (*Continued*)

| | | | | |
|---|---|---|---|---|
| Corporate liabilities | High share of loans, high debt/GDP (relationship banking) | High share of bonds, equities and MMIs, low debt/GDP | France high equity, Japan high bonds, UK high debt/GDP | France low loans, UK low bonds, Canada low equity, Italy low debt/GDP |
| General government assets | No strong predictions, possibly focus on bank deposits, loans, equity | No strong predictions, possibly focus on bonds and MMIs (securitised) | UK high loans | UK low bonds and MMIs |
| General government liabilities | Higher pension liabilities/ GDP due to generous social security | More securitised debt | UK high loans and deposits, Japan high bonds (due to Trust Fund Bureau), Canada high pension liabilities | |
| Foreign assets | No strong predictions, but foreigners would be expected to hold deposits, loans, reflecting financial system | No strong predictions, but foreigners would be expected to hold equities and bonds reflecting financial system | UK high deposit and loans (international financial centre), France and Japan highest equity | France, low loans |
| Foreign liabilities | No strong predictions, possibly more equity and bonds to balance portfolios | No strong predictions, possibly more deposits and loans to balance portfolios | Japan high loans | Japan low equity, France low bonds |

are indeed borne out, not least the importance of life and pension funds in the market-based countries. On the other hand, Japan has a large household asset and liability/GDP ratio, as does Germany on the liability side. Italy and Germany have large mutual funds, and France equity holdings, while the UK's direct equity holdings are relatively low. We note that in Table 5.5, where institutional assets are reallocated to households, these differences were much less marked for a number of countries. We consider this one of the most interesting results and it strongly suggests that Germany and Japan are the outliers. They have high deposits and low equity (as well as securities more generally), whereas the others are quite comparable in terms of household asset preferences if one allows for indirect as well as direct holdings of bonds, equities, deposits and money market paper.

In respect of companies, the strongest predictions are on the liability side, where the bank-based countries are expected to have a preponderance of loans, and high debt/GDP given the insurance offered by relationship banking (Allen and Gale, 2000). Market-based countries are expected to have high proportions of equities, and debt finance (at a lower level) in the form of bonds and money market instruments (MMIs). Again, these are largely visible in the data, but we note *inter alia* that French companies have high shares of equity and low loans, Japan high bonds, the UK low bonds and Canada low equity. The debt/GDP ratio is relatively high in the UK and low in Italy. Note that Germany and the US are not mentioned here as exceptions, and can again be seen as archetypal.

As noted in the table, the corporate asset side does not have strong theoretical predictions, although the bank-based systems might have more deposits given the predominance of banks (and compensating balance requirements) and equity (given cross-holdings). The market-based countries might need more liquidity (in MMIs and bonds) given the lack of relationship banks. In fact the UK has high equity holdings relative to assets, Canada and the US high deposits and Germany high bonds. Whereas Japan has high liquidity/GDP (perhaps owing to the cycle), the US has low liquidity/GDP.

On the side of general government, we see as expected that the bank-based countries have higher pension liabilities due to generous social security (Canada is one exception, as a market-based country also having high liabilities). Our expectation that market-based countries have more bonds on the liability side is not entirely borne out. The UK has a high level of loans and deposits on both sides of the balance sheet, in contrast to the US and Canada, while Japan appears to have a high share of bonds. In fact the Japanese public sector including public financial institutions has deposits outstanding to the non-public sectors via the post office system. This in turn holds bonds in the Trust Fund Bureau, omitted from the tables.

For the foreign sector, there are no strong predictions from theory. Hence we note in the table more as a stylised fact that in the bank-based systems, foreigners tend to hold more deposits and loans, while they would hold securities in the market-based ones. The deviations include the UK, with high deposits given the international financial centre it hosts, and France and Japan where foreigners have the highest share of equity, perhaps reflecting the small size of the domestic institutional sectors. Equally, we note that for foreign sector liabilities (gross foreign assets of the country) there is a tendency for the domestic sector to balance its portfolio, by holding market-based foreign instruments in the bank-based system and vice versa in the market based.

Moving to Table 11.2, in the financial sector we expect loans to predominate on the asset side in the bank-based systems and for the financial sector to be smaller overall. Bonds and equities should be more important in larger market-based systems. An indeterminate factor is whether deposits as assets of the financial sector will be larger in market-based systems due to needs for liquidity of institutional investors, or whether deposits in all countries are largely determined by the size of interbank markets, for which the theory has no strong predictions.

In fact, France and Japan have large financial sectors and the US and Canada relatively small ones. Canada has high loans and France high equities and MMIs, while France has low loans, and the UK low bonds and MMIs. The status of France as a transition system is indicated, while the UK does not have such developed bond and money markets as does North America. As regards deposits, these are not well correlated with the size of non-bank financial institutions, suggesting it is the size of the interbank market which is the distinguishing feature.

On the liability side for the financial sector, one expects more deposits for the bank-based systems and more life and pension funds, mutual funds and possibly securities for the market-based. The UK is a key hybrid here, having high deposits owing to the financial centre, low mutual funds and bonds, while France and Italy have high shares of mutual funds, France has developed money market financing and for Germany bond finance of financial institutions is important.

Some of these points carry over to the banking sector. The expectation on the asset side is for more deposits and possibly equities in bank-based countries (the latter reflecting shares held in the context of banking relationships), and a larger banking sector than in the market-based systems. Banks in the latter might be expected to hold more debt securities. Whereas most of these suggestions carry through, we have high bond shares

Table 11.2 *An assessment of balance sheets in the light of theory – financial sectors*

| Sector | Expectation from theory – bank based | Expectation from theory – market based | Positive deviation | Negative deviation |
|---|---|---|---|---|
| Financial sector assets | Loans predominate (banks), smaller overall financial sector | Bonds and equities predominate, possibly deposits (institutional investors), larger financial sector | Canada high loans, France quite high equities, MMIs, France and Japan large assets/GDP | France low loans, UK low bonds and MMIs, US and Canada low deposits, US and Canada small assets/GDP |
| Financial sector liabilities | More deposits | More life and pension funds, mutual funds, securities | UK high deposits (financial centre), France and Italy high mutual funds, France high MMIs, Germany high bonds | UK low mutual funds and bonds |
| Banking sector assets | More loans and equity (relationship banking), larger banking sector/GDP | More debt securities, smaller banking sector/GDP | Germany and Japan high bonds, Canada high loans, UK large assets/GDP | France low loans, UK and Canada low bonds, Italy low assets/GDP |
| Banking sector liabilities | More deposits | More bonds and MMIs | France high MMIs, Germany high bonds, UK high deposits | Italy low deposits |

Table 11.2 (*Continued*)

| | | | | |
|---|---|---|---|---|
| Insurance and pension assets and liabilities | More bonds, deposits, lower assets/GDP | More equities, possibly mutual funds, larger assets/GDP | Canada high bonds, Germany and France high mutual funds, large assets/GDP in Japan | Relatively small assets/GDP in Canada |
| Mutual fund assets and liabilities | More bonds, smaller sector | More equities, MMIs, larger sector | Large deposits and MMIs in France, large assets/GDP in France | Small assets/GDP in Canada and UK |

for banks in Germany and Japan but low in the UK and Canada; also a high loan share in Canada and low loans in France. The UK has an atypically large banking sector relative to GDP (reflecting again the financial centre) while Italy's is small, owing to lesser financial development than the rest of the G-7. If foreign currency bank assets and liabilities are omitted for the UK, the banking sector would be much more comparable with the other countries, and indeed smaller than Germany, Japan and France, albeit still twice as large as in the US and Canada.

Banking sector liabilities are not necessarily deposits in the bank-based systems and market-based instruments in the Anglo-Saxon countries. France has high shares of MMI financing, and Germany bond financing, while the UK has a high share of deposits, an instrument which for Italian banks is relatively unimportant. It can be argued that the high degree of bond finance of the German banking sector is still consistent with bank domination, in that companies borrow in the form of loans from banks, which then issue bonds to match the maturity of their balance sheets. Banks act as proxies for firms in the bond market.

Finally, looking at the institutional sectors, we anticipate that both life and pension funds on the one hand and mutual funds on the other will be larger in the market-based systems, while they will also be more equity-based, with less bonds and deposits on their balance sheets. Higher risk aversion as well as portfolio restrictions and a relatively greater importance of life insurance over pension funds mean that the opposite will be true for the bank-based countries. These again are generally true, but the long-term institutions are large in Japan as well as in the UK and US, and not in Canada. Canadian institutions hold relatively large proportions of bonds. The large size of the mutual fund sector in France, and its small size in the UK and Canada has already been noted. France also has a large money market mutual fund sector, because of which the mutual funds in that country hold a large share of bonds and MMIs relative to their assets.

Whereas the table and analysis focus on stocks and balance sheets, it is worth noting that there are also marked flow differences. Table 5.7 showed that, over 1995–2000, the flow of household borrowing is indeed highest in the UK, US and Canada. Table 5.6 showed that household sectors invest most heavily in mutual funds in the US, and in life and pension funds in the UK, but also in France. UK and US households decumulate equities while other sectors accumulate them, notably in Canada. After Japan, it is the UK household sector that accumulates most deposits. Moreover, as seen in Table 4.6, UK and Canadian firms raise more funds from equity issues than others, while US data are not comparable. But UK firms were also the largest borrowers from banks.

Concluding this section, we acknowledge that the division made in Section 1.5 is not watertight, and that France in particular may be in transition to a market-based system (see also Section 11.3), while Japan is also deeply affected by the current economic and financial crisis. Indeed, it is notable, in taking an overview of the tables, that the US and Germany are fairly rarely encountered, conforming as they do quite closely to the theoretical expectations. They are perhaps closest to the 'ideal type' of bank-dominated and market-based financial systems. Meanwhile, Italy could be seen as simply a less developed financial system than the others, to help explain some of its specific features.

## 11.2 ARE THERE INDICATIONS OF CONVERGENCE?

We calculated rough indicators of convergence in balance sheet structure for selected sectors, namely households, corporates (liabilities and liquidity), the financial and banking sectors. We suggest that these are at the heart of financial structure and financial intermediation, and summarise the degree to which financial systems differ in terms of balance sheet outcomes. We assessed convergence by standard deviations and coefficients of variation of portfolio shares for three groups, the G-7, the EU-4 (UK, France, Germany and Italy) and the EMU-3 (France, Germany and Italy). Our main focus is on the standard deviation. Note that standard deviations are a

Table 11.3 *Convergence of household sector financial asset portfolios*

| | | Standard deviation of portfolio shares | | | Coefficient of variation of portfolio shares | | |
|---|---|---|---|---|---|---|---|
| | | G7 | EU-4 | EMU-3 | G7 | EU-4 | EMU-3 |
| Deposits notes coin | 1970 | 14.9 | 11.5 | 4.0 | 0.31 | 0.21 | 0.07 |
| | 1980 | 14.1 | 11.4 | 1.3 | 0.26 | 0.19 | 0.02 |
| | 1990 | 10.1 | 8.6 | 7.9 | 0.26 | 0.21 | 0.18 |
| | 1998 | 14.7 | 7.9 | 6.4 | 0.46 | 0.26 | 0.19 |
| | 2000 | 14.2 | 6.1 | 6.2 | 0.48 | 0.22 | 0.21 |
| Money market inst | 1970 | 0.3 | 0.1 | 0.0 | 1.65 | 1.81 | 1.73 |
| | 1980 | 3.5 | 4.7 | 5.4 | 1.79 | 1.91 | 1.68 |
| | 1990 | 4.5 | 6.0 | 6.7 | 1.39 | 1.57 | 1.33 |
| | 1998 | 1.3 | 1.1 | 1.2 | 1.41 | 1.46 | 1.28 |
| | 2000 | 1.4 | 0.4 | 0.5 | 1.44 | 1.10 | 1.01 |
| Bonds | 1970 | 5.4 | 6.5 | 7.5 | 0.52 | 0.59 | 0.62 |
| | 1980 | 2.4 | 3.1 | 2.3 | 0.28 | 0.34 | 0.22 |
| | 1990 | 6.5 | 8.6 | 7.8 | 0.74 | 0.87 | 0.61 |
| | 1998 | 7.0 | 9.2 | 9.2 | 0.95 | 1.01 | 0.78 |
| | 2000 | 6.0 | 8.0 | 8.0 | 0.91 | 1.01 | 0.78 |
| Equity | 1970 | 9.4 | 10.5 | 11.2 | 0.44 | 0.52 | 0.63 |
| | 1980 | 6.8 | 4.1 | 4.3 | 0.51 | 0.39 | 0.46 |
| | 1990 | 7.2 | 8.7 | 10.7 | 0.43 | 0.49 | 0.60 |
| | 1998 | 9.2 | 8.2 | 9.2 | 0.44 | 0.39 | 0.41 |
| | 2000 | 9.9 | 10.0 | 10.9 | 0.44 | 0.41 | 0.40 |
| Mutual funds | 1970 | 1.0 | 0.8 | 0.0 | 1.27 | 2.00 | na |
| | 1980 | 0.9 | 1.2 | 1.4 | 1.07 | 1.31 | 1.73 |
| | 1990 | 4.7 | 6.0 | 6.3 | 1.11 | 1.13 | 0.91 |
| | 1998 | 5.7 | 5.4 | 4.4 | 0.78 | 0.54 | 0.37 |
| | 2000 | 6.0 | 4.9 | 4.3 | 0.71 | 0.44 | 0.34 |
| Life and pensions | 1970 | 8.7 | 8.2 | 5.0 | 0.46 | 0.58 | 0.47 |
| | 1980 | 12.1 | 14.2 | 6.6 | 0.57 | 0.83 | 0.63 |
| | 1990 | 14.3 | 18.0 | 6.8 | 0.52 | 0.79 | 0.47 |
| | 1998 | 14.8 | 19.6 | 6.8 | 0.47 | 0.68 | 0.35 |
| | 2000 | 13.4 | 17.2 | 6.6 | 0.42 | 0.61 | 0.32 |
| Memo: Assets/GDP ratio | 1970 | 40.6 | 40.3 | 12.5 | 0.34 | 0.39 | 0.15 |
| | 1980 | 34.4 | 13.9 | 5.5 | 0.28 | 0.14 | 0.06 |
| | 1990 | 40.3 | 32.7 | 22.6 | 0.23 | 0.21 | 0.16 |
| | 1998 | 49.9 | 58.1 | 23.5 | 0.22 | 0.27 | 0.13 |
| | 2000 | 44.3 | 51.8 | 34.5 | 0.19 | 0.23 | 0.17 |

Table 11.4 *Convergence of household sector liability portfolios*

| | | Standard deviation of portfolio shares | | | Coefficient of variation of portfolio shares | | |
|---|---|---|---|---|---|---|---|
| | | G7 | EU-4 | EMU-3 | G7 | EU-4 | EMU-3 |
| Consumer credit | 1970 | 11.3 | 8.1 | 8.6 | 0.65 | 0.49 | 0.47 |
| | 1980 | 11.4 | 9.9 | 12.0 | 0.60 | 0.49 | 0.57 |
| | 1990 | 12.8 | 13.1 | 14.8 | 0.66 | 0.58 | 0.59 |
| | 1998 | 7.6 | 7.7 | 8.9 | 0.47 | 0.56 | 0.71 |
| | 2000 | 7.6 | 7.3 | 7.6 | 0.47 | 0.54 | 0.65 |
| Housing loans | 1970 | 31.2 | 8.1 | 8.6 | 0.46 | 0.10 | 0.11 |
| | 1980 | 30.5 | 9.9 | 12.0 | 0.46 | 0.12 | 0.15 |
| | 1990 | 30.7 | 13.1 | 14.8 | 0.46 | 0.17 | 0.20 |
| | 1998 | 14.7 | 7.5 | 8.7 | 0.19 | 0.09 | 0.10 |
| | 2000 | 13.8 | 7.1 | 7.4 | 0.18 | 0.08 | 0.08 |
| Memo: Debt/GDP | 1970 | 14.9 | 13.0 | 15.8 | 0.51 | 0.59 | 0.74 |
| | 1980 | 18.1 | 18.1 | 22.2 | 0.47 | 0.63 | 0.77 |
| | 1990 | 19.7 | 20.0 | 18.8 | 0.37 | 0.46 | 0.51 |
| | 1998 | 21.0 | 24.9 | 26.3 | 0.37 | 0.51 | 0.62 |
| | 2000 | 21.4 | 26.0 | 26.5 | 0.36 | 0.50 | 0.60 |

function of the absolute size of the deviations and not the relative size. Hence, whereas there may be a greater deviation relative to the mean for a series with a small mean than a large mean, the standard deviation may show more divergence to the large mean series. We would contend that this is appropriate, as the main interest in convergence analysis is on the key items accounting for a significant share of portfolios. However, we also include the coefficient of variation (standard deviation/mean) as a memo item.

Table 11.3 shows the data for the household sector. According to the standard deviation data, shares of deposits, notes and coin are much more similar between EU countries than in the whole of the G-7 (as shown in Table 5.1), where this links partly to large deposits in Japan. There is evidence of convergence between the UK and the rest of the EU countries, as shown by comparing the second and third columns. Meanwhile there is more general convergence for money market instrument holdings. For bonds and equities, the series are volatile with little evidence of consistent convergence in any of the country groups. Both for the EMU-3 and EU-4, the standard deviation of equity is comparable at 10–11 per cent in 1970 and 2000 for example. Mutual funds were not important assets of the household sector before 1990 in most countries, hence it is interesting that, since then, there is some convergence in shares in the EU-4 and EMU-3,

Table 11.5 *Convergence of corporate sector liability portfolios*

| | | Standard deviation of portfolio shares | | | Coefficient of variation of portfolio shares | | |
|---|---|---|---|---|---|---|---|
| | | G7 | EU-4 | EMU-3 | G7 | EU-4 | EMU-3 |
| Money market inst | 1970 | 0.5 | 0.4 | 0.4 | 1.34 | 2.00 | 1.73 |
| | 1980 | 0.8 | 0.2 | 0.2 | 1.24 | 0.69 | 0.89 |
| | 1990 | 2.3 | 0.6 | 0.7 | 1.21 | 1.12 | 1.47 |
| | 1998 | 1.7 | 0.5 | 0.5 | 1.15 | 0.74 | 0.98 |
| | 2000 | 1.7 | 0.6 | 0.7 | 1.09 | 0.78 | 1.00 |
| Loans | 1970 | 23.5 | 19.6 | 13.3 | 0.58 | 0.45 | 0.26 |
| | 1980 | 20.4 | 17.3 | 14.0 | 0.47 | 0.38 | 0.27 |
| | 1990 | 22.5 | 17.7 | 20.8 | 0.52 | 0.41 | 0.46 |
| | 1998 | 16.2 | 11.4 | 11.8 | 0.52 | 0.36 | 0.34 |
| | 2000 | 14.6 | 12.3 | 13.9 | 0.50 | 0.42 | 0.44 |
| Bonds | 1970 | 7.1 | 2.4 | 2.6 | 0.74 | 0.38 | 0.45 |
| | 1980 | 7.2 | 1.3 | 1.2 | 0.94 | 0.37 | 0.32 |
| | 1990 | 6.7 | 1.0 | 0.6 | 0.80 | 0.25 | 0.16 |
| | 1998 | 6.5 | 1.9 | 1.3 | 0.81 | 0.57 | 0.52 |
| | 2000 | 6.2 | 2.6 | 1.4 | 0.82 | 0.87 | 0.77 |
| Equity | 1970 | 17.0 | 15.0 | 14.9 | 0.36 | 0.32 | 0.35 |
| | 1980 | 12.7 | 11.2 | 13.4 | 0.29 | 0.25 | 0.31 |
| | 1990 | 19.3 | 16.6 | 19.7 | 0.43 | 0.32 | 0.39 |
| | 1998 | 15.6 | 9.2 | 9.9 | 0.26 | 0.14 | 0.16 |
| | 2000 | 13.6 | 10.1 | 12.1 | 0.22 | 0.15 | 0.18 |
| Memo: Liabilities/ GDP ratio | 1970 | 18.7 | 25.0 | 28.8 | 0.18 | 0.25 | 0.30 |
| | 1980 | 25.6 | 18.3 | 20.3 | 0.27 | 0.22 | 0.23 |
| | 1990 | 37.4 | 46.7 | 52.4 | 0.28 | 0.34 | 0.41 |
| | 1998 | 59.7 | 76.8 | 85.5 | 0.33 | 0.41 | 0.50 |
| | 2000 | 89.8 | 111.0 | 129.0 | 0.42 | 0.46 | 0.58 |
| Memo: Debt/ GDP ratio | 1970 | 18.7 | 13.9 | 10.1 | 0.37 | 0.30 | 0.19 |
| | 1980 | 26.1 | 13.3 | 1.5 | 0.52 | 0.33 | 0.03 |
| | 1990 | 33.4 | 7.5 | 5.9 | 0.48 | 0.12 | 0.10 |
| | 1998 | 35.3 | 9.7 | 10.4 | 0.50 | 0.16 | 0.18 |
| | 2000 | 30.6 | 14.0 | 11.3 | 0.41 | 0.20 | 0.17 |
| Memo: Liquidity/ GDP ratio | 1970 | 11.4 | 9.3 | 9.7 | 0.71 | 0.57 | 0.52 |
| | 1980 | 13.0 | 6.6 | 5.8 | 0.72 | 0.39 | 0.30 |
| | 1990 | 16.1 | 6.5 | 7.5 | 0.72 | 0.32 | 0.39 |
| | 1998 | 11.2 | 6.3 | 3.6 | 0.56 | 0.34 | 0.23 |
| | 2000 | 10.7 | 7.2 | 4.2 | 0.48 | 0.32 | 0.22 |

but not at the G-7 level. For life and pension funds the much greater divergence in the G-7 and EU-4 relative to the EMU-3 reflects the lesser development of pension funds in the latter group, as highlighted above. Accordingly, G-7 and EU-4 columns have increased in divergence up to 1998, with only a slight convergence in 2000. Finally, the assets/GDP ratios have shown increasing divergence at the EU-4 and EMU-3 levels, albeit stable divergence in the G-7. Current standard deviations of 30–50 per cent show the major discrepancies in these aggregates.

Turning to household liabilities, Table 11.4 shows that, according to the standard deviation data, there is convergence in the relative use of consumer credit and mortgage credit by households in the G-7, EU-4 and EMU-3. On the other hand, the overall debt/GDP ratio has shown a growing divergence over time, which as we saw in Table 5.4 was partly linked to lower levels in Italy and France than elsewhere.

Corporate sector liabilities portfolios in Table 11.5 show a general convergence in the loans ratio according to the standard deviation data for all three country groups as well as for equities. This is quite an interesting result, since these are the key items in the balance sheet for most countries (as seen in Table 4.3, bonds are used mainly in the US, Japan and Canada). For both loans and equities, the lowest standard deviation in 2000 is for the EU-4 including the UK (this is also true for money market instruments).

Looking at the ratios to GDP, the overall liabilities/GDP ratio shows growing divergence according to the standard deviation data, for all the sectors shown. The greatest is in the EMU-3, reflecting the differing stocks of equity outstanding. Much lower and more stable are the debt/GDP ratios, which are arguably more relevant for monetary transmission and the overall behaviour of the corporate sector. Here both the EU-4 and EMU-3 standard deviations are comparable in 1970 and 2000 at 10–15 per cent, albeit with closer convergence apparent in 1990. There is a greater and growing divergence when Canada, the US and Japan are included in the G-7 column. Finally the corporate liquidity/GDP ratio on the assets side shows the strongest convergence in the EMU-3, although this was also apparent for the EU-4 up to 1998, and since 1990 in the G-7 also.

Whereas some claims on the corporate sector are held directly by households, the bulk of claims are intermediated by the financial sector. Tables 11.6–11.9 show the two sides of the financial sector and banking sector balance sheets. Table 11.6 shows that, in several cases, there is convergence in financial sector assets according to the standard deviation data in the EU-4 and EMU-3 but not for the G-7 as a whole. This is true since 1980 for both deposits and loans, although 1970 showed closer convergence. Up to 1998, there was convergence in bondholding in the

Table 11.6 *Convergence of financial sector financial asset portfolios*

| | | Standard deviation of portfolio shares | | | Coefficient of variation of portfolio shares | | |
|---|---|---|---|---|---|---|---|
| | | G7 | EU-4 | EMU-3 | G7 | EU-4 | EMU-3 |
| Deposits | 1970 | 8.2 | 8.0 | 9.5 | 0.79 | 0.55 | 0.71 |
| | 1980 | 11.0 | 10.9 | 13.4 | 0.89 | 0.60 | 0.73 |
| | 1990 | 12.5 | 10.8 | 11.0 | 0.96 | 0.52 | 0.61 |
| | 1998 | 10.1 | 8.2 | 7.8 | 0.77 | 0.42 | 0.46 |
| | 2000 | 10.0 | 8.0 | 7.2 | 0.77 | 0.41 | 0.43 |
| Money market inst | 1970 | 2.0 | 1.7 | 1.2 | 0.55 | 0.54 | 0.46 |
| | 1980 | 2.5 | 3.1 | 3.7 | 0.66 | 1.03 | 1.17 |
| | 1990 | 3.1 | 2.8 | 3.4 | 0.57 | 0.72 | 0.92 |
| | 1998 | 3.4 | 3.6 | 4.4 | 0.65 | 0.96 | 1.15 |
| | 2000 | 3.7 | 3.7 | 4.6 | 0.75 | 1.12 | 1.36 |
| Loans | 1970 | 11.0 | 6.7 | 5.9 | 0.18 | 0.10 | 0.09 |
| | 1980 | 11.1 | 14.9 | 18.2 | 0.19 | 0.26 | 0.31 |
| | 1990 | 11.8 | 14.2 | 13.6 | 0.23 | 0.29 | 0.25 |
| | 1998 | 11.3 | 11.0 | 11.3 | 0.29 | 0.31 | 0.29 |
| | 2000 | 10.9 | 10.4 | 11.4 | 0.28 | 0.30 | 0.31 |
| Bonds | 1970 | 9.2 | 5.9 | 7.0 | 0.60 | 0.58 | 0.64 |
| | 1980 | 7.4 | 6.6 | 8.1 | 0.46 | 0.54 | 0.65 |
| | 1990 | 7.3 | 4.5 | 3.8 | 0.40 | 0.32 | 0.24 |
| | 1998 | 5.1 | 6.0 | 6.1 | 0.23 | 0.29 | 0.27 |
| | 2000 | 7.2 | 7.5 | 4.9 | 0.35 | 0.45 | 0.25 |
| Equity | 1970 | 5.2 | 4.6 | 0.9 | 0.69 | 0.91 | 0.32 |
| | 1980 | 4.2 | 3.8 | 1.0 | 0.62 | 0.85 | 0.39 |
| | 1990 | 4.7 | 6.4 | 0.6 | 0.50 | 0.75 | 0.12 |
| | 1998 | 6.9 | 5.2 | 1.8 | 0.41 | 0.31 | 0.13 |
| | 2000 | 6.1 | 3.6 | 2.6 | 0.32 | 0.18 | 0.14 |
| Mutual funds | 1970 | 0.2 | 0.2 | 0.0 | 1.56 | 2.00 | na |
| | 1980 | 0.5 | 0.7 | 0.0 | 1.97 | 1.97 | 1.73 |
| | 1990 | 0.8 | 0.9 | 1.1 | 0.83 | 0.69 | 0.90 |
| | 1998 | 1.9 | 1.7 | 2.1 | 0.86 | 0.62 | 0.72 |
| | 2000 | 2.6 | 2.6 | 2.8 | 0.89 | 0.63 | 0.60 |
| Central Bank reserves | 1970 | 2.6 | 3.1 | 3.0 | 1.06 | 1.05 | 0.75 |
| | 1980 | 2.7 | 2.9 | 1.5 | 1.10 | 0.74 | 0.29 |
| | 1990 | 0.9 | 0.9 | 0.2 | 0.80 | 0.68 | 0.13 |
| | 1998 | 0.6 | 0.4 | 0.4 | 0.91 | 1.01 | 0.70 |
| | 2000 | 0.7 | 0.3 | 0.2 | 1.22 | 0.76 | 0.34 |

Table 11.7 *Convergence of financial sector liability portfolios*

| | | Standard deviation of portfolio shares | | | Coefficient of variation of portfolio shares | | |
|---|---|---|---|---|---|---|---|
| | | G7 | EU-4 | EMU-3 | G7 | EU-4 | EMU-3 |
| Deposits | 1970 | 8.4 | 4.1 | 4.9 | 0.13 | 0.06 | 0.07 |
| | 1980 | 8.1 | 2.1 | 2.5 | 0.12 | 0.03 | 0.04 |
| | 1990 | 9.6 | 5.8 | 6.5 | 0.18 | 0.10 | 0.11 |
| | 1998 | 11.2 | 4.2 | 4.5 | 0.28 | 0.09 | 0.10 |
| | 2000 | 11.6 | 3.9 | 4.7 | 0.30 | 0.09 | 0.11 |
| Money market inst | 1970 | 2.0 | 2.1 | 0.5 | 1.12 | 1.46 | 1.16 |
| | 1980 | 2.3 | 0.2 | 0.2 | 1.58 | 0.69 | 0.88 |
| | 1990 | 3.2 | 3.6 | 3.1 | 0.94 | 1.15 | 1.68 |
| | 1998 | 2.8 | 2.5 | 2.8 | 0.91 | 1.04 | 1.49 |
| | 2000 | 2.8 | 2.6 | 2.9 | 0.92 | 0.92 | 1.27 |
| Loans | 1970 | 6.7 | 8.2 | 8.7 | 1.18 | 1.01 | 0.86 |
| | 1980 | 5.3 | 6.5 | 7.0 | 1.03 | 0.96 | 0.85 |
| | 1990 | 3.4 | 3.8 | 4.6 | 0.83 | 0.68 | 0.87 |
| | 1998 | 6.2 | 4.7 | 4.7 | 0.90 | 0.90 | 1.21 |
| | 2000 | 6.2 | 5.0 | 4.8 | 0.87 | 0.91 | 1.21 |
| Bonds | 1970 | 4.9 | 6.1 | 4.5 | 0.76 | 0.77 | 0.43 |
| | 1980 | 5.2 | 6.8 | 5.3 | 0.70 | 0.82 | 0.49 |
| | 1990 | 5.6 | 5.9 | 4.8 | 0.62 | 0.68 | 0.44 |
| | 1998 | 6.7 | 7.3 | 7.0 | 0.66 | 0.69 | 0.54 |
| | 2000 | 6.7 | 6.8 | 7.1 | 0.68 | 0.69 | 0.61 |
| Equity | 1970 | 4.5 | 2.7 | 3.2 | 0.72 | 0.56 | 0.72 |
| | 1980 | 2.7 | 2.6 | 3.1 | 0.57 | 0.53 | 0.66 |
| | 1990 | 4.8 | 4.1 | 4.4 | 0.66 | 0.49 | 0.48 |
| | 1998 | 3.8 | 3.6 | 4.2 | 0.41 | 0.35 | 0.38 |
| | 2000 | 4.4 | 4.3 | 4.8 | 0.42 | 0.36 | 0.38 |
| Mutual funds | 1970 | 1.3 | 0.6 | 0.0 | 1.10 | 2.00 | na |
| | 1980 | 1.1 | 0.7 | 0.7 | 0.96 | 1.16 | 1.73 |
| | 1990 | 3.5 | 4.1 | 4.4 | 0.67 | 0.83 | 0.73 |
| | 1998 | 5.8 | 5.0 | 2.8 | 0.54 | 0.46 | 0.22 |
| | 2000 | 5.9 | 4.9 | 2.0 | 0.50 | 0.41 | 0.14 |
| Life and pension claims | 1970 | 8.5 | 5.7 | 4.1 | 0.61 | 0.66 | 0.65 |
| | 1980 | 9.0 | 8.1 | 5.0 | 0.63 | 0.88 | 0.87 |
| | 1990 | 9.7 | 8.6 | 4.4 | 0.53 | 0.69 | 0.52 |
| | 1998 | 8.7 | 8.8 | 3.8 | 0.45 | 0.56 | 0.33 |
| | 2000 | 7.2 | 6.5 | 3.0 | 0.38 | 0.43 | 0.25 |
| Central Bank reserves | 1970 | 0.1 | 0.1 | 0.1 | 2.65 | 2.00 | 1.73 |
| | 1980 | 0.2 | 0.3 | 0.4 | 2.65 | 2.00 | 1.73 |
| | 1990 | 0.4 | 0.5 | 0.6 | 2.65 | 2.00 | 1.73 |
| | 1998 | 0.0 | 0.0 | 0.0 | na | na | na |
| | 2000 | 0.0 | 0.0 | 0.0 | na | na | na |

Table 11.8 *Convergence of banking sector financial asset portfolios*

| | | Standard deviation of portfolio shares | | | Coefficient of variation of portfolio shares | | |
|---|---|---|---|---|---|---|---|
| | | G7 | EU-4 | EMU-3 | G7 | EU-4 | EMU-3 |
| Deposits | 1970 | 9.3 | 10.0 | 10.7 | 0.78 | 0.64 | 0.81 |
| | 1980 | 12.6 | 13.4 | 15.9 | 0.93 | 0.67 | 0.87 |
| | 1990 | 17.0 | 17.2 | 18.2 | 1.09 | 0.68 | 0.88 |
| | 1998 | 14.5 | 14.4 | 14.6 | 0.89 | 0.59 | 0.72 |
| | 2000 | 13.9 | 13.2 | 13.4 | 0.88 | 0.56 | 0.67 |
| Money market inst | 1970 | 2.4 | 2.2 | 1.5 | 0.60 | 0.61 | 0.53 |
| | 1980 | 3.5 | 3.5 | 4.2 | 0.83 | 1.06 | 1.19 |
| | 1990 | 3.5 | 2.2 | 2.0 | 0.70 | 0.63 | 0.71 |
| | 1998 | 3.8 | 4.4 | 5.4 | 0.80 | 0.99 | 1.24 |
| | 2000 | 3.6 | 4.0 | 4.9 | 0.84 | 1.07 | 1.37 |
| Loans | 1970 | 9.9 | 10.2 | 12.5 | 0.15 | 0.15 | 0.19 |
| | 1980 | 14.7 | 20.0 | 23.7 | 0.23 | 0.33 | 0.40 |
| | 1990 | 13.5 | 15.6 | 18.0 | 0.21 | 0.27 | 0.30 |
| | 1998 | 12.5 | 12.6 | 15.0 | 0.23 | 0.26 | 0.29 |
| | 2000 | 12.9 | 12.9 | 15.6 | 0.24 | 0.26 | 0.31 |
| Bonds | 1970 | 9.7 | 9.0 | 9.9 | 0.73 | 1.07 | 0.95 |
| | 1980 | 9.2 | 10.2 | 10.9 | 0.74 | 1.06 | 0.89 |
| | 1990 | 8.3 | 6.6 | 6.7 | 0.69 | 0.64 | 0.55 |
| | 1998 | 6.9 | 5.8 | 6.8 | 0.43 | 0.40 | 0.44 |
| | 2000 | 7.3 | 6.0 | 6.0 | 0.49 | 0.49 | 0.43 |
| Equity | 1970 | 3.1 | 0.5 | 0.2 | 1.02 | 0.27 | 0.13 |
| | 1980 | 3.7 | 0.9 | 0.2 | 1.06 | 0.68 | 0.13 |
| | 1990 | 1.5 | 0.5 | 0.5 | 0.56 | 0.26 | 0.26 |
| | 1998 | 2.2 | 2.9 | 2.0 | 0.44 | 0.49 | 0.28 |
| | 2000 | 3.9 | 4.2 | 3.1 | 0.53 | 0.53 | 0.32 |
| Mutual funds | 1970 | 0.2 | 0.0 | 0.0 | 2.31 | na | na |
| | 1980 | 0.5 | 0.6 | 0.0 | 2.06 | 1.99 | 1.73 |
| | 1990 | 0.4 | 0.3 | 0.3 | 1.13 | 1.21 | 1.02 |
| | 1998 | 1.8 | 1.0 | 1.0 | 1.40 | 1.12 | 0.86 |
| | 2000 | 1.6 | 1.3 | 1.3 | 1.18 | 1.04 | 0.77 |
| Central Bank reserves | 1970 | 2.7 | 2.8 | 2.4 | 0.94 | 0.93 | 0.60 |
| | 1980 | 3.0 | 3.2 | 1.6 | 1.04 | 0.73 | 0.28 |
| | 1990 | 1.2 | 1.4 | 1.4 | 0.98 | 1.16 | 0.87 |
| | 1998 | 1.2 | 0.6 | 0.6 | 1.25 | 1.06 | 0.76 |
| | 2000 | 1.5 | 0.5 | 0.4 | 1.36 | 0.80 | 0.41 |

Table 11.9 *Convergence of banking sector liability portfolios*

| | | Standard deviation of portfolio shares | | | Coefficient of variation of portfolio shares | | |
|---|---|---|---|---|---|---|---|
| | | G7 | EU-4 | EMU-3 | G7 | EU-4 | EMU-3 |
| Deposits | 1970 | 13.6 | 9.6 | 9.9 | 0.17 | 0.12 | 0.13 |
| | 1980 | 13.4 | 10.7 | 7.8 | 0.17 | 0.13 | 0.10 |
| | 1990 | 13.0 | 11.3 | 13.2 | 0.17 | 0.14 | 0.17 |
| | 1998 | 11.1 | 9.9 | 7.5 | 0.16 | 0.14 | 0.11 |
| | 2000 | 11.8 | 11.2 | 8.0 | 0.17 | 0.16 | 0.12 |
| Money market inst | 1970 | 3.4 | 3.2 | 0.5 | 1.32 | 1.57 | 1.19 |
| | 1980 | 3.6 | 0.2 | 0.2 | 1.58 | 1.02 | 0.96 |
| | 1990 | 4.7 | 5.3 | 4.0 | 0.96 | 1.19 | 1.69 |
| | 1998 | 4.4 | 4.1 | 3.9 | 0.95 | 1.05 | 1.50 |
| | 2000 | 4.6 | 4.1 | 3.8 | 0.95 | 0.94 | 1.24 |
| Loans | 1970 | 13.0 | 8.9 | 9.1 | 1.34 | 1.15 | 0.89 |
| | 1980 | 14.9 | 7.7 | 7.7 | 1.51 | 1.18 | 0.89 |
| | 1990 | 16.0 | 3.3 | 3.7 | 1.94 | 1.29 | 1.09 |
| | 1998 | 14.9 | 2.9 | 3.3 | 1.63 | 1.58 | 1.41 |
| | 2000 | 14.7 | 2.9 | 3.3 | 1.60 | 1.52 | 1.33 |
| Bonds | 1970 | 5.4 | 6.5 | 7.0 | 1.00 | 1.32 | 1.08 |
| | 1980 | 6.5 | 8.5 | 9.3 | 1.20 | 1.40 | 1.17 |
| | 1990 | 7.5 | 9.5 | 10.3 | 1.10 | 1.10 | 0.96 |
| | 1998 | 9.6 | 10.9 | 10.2 | 0.95 | 0.74 | 0.56 |
| | 2000 | 8.7 | 10.0 | 9.7 | 0.91 | 0.73 | 0.58 |
| Equity | 1970 | 2.6 | 2.9 | 3.5 | 1.06 | 0.79 | 0.92 |
| | 1980 | 2.2 | 2.9 | 3.6 | 0.62 | 0.72 | 0.84 |
| | 1990 | 2.7 | 3.1 | 3.3 | 0.66 | 0.59 | 0.56 |
| | 1998 | 4.7 | 5.4 | 6.0 | 0.75 | 0.65 | 0.64 |
| | 2000 | 6.1 | 7.1 | 6.5 | 0.85 | 0.71 | 0.53 |
| Central Bank reserves | 1970 | 0.2 | 0.2 | 0.2 | 1.96 | 1.39 | 1.12 |
| | 1980 | 0.3 | 0.4 | 0.4 | 2.57 | 1.94 | 1.67 |
| | 1990 | 0.5 | 0.6 | 0.7 | 2.62 | 1.98 | 1.71 |
| | 1998 | 0.0 | 0.0 | 0.0 | na | na | na |
| | 2000 | 0.0 | 0.0 | 0.0 | na | na | na |

G-7, and for the whole period in the EU-4. Standard deviations for equity are lowest in the EMU-3. However, there is some growth in divergence. All the groups show a growing divergence of mutual fund holding.

In Table 11.7, there is some convergence for loans, notably in the EU-4 and EMU-3, and for deposits since 1990. For bonds there is some divergence, in contrast to the asset side, notably for the G-7 and EMU-3.

Finally life and pension claims show more divergence in recent years for the EU-4, while there is convergence in the EMU-3.The standard deviation for the G-7 is roughly constant.

Looking briefly at the banking sector assets (Table 11.8), the standard deviations are higher than for the financial sector in the case of loans in the EU-4 and EMU-3, where portfolio shares are more closely convergent. Deposit shares are quite heterogeneous and only slightly convergent in the G-7 and EU-4. Standard deviations of money market instruments are flat and those for equities and bonds are rising in virtually all cases. On the liability side, Table 11.9 shows some convergence for deposits and loans since 1990, especially for the EU-4 and EMU-3, and some divergence for bond issuance. Interestingly, the share of equities outstanding rises in terms of standard deviation despite the Basel accord enforcing minimum capital–risk asset ratios. Given risk-based capital has indeed converged, the data probably reflect differences in the ratio of risk weighted assets to actual assets across countries.

## 11.3 EQUITY MARKETS AND CORPORATE FINANCE IN FRANCE AND THE G-7

In the light of Section 11.1 and Schmidt *et al.* (2001), which saw France as a hybrid system, a further specific topic of interest is the status of French corporate finance relative to the rest of the G-7. Does it stand out as an outlier or is it comparable to other countries and, if so, is it bank- or market-based? This illustrates the broader use to which the data may be put. In terms of corporate finance itself, Table 4.3 showed that shares of loans, bonds and equities in corporate liabilities were comparable to those in the UK and US, with the share of equity being well above that in Germany, Japan, Canada and Italy. The ratios to GDP shown in Table 4.4 showed that French liabilities as a whole were the highest in the G-7, but this was largely a consequence of the share of equity. The debt/GDP ratio was below that for the UK and Japanese corporate sectors, albeit above those of the US, Germany, Canada and Italy. On the asset side (Table 4.2), the level of corporate liquidity at 21 per cent of GDP is around the average for the G-7.

If we consider household sector assets, the share of directly held equity at 38 per cent is well above the rest of the G-7 (Table 5.1). For the US, Canada and Italy the ratio is 20–30 per cent and for the UK, Japan and Germany it is below 20 per cent. On the other hand, the share of insurance and pension funds is well below that in the Anglo Saxon countries, and is indeed mainly life insurance. We see in Table 10.1 that the French life and pension sector holds mainly bonds (45 per cent) and only 24 per cent equity. A similar picture emerges for mutual funds, which account for 9 per cent of household assets, and where equity holdings are just over 30 per cent.

Table 5.5, which aggregates institutional assets with those of households, shows that French equity holdings are comparable to the UK, US and Canada, while bond holdings are in line with the UK and below other G-7 countries. Liquidity is comparable to all of the G-7 except Germany and Japan, where it is much higher.

Concerning the holdings of equity by sector, Table 4.7 shows that intercorporate cross-holdings of shares are the highest in France at 25 per cent; of the remainder, 20–30 per cent each are with the foreign sector, financial sector and households. Foreign holdings are the highest in the G-7 except for the UK (37 per cent). Financial sector holdings, with Italy, are the lowest in the G-7, and are mainly (9 per cent) held by banks. The share of institutional investors is one of the lowest in the G-7, reflecting the low level of development of pension funds in France.

The proportion of unquoted shares in France and Italy is far above that elsewhere (Tables 4.8 and 4.9). There it is shown that nearly 70 per cent of the equity outstanding for French companies is unquoted and the share for Italy is 50 per cent; elsewhere it is below 30 per cent. Nevertheless, the stock of equity for French quoted companies is still over 100 per cent of GDP, above that in Germany, Japan and Italy, albeit well below that in the UK and the US. A similar pattern emerges both for the total stock of domestic shares and for shares outstanding from the non-financial corporate sector.

In Table 4.10 the data were shown for the holders of quoted and unquoted shares. It is apparent that French quoted shares are held to a considerable extent by foreign investors – 37 per cent, while foreign holdings of unquoted shares is only 22 per cent. Domestic households and companies hold the bulk of unquoted shares, while financial institutions hold 28 per cent of quoted but only 16 per cent of unquoted. These figures are most closely comparable to the UK, notably in respect of holdings by households (around 10 per cent of quoted and 30 per cent of unquoted in each case). One difference is that foreigners hold 40 per cent of unquoted UK shares as well as 36 per cent of quoted. UK companies are less important holders of both types of share than in France, and financial institutions more so, reflecting the size of the institutional sector. On the other hand it is apparent that the life and pension sector in the UK is unwilling to hold unquoted shares, accounting for only 1 per cent against 38 per cent of quoted shares (see Davis and Steil, 2001, for a discussion of reasons for this). Table 5.2 meanwhile shows that households' direct holdings of equity are 88 per cent of GDP in France, 28 per cent in Germany, 52 per cent in the UK and 69 per cent in the US.

The implications of these patterns for corporate governance may warrant further investigation, see also Section 1.3. With unquoted shares it is harder to mount hostile takeovers, and effective monitoring by institutions may also be weakened. More generally, these data link in an interesting manner to the work of Schmidt *et al.* (2001). They suggest that in France the corporate governance system is a hybrid between the Anglo Saxon and Continental traditions. Traditionally, hostile takeovers have been difficult owing to state 'golden shares' and corporate cross holdings. The 'state, the bureaucracy and the network of the business and civil service elite' did until recently maintain oversight on the otherwise substantial powers of company managers. But now the authors suggest that, owing to reform, deregulation and denationalisation, there is a potential for dysfunction since the public sector no longer seeks to direct industry, while banks, which have a major shareholding, do not do so either, and domestic institutional investors are weak. Vivendi is a recent example. Activism by foreign shareholders could arguably help ensure consistency in this context, although development of domestic pension funds is clearly also desirable.

## 11.4 IS THERE ANY EVIDENCE THAT THE BALANCE SHEETS AFFECT OVERALL ECONOMIC BEHAVIOUR OR PERFORMANCE?

Effects of different balance sheets and financial structure on the economy may be divided into macro and micro aspects. Beginning with the former, the corpus of work on international comparisons of balance sheets' impact on the monetary transmission mechanism is very extensive and it is not the function of this book to summarise it. Nevertheless, we consider it appropriate to summarise two recent research papers from NIESR that touch on the issue of whether macro behaviour differs as a consequence of financial structures across the G-7. The references in the papers give access to further material.

Byrne and Davis (2001) analysed disaggregated wealth in consumption functions for G7 countries. They found that, contrary to other empirical work, illiquid financial wealth (securities, pensions and mortgage debt), tends to be a more significant long-run determinant of consumption than liquid financial wealth across the G-7. They suggested that this pattern reflects a shift from liquidity constrained to life-cycle behaviour following financial liberalisation. Results were robust in SURE analysis, tested in a nested manner, using varying definitions of liquid assets and using non-property income instead of personal disposable income. Wald tests indicated similar long-run behaviour for all EU countries including the UK, despite the differences in financial structure.

Ashworth and Davis (2001) noted that standard theories of investment behaviour have concentrated on the neoclassical and Tobin's Q approaches, with most empirical work on aggregate data focusing on the former. In contrast, a separate literature on monetary transmission, centred on the credit channel and financial accelerator effects as discussed in Chapter 4, has highlighted the potential impact of credit market imperfections in constraining the investment behaviour of firms. In their paper they presented evidence at a macro level for the G7 countries that a broad range of financial variables, consistent with the valuation ratio, financial accelerator and credit channel approaches, are relevant determinants of business fixed investment above those variables normally included in traditional macroeconomic investment functions. The results indicated a wider incidence of these financial effects on investment than the existing literature, focused as it is on the US, would otherwise indicate. Again, there were similar coefficients for the debt–equity ratio in the UK, Germany and France consistent with a similar transmission process in respect of the financial accelerator despite differences in financial structure. A given shift in the debt–equity ratio has a similar impact on investment, in other words.

Answering the question whether the balance sheets affect performance at an economy-wide level is partly a question of addressing the interest rate sensitivity of the different economies. Does a bank-dominated financial system lead to a lesser interest rate sensitivity, owing to the credit insurance provided to borrowers, or is it comparable or larger owing to the higher gearing in these systems? Macro studies tend to find that there is no simple ordering of the interest rate sensitivity of the different economies. Germany is as or more sensitive than the UK, while France and Italy are somewhat less so, according to NiGEM and a number of other modellers. See also van Els *et al.* (2002) who show that, of the EMU countries, Germany is one of the most interest rate sensitive.

On the micro side, research on the best form of corporate finance and governance is inconclusive (Mayer, 1996). Whereas relationship banking systems are good at monitoring and controlling debt exposures, they may also provide such funds beyond the firms' investment opportunities, leading to overinvestment when funds are abundant. Takeovers mitigate such problems in arm's-length systems, although such systems may be inferior when funds are scarce. In other words, whereas relationship based systems are good at control and monitoring, arm's-length systems are better at governance. In a similar vein, relationship banking systems ease the renegotiation of contracts, which helps overcome liquidity problems but worsens the issue of discipline, leading to so-called soft budget constraints. Arm's-length systems can stop unprofitable projects more readily, given lack of long term monitoring, while liquidity difficulties are worsened. There are legal preconditions for an arm's-length system, in that only where the rights of investors are well protected is anything other than relationship banking feasible (La Porta *et al.*, 1999).

Taking a broader view, Allen (1993) and Allen and Gale (1997) suggest that Anglo-American capital markets dominated by institutional investors may have a disadvantage in terms of risk sharing, whereby competition and opportunities for arbitrage constrain intermediaries to carry out only cross-sectional risk sharing – exchanges of risk among individuals at a given point in time. This leaves individuals and companies vulnerable to undiversifiable risks arising over time, for example, owing to macroeconomic shocks, which cannot be eliminated by portfolio diversification. In contrast, financial systems in which long-lived banks have some monopoly power over savers facilitate the elimination of such intertemporal risks by accumulation of reserves and smoothing of returns over time. Firms may then obtain rescue finance in recessions, for example.

These benefits may be lost as openness to global markets increases via pension fund growth, as discussed further below. (There is an obvious application to the current situation in Germany and Japan.) Also collapse of relationship banks may be highly damaging to the economy, given the dependence of the economy on these institutions. The banking crises in Scandinavia and Japan (Davis, 1995b) were certainly highly damaging to the real economy.

Meanwhile, in Anglo-American countries, the so-called multiple avenues of intermediation are said to cushion the effect of crises in either banks or securities markets on corporate financing (Greenspan, 1999). Arguably, most securities market crises tended to harm householders' wealth but not the infrastructure underlying securities market functioning. (It is market liquidity crises that may be more serious in this regard than price volatility, see Davis, 2001c). Furthermore, in Anglo-American countries, the focus on cross-sectional risk sharing may help to explain the intense focus on risk management via derivatives (Allen and Santomero, 1999).

Of course it may be that the benefits of relationship banking in terms of lower agency costs and possibly also costs of bankruptcy are totally offset by higher debt–equity ratios,[56] and generally there is little evidence that

56 Certainly, debt–equity ratios tend to be higher in bank-dominated than market-oriented systems, see Section 4.5.

bank-based systems are better for overall economic performance (Levine, 2000). Moreover, the relationship-banking system requires that bank margins should widen in a recovery to recoup the insurance premia, which may not be compatible with a competitive financial system. Whereas relationship banking exists in both French and German law based countries, it may be expected to be more stable in the latter, given the better creditor protection that prevails. Relationship banking applies even in market-based systems such as the US to small firms (Berger and Udell, 1995), in that small firms for which public information is not available tend to depend on a relationship with a single bank. There are also issues linked to the differing abilities of bank- and market-based systems to finance different types of firm, as discussed in Sections 4.2 and 4.3.

A reasonable conclusion may be that of Allen and Gale (2000), who suggested that 'since neither markets nor intermediaries work in exactly the way theory suggests, we would do well to exercise some humility in making recommendations about policies to reform our financial systems'.

What of the impact of a given size and development of the financial sector, independently from its bank or market orientation? A number of papers have sought to address the relation of financial development and economic growth. In a pioneering study, King and Levine (1993) used four measures of financial structure, namely the size of liquid liabilities, the role of banks relative to the central bank in allocating credit, credit allocation to private business versus total credit to the non-financial sector and the ratio of credit to private firms to GDP. Across a large sample of countries, the financial variables were found to have a strong relation to three growth variables, namely capital accumulation, economic growth and productivity growth, even controlling for other influences on growth such as education and government expenditure. Levine and Zervos (1998) sought to extend the analysis to allow for the role of stock market development, finding that stock market liquidity (but not size, international integration or volatility) as well as banking development were related to growth.

An implication of this and related papers is that the overall development of financial services is important to growth and not its bias to bank or market financing (Levine, 1997). Extensions such as Levine (1999) have additionally allowed for the role of certain legal aspects (linked to creditor and investor rights, contract enforcement and accounting standards) in financial development, and found that these are crucial for economic growth more generally. This influence may operate, *inter alia*, by influencing the proportion of firms that have access to external finance (Demirgüç-Kunt and Maksimovic, 1998, 2000).

# Conclusion

We have seen that the literature focuses most closely on the overall financial structure, with an underlying emphasis on the way in which household savings are directed to the corporate sector via financial intermediaries. The theory distinguished bank-based and market-based financial systems, while noting that some, such as in France, appear to be in transition and hence are hard to categorise. The sectoral literature focuses mainly on the assets of the household sector and the liabilities of companies. Other sectors are much less studied in terms of their asset allocation, although we may note that there are numerous performance studies of mutual funds and pension funds, see Davis and Steil (2001), as well as studies of bank efficiency, such as Altunbas *et al.* (2001).

One point of note from the survey is that the system analyses tend to assume rather different behaviour between financial systems, but the sector analyses assert that behaviour of households, companies etc. in terms of underlying fundamentals is quite similar. This may suggest an important role for exogenous factors such as law, regulation and taxation overlaying similar sectoral behaviour, although cultural differences should not be disregarded. Another tension is between the theoretical analyses and the balance sheets data, where analysis of the latter raises questions concerning the extent to which financial systems can be neatly categorised into bank- and market-dominated.

Certainly, there are notable differences, with some 'clustering' of France, Italy and Germany and of the US and UK, although Germany and the US are the true archetypes, and France and the UK share many features (see Byrne and Davis, 2002). Canada is close to the Anglo-Saxon group and Japan to the Continental one, but both have idiosyncratic features. To a degree, this may relate to the presence of a transition from one type of system to another – an aspect which is barely covered in the analytical literature (see Section 11.3). But even in steady state there are some aspects (which may link to history and path dependence) which do not fit neatly into the frameworks presented here. Meanwhile, much convergence in non-financial sector balance sheets has taken place in recent years, with, in particular, growing holdings of household assets in the form of claims on institutional investors in Continental Europe and Japan, and companies issuing securities rather than relying solely on bank lending.

The contribution of this book goes well beyond these traditional differences in financial structure, by showing the balance sheets of the public, foreign and financial sectors as well as subsectors of finance, namely banks, life and pension funds, and mutual funds. We have seen that the differences between these sectors are marked, and by no means correspond precisely to the traditional bank-dominated/market-oriented split proposed for households and companies. Two highlights may be noted, namely the US and UK banking sectors, whose sizes are at the two extreme ends of the spectrum, and the highly variable size of foreign sector claims and their net deficit or surplus position. On the other hand, some tentative evidence of convergence in financial structure is apparent for a number of country groups, sectors and instruments, notably within the EU. Whereas this movement should not be exaggerated, it gives some support to the idea of future convergence in financial structure on a market-based paradigm, driven by factors such as EMU, globalisation of financial markets and the need for pension funding given the ageing of the population.

The policy issues arising from the analysis are manifold, so we highlight just a few:

- Are there mechanisms currently at work leading to a likely convergence of financial systems, notably the vulnerability of relationship banking systems to increased banking competition, globalisation and institutionalisation? Can different financial systems coexist, especially in a common currency zone such as EMU? How strong is path dependence?
- More generally, which systems are more vulnerable to systemic financial crises? What shock absorbers are available?
- Is it of policy concern (e.g. for reasons of corporate governance) if equity is widely held by foreigners, as is the case in France and the UK? Does it impact on the cost of equity?
- What is the implication of a high share of unquoted shares as in France? How can one increase the proportion of shares which are tradable?
- For a system in transition from bank-based to market-based, is there a

risk that corporate governance mechanisms of the traditional sort may wither, while there is resistance to full implement-ation of the takeover sanction, leading to a vacuum, poor investment decisions and possible rationing of external finance?

- How much competition is desirable, given it may undermine relationship banking and related time-series risk sharing?
- What are the implications of differences – and potential convergence – for monetary transmission?
- How can one best measure overall convergence with the Eurozone (for the UK) and within the Eurozone (for France, Germany and Italy)? What judgement can one make regarding systems which have similar balance sheets but different underlying legal or regulatory provisions? Is more legal convergence desirable (for example, an EU Takeover Directive)?
- How important is the net overseas position and its composition for domestic monetary and financial stability?
- A key policy aspect in Japan arises from the potential concerns about monetisation of government debt, bankruptcy of the corporate sector, and systemic collapse of the banking and life insurance sectors. Evidence for all of these risks are present in the tables.
- More generally, how might heavily indebted corporate and household balance sheets cope with deflation? (See Fisher, 1933, on the Great Depression.)
- More work is needed to assess the impact of financial structure on the behaviour and performance of economies generally.

# References


Agell, J. and Persson, M. (1992), 'Does debt management matter?' in Agell, J., Persson, M. and Friedman, B. M. (eds), *Does Debt Management Matter?* Oxford, Clarendon Press.

Allen, F. (1993), 'Stock markets and resource allocation', in Mayer, C. and Vives, X. (eds), *Capital Markets and Financial Intermediation*, Cambridge, Cambridge University Press.

Allen, F. and Gale, D. (1997), 'Financial markets, intermediaries and intertemporal smoothing', *Journal of Political Economy*, 105, pp. 523–46.

(2000), *Comparing Financial Systems*, Cambridge, Mass., MIT Press.

Allen, F. and Santomero, A. M. (1998), 'The theory of financial intermediation', *Journal of Banking and Finance*, 21, pp. 1461–85.

(1999), 'What do financial intermediaries do?', Working Paper No. 99-30-B, Financial Institutions Centre, The Wharton School, University of Pennsylvania.

Altunbas, Y., Gardener, E. P. M., Molyneux, P. and Moore, B. (2001), 'Efficiency in European banking', *European Economic Review*, 45, pp. 1931–56.

Ambachtsheer, K. (1988), 'Integrating business planning with pension fund planning', in Arnott, R. and Fabozzi, F. (eds), *Asset Allocation; A Handbook*, Chicago, Probus.

Ameriks, J. and Zeldes, S. P. (2000), 'How do households' portfolio shares vary with age?', Working Paper, Columbia University and TIAA-CREF.

Ando, A. and Modigliani, F. (1963), 'The life cycle hypothesis of saving: aggregate', *American Economic Review*, 103, pp. 55–84.

Arrow, K. J. (1964), 'The role of securities in the optimal allocation of risk bearing', *Review of Economic Studies*, 31, pp. 91–6.

Ashworth, P. and Davis, E. P. (2001), 'Some evidence on financial factors in the determination of aggregate business investment for the G7 countries', Discussion Paper no. 187, London, National Institute of Economic and Social Research.

Attanasio, O. and Brugiavini, A. (1999), 'Social security and household saving', mimeo, UCL and University of Venice.

Attanasio, O. and De Leire, T. (1994), 'IRAs and household savings revisited; some new evidence', Working Paper No. 4900, National Bureau of Economic Research.

Bank of Japan (2000), 'Points of international comparison of the flow of funds accounts', Research Paper, Research and Statistics Department, Bank of Japan, 28 December.

Banks, J., Blundell, R. and Dilnot, A. (1994), 'Tax-based savings incentives in the UK', paper delivered to the conference on 'International Comparisons of Household Savings', Paris, OECD, 19 May 1994.

Banks, J. and Tanner, S. (2001), 'Household portfolios in the UK', in Guiso, L. Haliassos, M. and Jappelli, T. (eds), *Household Portfolios*, Cambridge, Mass., MIT Press.

Barro, R. (1974), 'Are government bonds net wealth?', *Journal of Political Economy*, 81, pp. 1095–117.

Bergantino, S. M. (1998), 'Life cycle investment behavior, demographics, and asset prices', PhD Dissertation, Massachusetts Institute of Technology.

Berger, A. and Udell, G. (1995), 'Relationship banking and lines of credit in small firm finance', *Journal of Business*, 68, pp. 351–81.

Bernanke, B. S. (1993), 'Credit in the macroeconomy', *Quarterly Review*, Federal Reserve Bank of New York, Spring, pp. 50–70.

Bernanke, B. S., Gertler, M. and Gilchrist, S. (1996), 'The financial accelerator and the flight to quality', *Review of Economics and Statistics*, 78, pp. 1–15.

Bernanke, B. S. and Lown, C. S. (1991), 'The credit crunch', *Brookings Papers on Economic Activity*, 2, pp. 205–47.

Bernard, H. and Bisignano, J. (2000), 'Information, liquidity and risk in the international interbank market; implicit guarantees and private credit market failure', Bank for International Settlements Working Paper No 86.

Bernheim, B. D. (1991), 'How strong are bequest motives? Evidence based on estimates of the demand for life insurance and annuities', NBER Working Paper No. 2942.

Bertaut, C. and Starr-McCluer, M. (2001), 'Household portfolios in the United States', in Guiso, L., Haliassos, M. and Jappelli,T. (eds), *Household Portfolios*, Cambridge, Mass., MIT Press.

Bertrand, A. (2000), 'Main features of financial accounts in OECD countries', *Financial Market Trends*, Paris, OECD, pp. 149–76.

Bhattacharya, S. (1979), 'Imperfect information, dividend policy and the bird in hand fallacy', *Bell Journal of Economics*, 10, pp. 259–70.

Bhattacharya, S. and Chiesa, G. (1995), 'Proprietary information, financial intermediation and research incentives', *Journal of Financial Intermediation*, 4, pp. 328–57.

Bhattacharya, S. and Thakor, A. V. (1993), 'Contemporary banking theory', *Journal of Financial Intermediation*, 3, pp. 2–50.

Black, F. (1976), 'Studies of stock price volatility changes', *Proceedings of the Business and Economic Statistics Section*, American Statistical Association, 1, pp. 177–81.

(1980), 'The tax consequences of long-run pension policy', *Financial Analysts Journal*, September-October, pp. 17–23.
Blake, D. (1999), 'Portfolio choice models of pension funds and life assurance companies, similarities and differences', *Geneva Papers on Risk and Insurance*, 24, pp. 327–57.
Blake, D. and Orszag, M. (1999), 'Annual estimates of personal wealth holdings in the UK since 1948', *Applied Financial Economics*, 9, pp. 397–421.
Blanchard, O. J. (1993), 'The vanishing equity premium', in O'Brien, R. (ed.), *Finance and the International Economy*, 7, Oxford University Press.
(1999), *Lectures in Macroeconomics*, Prentice Hall.
Bodie, Z. (1990), 'Pensions as retirement income insurance', *Journal of Economic Literature*, 28, pp. 28–49.
Bodie, Z. and Davis, E. P. (eds) (2000), *The Foundations of Pension Finance*, London, Edward Elgar.
Bodie, Z., Kane, A. and Marcus, A. J. (1999), *Investments*, Illinois, Irwin, Homewood.
Bolton, P. and Freixas, X. (2000), 'Equity, bonds and bank debt: capital structure and financial market equilibrium under asymmetric information', *Journal of Political Economy*, 108, 2, April, pp. 324–51.
Borio, C.V., Chincarini, L. and Tsatsaronis, K. (1997), 'Institutional investors, asset management and financial markets', mimeo, Bank for International Settlements, Basel.
Börsch-Supan, A. and Eymann, A. (2001), 'Household portfolios in Germany', in Guiso, L. Haliassos, M. and Jappelli, T. (eds), *Household Portfolios*, Cambridge, Mass., MIT Press.
Brandt, M. W. (1999), 'Estimating portfolio and consumption choice: a conditional Euler equation approach', *Journal of Finance*, LIV, pp. 1609–45.
Brealey, R. and Myers, S. (2002), *Principles of CorporateFinance*, Irwin/McGraw Hill.
Browning, M. and Lusardi, A. (1996), 'Household saving: micro theories and macro facts', *Journal of Economic Literature*, XXXIV, pp. 1797–1855.
Bruinshoofd, A. and Kool, C. (2001), 'The determinants of corporate liquidity in the Netherlands', mimeo, Maastricht University.
Buckberg, E. (1996), 'Institutional investors and asset pricing in emerging markets', Working Paper WP/96/2, International Monetary Fund.
Byrne, J. P. and Davis, E. P. (2001), 'Disaggregate wealth and aggregate consumption: an investigation of empirical relationships for the G7', *Oxford Bulletin of Economics and Statistics* (*forthcoming*).
(2002), 'A comparison of balance sheet structures in major EU countries', *National Institute Economic Review*, April, pp. 83–95.
Campbell, J. Y. (1995), 'Some lessons from the yield curve', *Journal of Economic Perspectives*, 9, pp. 129–52.
(1999), 'Comment on Hess, G.D. (1999), The maturity structure of government debt and asset substitutability in the United Kingdom', in Chrystal, K. A. (ed.), *Government Debt Structure and Monetary Conditions*,

London, Bank of England.
Campbell, J. Y. and Viceira, L. M. (2001), 'Who should buy long-term bonds?', *American Economic Review*, 91, pp. 99–127.
Canner, N., Mankiw, N. G. and Weil, D. N. (1997), 'An asset allocation puzzle', *American Economic Review*, 87, pp. 181–91.
Carlin, W. and Mayer, C. (1999), 'Finance, investment and growth', London, Centre for Economic Policy Research Discussion Paper No. 2233.
Chai, J. and Johnston, R. B. (2000), 'An incentive approach to identifying financial system vulnerabilities', IMF Working paper No. WP/00/211.
Chiuri, M. C. and Jappelli, T. (2000), 'Financial market imperfections and home ownership: a comparative study', CSEF Working Paper No. 44.
Christiano, L. J., Eichenbaum, M. and Evans, C. (1996), 'The effects of monetary policy shocks; some evidence from the flow of funds', *Review of Economics and Statistics*, 78, pp. 16–34.
Coase, R. H. (1937), 'The nature of the firm', *Economica*, 4, pp. 386–405.
Corbett, J. and Jenkinson, T. (1997), 'How is investment financed? A study of Germany, Japan, the UK and the US', *The Manchester School*, 65, pp. 69–93.
Cuthbertson, K. (1996), *Quantitative Financial Economics; Stocks, Bonds and Foreign Exchange*, Chichester, Wiley.
Dang, T. T., Antolin, P. and Oxley, H. (2001), 'Fiscal implications of ageing – projections of age related spending', OECD Economics Department Working paper No. 305.
Danielsson, J., Embrechts, P., Goodhart, C., Keating, C., Renault, O., Muennich, F., Shin, H.-S. (2001), 'An academic response to Basel II', LSE Financial Markets Group Special Paper No. 130.
Davis, E. P. (1986), 'Portfolio behaviour of the non financial private sectors in the major economies', Bank for International Settlements, Economic Paper No. 17.
(1988), 'Financial market activity of life insurance companies and pension funds', Bank for International Settlements, Economic Paper No. 21.
(1995a), *Pension Funds, Retirement-Income Security and Capital Markets – An International Perspective*, Oxford, Oxford University Press.
(1995b), *Debt, Financial Fragility and Systemic Risk, Revised and Expanded Version*, Oxford, Oxford University Press.
(1995c), 'Financial fragility in the early 1990s, what can be learnt from international experience?', Special Paper No. 76, LSE Financial Markets Group.
(1999a), *Financial Data Needs for Macroprudential Surveillance – What are the Key Indicators of Risk to Domestic Financial Stability?*, Handbooks in Central Banking – Lecture Series No. 2, Center for Central Banking Studies, Bank of England.
(1999b), 'Institutionalization and EMU; implications for European financial markets', *International Finance*, 2, pp. 33–61.
(2000), 'Pension funds, financial intermediation and the new financial landscape', *Kredit und Kapital*, 33, pp. 229–52.

(2001a), 'Portfolio regulation of life insurance companies and pension funds', *Financial Market Trends*, Paris, OECD.
(2001b), 'Multiple avenues of intermediation, corporate finance and financial stability', IMF Working Paper No. 01/115.
(2001c), 'Financial stability in the euro area, some lessons from US financial history', in Balling, M. *et al.* (eds), *Adapting to Financial Globalisation*, London, Routledge.
(2002a), 'Institutional investors, corporate governance, and the performance of the corporate sector' (*forthcoming*), *Economic Systems*.
(2002b), 'Issues in the regulation of annuities markets', Discussion Paper No. 26/02, Centre for Research on Pensions and Welfare, University of Turin.
(2002c), 'Prudent person rules or quantitative restrictions? The regulation of long-term institutional investors' portfolios', *Journal of Pension Economics and Finance*, 1, July.
(2002d), 'Ageing and financial stability', in Herrmann, H. and Auerbach, A. (eds), *Ageing and Financial Markets*, Springer Verlag-Deutsche Bundesbank.
Davis, E. P. and Ioannidis, C. (2002), 'Does the availability of bank and bond finance smooth overall corporate financing?', Brunel University Working Paper.
Davis, E. P. and Li, C. (2002), 'Demographics and asset prices in the major industrial countries', Brunel University Working Paper.
Davis, E. P. and Madsen, J. (2001), 'Productivity and equity returns; a century of evidence for 9 OECD countries', Working Paper 01-12, Brunel University.
Davis, E. P. and Mayer, C. P. (1991), 'Corporate finance in the euromarkets and the economics of intermediation', London, Centre for Economic Policy Research Discussion Paper No. 570.
Davis E. P. and Steil, B. (2001), *Institutional Investment*, Cambridge, Mass., MIT Press.
Davis E. P. and Tuori, K. (2000), 'The changing structure of banks' income, an empirical investigation', Brunel University Working Paper No. 00-11.
Debreu, G. (1959), *Theory of Value*, New York.
Demirgüç-Kunt, A. and Levine, R. (2000), 'Bank-based and market-based financial systems; cross-country comparisons', paper presented at the World Bank conference on 'Financial structure and economic development', 10–11 February.
Demirgüç-Kunt, A. and Maksimovic, V. (1998), 'Law, finance and firm growth', *Journal of Finance*, 53, pp. 2107–37.
(2000), 'Funding growth in bank-based or market-based financial systems, evidence from firm level data', paper presented at the World Bank conference on 'Financial structure and economic development', 10–11 February.
Deutsche Bundesbank (1999), 'Corporate financing in Germany and France; a comparative analysis', *Deutsche Bundesbank Monthly Review*, October, pp. 29–46.
Dewatripont, M. and Maskin, E. (1995), 'Credit efficiency in centralized and decentralized economies', *Review of Economic Studies*, 62, pp. 541–55.

Diamond, D. (1984), 'Financial intermediation and delegated monitoring', *Review of Economic Studies*, 51, pp. 393–414.

(1991), 'Monitoring and reputation; the choice between bank loans and directly placed debt', *Journal of Political Economy*, 99, pp. 689–721.

Diamond, D. and Dybvig, P. (1983), 'Bank runs, deposit insurance and liquidity', *Journal of Political Economy*, 91, pp. 401–19.

Dickinson, G. M. (1998), 'Issues in the effective regulation of the asset allocation of life insurance companies', in Blommestein, H. and Funke, N. (eds), *Institutional Investors in the New Financial Landscape*, Paris, OECD.

Disney, R. (2000), 'Declining public pensions in an era of demographic ageing: will private pensions fill the gap?', *European Economic Review*, 44, pp. 957–73.

Edey, M. and Hviding, K. (1995), 'An assessment of financial reform in OECD countries', Economics Department Working Paper No. 154, Paris, OECD.

Edison, H. and Sløk, T. (2001), 'Wealth effects and the new economy', IMF Working Paper No. 77.

Edwards, J. and Fischer, K. (1994), *Banks, Finance and Investment in Germany*, Cambridge, Cambridge University Press.

EMI (1998), *Convergence Report*, Frankfurt, European Monetary Institute.

Erb, C. B., Harvey, C. R. and Viskanta, T. E. (1997), 'Demographics and international investment', *Financial Analysts Journal*, 53, July/August, pp. 14–28.

Evanoff, D. D. and Wall, L. D. (2002), 'Measures of the riskiness of banking organizations: subordinated debt yields, risk-based capital, and examination ratings', *Journal of Banking and Finance*, 26, pp. 989–1009.

Fama, E. F. (1980), 'Banking in the theory of finance', *Journal of Monetary Economics*, 6, pp. 39–58.

Fama, E. F. and Schwert, G. W. (1977), 'Asset returns and inflation', *Journal of Finance*, 5, pp. 115–46.

Fauver, L., Houston, J. and Naranjo, A. (1999), 'Capital market development, legal systems and the value of corporate diversification: a cross country analysis', mimeo, University of Florida.

Fazzari, S., Hubbard, R. G. and Petersen, B. (1988), 'Financing constraints and corporate investment', *Brookings Papers on Economic Activity*, 1, pp. 141–95.

Feldstein, M. S. (1974), 'Social security, inducement retirement and aggregate capital accumulation', *Journal of Political Economy*, 82, pp. 905–26.

(1977), 'Social security and private saving; international evidence in an extended life cycle model', in Feldstein, M. and Inman, R. (eds), *The Economics of Public Services*, International Economic Association.

(1978), 'Do private pensions increase national savings?' *Journal of Public Economics*, 10, pp. 277–93.

(1995), 'Social security and saving, new time series evidence', NBER Working Paper No. 5054.

Fisher, I. (1933), 'The debt-deflation theory of great depressions', *Econometrica*,

1, pp. 337–57.
Flavin, T. J. and Wickens, M. R. (2000), 'Global asset allocation and time varying risk', unpublished manuscript, Maynooth University.
Fleming, M. J. (2000), 'Financial markets implications of the Federal Debt paydown', *Brookings Papers on Economic Activity*, 2, pp. 221–52.
Frankel, J. (1985), 'Portfolio crowding-out empirically estimated', *Quarterly Journal of Economics*, 100, pp. 1041–65.
Franks, J. and Mayer, C. (1994), 'Ownership and control', in Siebert , H. (ed.), *Trends in Business Organization*, Tübingen, Mohr Siebeck.
Freixas, X. and Rochet, J. C. (1999), *The Microeconomics of Banking*, Cambridge, Mass., MIT Press.
French, K. R. and Poterba, J. M. (1991), 'Investor diversification and international equity markets', *American Economic Review*, 81, pp. 222–6.
Friedman, B. M. (1977), 'Financial flow variables and the short-run determination of long-run interest rates', *Journal of Political Economy*, 85, pp. 661–85.
Friedman, M. (1957), *A Theory of the Consumption Function*, Princeton, New Jersey, Princeton University Press.
Froot, K. A., O'Connell, P. and Seasholes, M. (1999), 'The portfolio flows of international investors', Harvard Business School Working Paper, August.
Frost, A. J. and Henderson, I. J. S. (1983), 'Implications of modern portfolio theory for life insurance companies' and 'Modern portfolio theory and financial institutions', in Corner, D. and Mayes, D. G. (eds), London, Macmillan.
Gale, D. (1990), 'The efficient design of public debt', in Dornbusch, R. and Draghi, M. (eds), *Public Debt Management: Theory and History*, Cambridge, Cambridge University Press.
Gale, D. and Hellwig, M. (1985), 'Incentive-compatible debt contracts, the one period problem', *Review of Economic Studies*, 52, pp. 647–63.
Gale, W. G. (1998), 'The effects of pensions on household wealth: a re-evaluation of theory and evidence', *Journal of Political Economy*, 106, pp. 706–23.
Gertler, M. and Gilchrist, S. (1992), 'The cyclical behavior of short term business lending; implications for financial propagation mechanisms', mimeo.
(1994), 'Monetary policy, business cycles, and the behavior of small manufacturing firms', *Quarterly Journal of Economics*, 59, pp. 309–40.
Gertler, M. and Hubbard, R. G. (1989), 'Taxation, corporate capital structure and financial distress', NBER Working Paper No. 3202.
Giavazzi, F. and Pagano, M. (1995), 'Non Keynesian effects of fiscal policy changes; international evidence and the Swedish experience', Working Paper No. 1284, London, Centre for Economic Policy Research.
Goldsmith, R. W. (1969), *Financial Structure and Development*, Yale University Press.
Gordon, R. H. and Malkiel, B. G. (1981), 'Corporation finance', in Aaron, H. A. and Pechman, J. A. (eds), *How Taxes Affect Economic Behaviour*, Washington, DC, Brookings Institution.
Gorton, G. and Schmidt, F. A. (1996), 'Universal banking and the performance

of German firms', NBER Working Paper No. 5453.

Greenbaum, S. and Thakor, A. (1995), *Contemporary Financial Intermediation*, New York, Prentice Hall.

Greenspan, A. (1999), 'Do efficient financial markets mitigate financial crises?', speech to the Financial Markets Conference at the Federal Reserve Bank of Atlanta, 19 October.

Grubel, H. (1968), 'Internationally diversified portfolios: welfare gains and capital flows', *American Economic Review*, 58, pp. 1299–314.

Guariglia, A. (1999), 'The effects of financial constraints on inventory investment; evidence from a panel of UK firms', *Economica*, 66, pp. 43–62.

Guiso, L. (2001), 'Comment', in Guiso, L. Haliassos, M. and Jappelli, T. (eds), *Household Portfolios*, Cambridge, Mass., MIT Press.

Guiso, L. and Jappelli, T. (2001), 'Household portfolios in Italy', in Guiso, L. Haliassos, M. and Jappelli, T. (eds), *Household Portfolios*, Cambridge, Mass., MIT Press.

Gurley, J. and Shaw, E. (1960), *Money in a Theory of Finance*, Washington D.C., Brookings.

Haliassos, M. and Bertaut, C. C. (1995), 'Why do so few hold stocks?', *Economic Journal*, 105, pp. 1110–29.

Haliassos, M. and Michaelides, A. (2000), 'Calibration and computation of household portfolio models', in Guiso, L., Haliassos, M. and Jappelli, T. (eds), *Household Portfolios*, Cambridge, Mass., MIT Press.

Harris, M. and Raviv, A. (1990), 'Capital structure and the informational role of debt', *Journal of Finance*, 45, pp. 321–50.

Harvey, C. (1991), 'The world price of covariance risk', *Journal of Finance*, 46, pp. 111–57.

Hayashi, F. (1985), 'Tests for liquidity constraints: a critical survey', NBER Working Paper No. 1720.

Hepp, S. (1992), 'Comparison of investment behaviour of pension plans in Europe – implications for Europe's capital markets', in Mortensen, J. (ed.), *The Future of Pensions in the European Community*, London, Brassey's, for the Centre for European Policy Studies, Brussels.

Hess, G. D. (1999), 'The maturity structure of government debt and asset substitutability in the United Kingdom', in Chrystal, K.A. (ed.), *Government Debt Structure and Monetary Conditions*, London, Bank of England.

Holland, T. E. (1969), 'Operation twist and the movement of interest rates and related economic time series', *International Economic Review*, 10, pp. 260–5.

Holmstrom, B. and Tirole, J. (1997), 'Financial intermediation, loanable funds and the real sector', *Quarterly Journal of Economics*, 112, pp. 663–91.

Horiuchi, A. and Okazaki. R. (1994), 'Capital markets and the banking sector: efficiency of Japanese banks in reducing agency costs', in Sato, R., Levich, R. M. and Ramachandran, R. V. (eds), *Japan, Europe and International Financial Markets: Analytical and Empirical Perspectives*, Cambridge, Cambridge University Press.

Hoshi, T. and Kashyap, A. (1999), 'The Japanese banking crisis – where did it

come from and how will it end?', NBER Working Paper No. 7250.
Hoshi, T., Scharfstein, D. and Singleton, K. J. (1993a), 'Japanese corporate investment and Bank of Japan guidance of commercial bank lending', in Singleton, K. (ed.), *Japanese Monetary Policy*, University of Chicago Press.
Hoshi, T., Kashyap, A. and Scharfstein, D. (1993b), 'The choice between public and private debt; an analysis of post deregulation corporate financing in Japan', NBER Working Paper No. 4211.
Hu, C. X. (1999), 'Leverage, monetary policy and firm investment', *Federal Reserve Bank of San Francisco Economic Review*, 2/1999, pp. 32–9.
Huang, H. and Xu, C. (1998), 'Institutions, innovations and growth', mimeo, London School of Economics.
Hubbard, R. G. (1986), 'Pension wealth and individual saving, some new evidence', *Journal of Money, Credit and Banking*, 18, pp. 167–78.
(1987), 'Uncertain lifetimes, pensions and individual saving', in Bodie, Z., Shoven, J. B. and Wise, D. A. (eds), *Issues in Pension Economics*, Chicago, University of Chicago Press.
Hutchinson, M. and McDill, K. (1999), 'Are all banking crises alike? The Japanese experience in international comparison', NBER Working Paper No. 7253.
IMF (1996), *World Economic Outlook, May 1996*, Washington D.C., International Monetary Fund.
Investment Company Institute (1998), *Mutual Fund Fact Book*, Washington D.C., The Investment Company Institute.
Jappelli, T. and Pagano, M. (1994), 'Saving, growth and liquidity constraints', *Quarterly Journal of Economics*, 109, pp. 83–109.
Jensen, M. C. (1993), 'The modern industrial revolution, exit, and the failure of internal control mechanisms', *Journal of Finance*, 48, pp. 831–80.
Jensen, M. C. and Meckling, W. (1976), 'Theory of the firm, managerial behavior, agency costs and ownership structure', *Journal of Financial Economics*, 3, pp. 305–60.
Joines, D. H. and Manegold, J. G. (1995), 'IRA and saving; evidence from a panel of taxpayers', mimeo, University of Southern California.
Kaplan, S. (1994), 'Top executive rewards and firm performance, a comparison of Japan and the United States', *Journal of Political Economy*, 102, pp. 510–46.
Kaplan, S. and Stein, J. (1993), 'The evolution of buy-out pricing and financial structure in the 1980s', *Quarterly Journal of Economics*, 108, pp. 313–57.
Kashyap, A. K. (1999), 'Comment', in Chrystal, K. A. (ed.), *Government Debt Structure and Monetary Conditions*, London, Bank of England.
Kashyap, A. K., Stein, J. C. and Lamont, D. (1994), 'Credit conditions and the cyclical behavior of inventories', *Quarterly Journal of Economics*, 109, pp. 565–92.
Keeley, M. C. (1990), 'Deposit insurance, risk and market power in banking', *American Economic Review*, 80, pp. 1183–200.
Kim, C. S., Mauer, D. C. and Sherman, A. E. (1998), 'The determinants of corporate liquidity, theory and evidence', *Journal of Financial and*

*Quantitative Analysis*, 33, pp. 335–59.
King, R. G. and Levine, R. (1993), 'Finance and growth, Schumpeter might be right', *Quarterly Journal of Economics*, 108, pp. 713–37.
Kiyotaki, N. and Moore, J. (1997), 'Credit cycles', *Journal of Political Economy*, April, 105, pp. 211–48.
Kreps, D. (1990), 'Corporate culture and economic theory', in Alt, J. and Shepsle, K. (eds), *Perspectives on Positive Political Economy*, Cambridge, Cambridge University Press.
La Porta, R., Lopez-Silanes, F. and Schleifer, A. (1999), 'Corporate ownership around the world', *Journal of Finance*, 54, pp. 471–517.
(2000), 'Investor protection and corporate governance', *Journal of Financial Economics*, 58, pp. 3–27.
Lancaster, K. (1971), *Consumer Demand: A New Approach*, New York, Columbia University Press.
Leibowitz, M. L. and Kogelman, S. (1991), 'Asset allocation under shortfall constraints', *Journal of Portfolio Management*, Winter, pp. 18–23.
Leland, H. and Pyle, D. (1977), 'Information asymmetries, financial structures and financial intermediaries', *Journal of Finance*, 32, pp. 371–87.
Levine, R. (1997), 'Financial development and economic growth: views and agenda', *Journal of Economic Literature*, 35, June, pp. 688–726.
(1999), 'Law, finance and economic growth', *Journal of Financial Intermediation*, 8, pp. 8–35.
(2000), 'Bank based or market based financial systems – which is better?', paper presented at the World Bank conference on 'Financial structure and economic development', 10–11 February.
Levine, R. and Zervos, S. (1998), 'Stock markets, growth and economic development', *American Economic Review*, 88, pp. 537–58.
Levy, H. and Sarnat, M. (1970), 'International diversification of investment portfolios', *American Economic Review*, 60, pp. 668–75.
Lewis, K. K. (1995), 'Puzzles in international financial markets', in Grossman, G. and Rogoff, K. (eds), *Handbook of International Economics vol III*, Amsterdam, Elsevier.
Lucas, R. E. and Stokey, N. (1983), 'Optimal fiscal and monetary policy in an economy without capital', *Journal of Monetary Economics*, 12, pp. 55–93.
Ludvigson, S. and Steindel, C. (1999), 'How important is the stock market effect on consumption?', *Economic Policy Review*, July, Federal Reserve Bank of New York.
Lund, M. and Wright, J. (1998), 'The financing of small firms in the United Kingdom', *Bank of England Quarterly Bulletin*, November, pp. 195–201.
Mankiw, G. N. and Weil, D. N. (1989), 'The baby boom, the baby bust and the housing market', *Regional Science and Urban Economics*, 19, pp 235–58.
Markowitz, H. (1952), 'Portfolio selection', *Journal of Finance*, 7, pp. 77–91.
Mayer, C. (1988), 'New issues in corporate finance', *European Economic Review*, 32, pp. 1167–89.
(1996), 'Corporate governance, competition and performance', Economics

Department Working Paper No. 164, Paris, OECD.
Mehra, R. and Prescott, E. C. (1985), 'The equity premium: a puzzle', *Journal of Monetary Economics*, 15, pp. 145–61.
Merton, R. C. and Bodie, Z. (1995), 'A conceptual framework for analysing the financial environment', in Crane, D. B. *et al.* (eds), *The Global Financial System, a Functional Perspective*, Harvard Business School Press.
Metais, J. (1997), 'The banking industry in the nineties, do emerging trends challenge the theory?', in Revell, J. (ed.), *The Recent Evolution of Financial Systems*, Basingstoke, Macmillan.
Miles, D. and Patel, B. (1996), 'Saving and wealth accumulation in Europe, the outlook into the next century', Merrill Lynch, Financial Research, 3 June.
Miller, M. H. (1977), 'Debt and taxes', *Journal of Finance*, 32, pp. 261–97.
Mishkin, F. S. (1991), 'Asymmetric information and financial crises: a historical perspective', in Hubbard, R. G. (ed.), *Financial Markets and Financial Crises*, Chicago, University of Chicago Press.
(2001), 'Financial policies and the prevention of financial crises in emerging market economies', NBER Working Paper No. 8087.
Mitra-Stiff, P. (1995), 'Empirical studies in international equity markets', unpublished doctoral dissertation, Princeton University.
Modigliani, F. and Miller, M. H. (1958), 'The cost of capital, corporation finance and the theory of investment', *American Economic Review*, 48, pp. 261–97.
Modigliani, F. and Sutch, R. (1967), 'Debt management and the term structure of interest rates: an empirical examination of recent experiences', *Journal of Political Economy*, 75, pp. 569–89.
Morck, R., Schleifer, A. and Vishny, R. (1988), 'Management ownership and market valuation, an empirical analysis', *Journal of Financial Economics*, 20, pp. 293–315.
Morgan, D. P. (1994), 'Bank credit commitments, credit rationing and monetary policy', *Journal of Money, Credit and Banking*, 26, pp. 87–101.
Munnell, A. H. (1986), 'Private pensions and savings: new evidence', *Journal of Political Economy*, 84, pp. 1013–32.
(1987), 'The impact of public and private saving schemes on saving and capital formation', in 'Conjugating public and private, the case of pensions', *International Social Security Association, Studies and Research*, 24, pp. 219–36.
Myers, S. (1977), 'Determinants of corporate borrowing', *Journal of Financial Economics*, 5, pp. 147–75.
Myers, S. and Majluf, N. (1984), 'Corporate financing and investment decisions when firms have information that investors do not have', *Journal of Financial Economics*, 13, pp. 187–221.
Nakagawa, S. (1999), 'Why has Japan's household savings rate remained high during the 1990s?', reprinted from *Bank of Japan Monthly Bulletin*, April.
National Institute of Economic and Social Research (NIESR) (1997), *The Single Market Review, Subseries III Dismantling of Barriers, Volume 5: Capital Market Liberalisation*, European Commission.
Obstfeld, M. (1998), 'The global capital market: benefactor or menace', *Journal*

*of Economic Perspectives*, 12, pp. 9–30.

OECD (2000), *Issues Paper on Investment Regulation*, Paper No. DAFFE/AS(2000)3, Insurance Committee, Paris, OECD.

Oliner, S. D. and Rudebusch, G. D. (1996), 'Is there a broad credit channel of monetary policy?', *Federal Reserve Bank of San Francisco Economic Review*, 1/1996, pp. 3–13.

Opler, T., Pinkowitz, L., Stulz, R. and Williamson, R. (1999), 'The determinants and implications of corporate cash holdings', *Journal of Financial Economics*, 52, pp. 3–46.

*Oxford Review of Economic Policy* (1999), 'Financial stability', OXREP.

Oyama, T. and Yoshida, K. (1999), 'Does Japan save too little or do other countries save too much?', Working Paper 99-5, Research and Statistics Department, Bank of Japan.

Pesando, J. E. (1992), 'The economic effects of private pensions', in *Private Pensions and Public Policy*, Paris, OECD.

Poterba, J. M. (1998), 'Population age structure and asset returns: an empirical investigation', NBER Working Paper No. 6774.

Poterba, J. M. and Samwick, A. A. (1997), 'Household portfolio allocation over the life cycle', NBER Working Paper No. 6185.

Poterba, J. M., Venti, S. F. and Wise, D. A. (1993), 'Do 401(K) contributions crowd out other personal saving?', NBER Working Paper No. 4391.

(1996), 'Personal retirement saving programmes and asset accumulation; reconciling the evidence', NBER Working Paper No. 5599.

Rajan, R. and Zingales, L. (1998a), 'Financial dependence and growth', *American Economic Review*, 88, pp. 559–86.

(1998b), 'Which capitalism, lessons from the Asian crisis', *Journal of Applied Corporate Finance*, 11, Fall.

(2000), 'The great reversals; the politics of financial development in the 20th century', Working paper No. 265, Economics Department, OECD.

Reinhart, V. and Sack, B. (2000), 'The economics consequences of disappearing government debt', *Brookings Papers on Economic Activity*, 2, pp. 163–220.

Repullo, R. and Suarez, J. (2000), 'Entrepreneurial moral hazard and bank monitoring: a model of the credit channel', *European Economic Review*, 44, pp. 1931–50.

Ritter, J. (1991), 'The long term performance of IPOs', *Journal of Finance*, 46, pp. 3–27.

Roll, R. (1986), 'The hubris theory of corporate take-overs', *Journal of Business*, 59, pp. 197–216.

Roseveare, D., Leibfritz, W., Fore, D. and Wurzel, E. (1996), 'Aging populations, pension systems and government budgets: simulation for 20 OECD countries', Economics Department Working Paper No. 168, Paris, OECD.

Rybczynski, T. (1997), 'A new look at the evolution of the financial system', in Revell, J. (ed.), *The Recent Evolution of Financial Systems*, Basingstoke, Macmillan.

Saidenberg, M. and Strahan, P. (1999), 'Are banks still important for financing large businesses?', *Current Issues in Economics and Finance*, Federal Reserve Bank of New York, August, 5, 12.

Schleifer, A. and Vishny, R. W. (1997), 'A survey of corporate governance', *Journal of Finance*, 52, pp. 737–83.

Schmidt, R. H., Hackethal, A. and Tyrell, M. (1999), 'Disintermediation and the role of banks in Europe, an international comparison', *Journal of Financial Intermediation*, 8, pp. 36–67.

Schmidt, R. H., Hackethal, A. and Tyrell, M. (2001), 'The convergence of financial systems in Europe, main findings of the DFG project', University of Frankfurt.

Scholtens, B. (1997), 'Bank and market based financial systems – fact or fiction?', *BNL Quarterly Review*, 202, pp. 301–23.

Scholtens, B. and van Wensveen, D. (2000), 'A critique of the theory of financial intermediation', *Journal of Banking and Finance*, 24, pp. 1243–51.

Senior, S. and Westwood, R. (2000), 'The external balance sheet of the United Kingdom: implications for financial stability', *Bank of England Quarterly Bulletin*, 40, pp. 351–64.

Shiller, R. E. (2000), *Irrational Exuberance*, Cambridge, Mass., MIT Press.

Singh, A. (1995), 'Corporate financing patterns in industrializing countries; a comparative international study', Technical Paper No. 2, Washington DC, IFC.

Solomou, S. and Weale, M. (1997), 'Personal sector wealth in the United Kingdom, 1920–56', *Review of Income and Wealth*, 43, pp. 297–318.

Stiglitz, J. and Weiss, A. (1981), 'Credit rationing in markets with imperfect information', *American Economic Review*, 71, pp. 393–410.

Tanzi, V. and King, J. (1995), 'The taxation of financial assets, a survey of issues and country experiences', IMF Working Paper No. 95/46.

Tesar, L. L. and Werner, I. (1995), 'Home bias and high turnover', *Journal of International Money and Finance*, 14, pp. 467–92.

Thompson, M. and Yurkuat, K. (1999), 'Rewards in a global context', *Compensation and Benefits Review*, 31, July/August.

Tobin, J. (1958), 'Liquidity preference as behavior towards risk', *Review of Economic Studies*, 25, pp. 68–85.

(1963), 'An essay on the principle of debt management', in *Fiscal and Debt Management Policies*, prepared for the Commission on Money and Credit, Englewood Cliffs, Prentice-Hall.

(1969), 'A general equilibrium approach to monetary theory', *Journal of Money, Credit and Banking*, 1, pp. 15–29.

(1972), 'Wealth, liquidity and the propensity to consume', in Strumpel, B. *et al.* (eds), *Human Behaviour in Economic Affairs*, Amsterdam, Elsevier.

Tobin, J. and Golub, S. (1998), *Money, Credit and Capital*, New York, McGraw-Hill.

Trzcinka, C. (1997), *Institutional Investing*, Paris, OECD.

(1998), 'The conflicting views and management practices of institutional equity investing', *Financial Markets, Institutions and Instruments*, 7, pp. 20–53.

Tsuru, K. (2000), 'Finance and growth, some theoretical considerations and a review of the empirical literature', OECD Economics Department Working Paper No. 228.

Van Els, P., Locarno, A., Morgan, J. and Villetelle, J.-P. (2002), 'Monetary policy transmission in the euro area; what do aggregate and national structural models tell us?', ECB Working Paper.

Venti, S. F. and Wise, D. A. (1994), 'RRSPs and savings in Canada', paper presented at a conference 'Public policies that affect private saving', Paris, OECD, 19 May.

Vermeulen, P. (2000), 'Business fixed investment: evidence of a financial accelerator in Europe', ECB Working Paper No. 37.

Walkling, R. and Long, M. (1984), 'Agency theory, managerial welfare and take-over bid resistance', *Rand Journal of Economics*, 15, pp. 54–68.

Wallace, M. S. and Warner, J. T. (1996), 'Do excess holding period returns depend on the composition of outstanding federal debt?', *Journal of Money Credit and Banking*, 28, pp. 132–9.

Wheeler, G. (1997), 'Sovereign debt management in New Zealand', in Nars, K. (ed.), *Excellence in Debt Management: The Strategies of Lending International Borrowers*, Euromoney Publications.

Yoo, P. S. (1994), 'Age dependent portfolio selection', Federal Reserve Bank of St. Louis Working Paper No. 94-003A.

Zingales, L. (1995), 'What determines the value of corporate votes?', *Quarterly Journal of Economics*, 110, pp. 1075–110.

# Author index

# Subject index

9 780521 831802